LEAN AND LUSCIOUS

FAVORITES

Other books in the LEAN AND LUSCIOUS series

Lean and Luscious
More Lean and Luscious
Lean and Luscious and Meatless

Also by Bobbie Hinman

Meatless Gourmet: Favorite Recipes from Around the World
Meatless Gourmet: Easy Lowfat Favorites

Also by Millie Snyder

Light Fantastic! Over 200 Fun, Flavorful, and Fat-Reduced Recipes

LEAN AND LUSCIOUS FAVORITES

BOBBIE HINMAN & MILLIE SNYDER

Illustrator: Vonnie Winslow Crist

PRIMA PUBLISHING

Library of Congress Cataloging-in-Publication Data

Hinman, Bobbie.
    Lean and luscious favorites/ Bobbie Hinman, Millie Snyder.
       p.   cm.
    Includes index.
    ISBN 0-7615-0644-4
    1. Low-fat diet—Recipes.   I. Snyder, Millie.   II. Title.
RM237.7.H557   1997
641.5'638—dc21   97-28462
                                                    CIP

97 98 99 00 01 AA 10 9 8 7 6 5 4 3 2 1

Printed in the United States of America

How to Order:
Single copies may be ordered from Prima Publishing, P.O. Box 1260BK, Rocklin, CA 95677; telephone (916) 632-4400. Quantity discounts are also available. On your letterhead, include information concerning the intended use of the books and the number of books you wish to purchase.

Visit us online at http://www.primapublishing.com

This book is dedicated to all of the wonderful people who continue to use and enjoy our recipes.

Enjoy and be healthy!

Important

This book is not intended as a promotion or recommendation for any specific diet, nor as a substitute for your physician's advice. Its purpose is to show you how you can follow a balanced diet that is low in fat and high in fiber, and still enjoy tasty meals.

Contents

Introduction: About Our Book   ix
    What Is a Balanced Diet?   ix
    Can Food *Really* Be Both Lean *and* Luscious?   xi
    Food Families   xii
    How to Use the Nutritional Information Found
      in This Book   xv

Appetizers, Dips, and Spreads   1
Soups   21
Salads and Salad Dressings   41
Poultry   65
Fish and Seafood   85
Beef, Pork, and Lamb   107
Beans and Tofu   125
Pasta and Pasta Sauces   153
Eggs and Cheese   171
Sandwiches   191
Vegetables   206
Starchy Vegetables   230
Grains   248
Fruits   269
Breads and Muffins   290
Desserts   317
Sauces and Toppings   363

Index   375

Introduction:
About Our Book

Lean and Luscious debuted in 1985 as a collection of recipes created to allow you to enjoy your favorite foods without adding unnecessary calories or fat. The first book was followed by *More Lean and Luscious*, then came *Lean and Luscious and Meatless*. All three books have been very successful, showing us that more and more people are interested in preparing meals that are both healthful and delicious. To keep up with scientific breakthroughs, we have adapted our cooking styles over the years, to make use of the latest information on health and diet.

We are very excited about this recipe collection. We have chosen our own personal favorites, along with those of our families and friends. It is our wish that you will enjoy these recipes and that they will help you to create a new way of cooking and eating. Our quick, easy-to-prepare dishes will transform ordinary meals into culinary delights, while teaching you and your family new, more healthful eating habits.

As always, for each recipe we include a calorie count as well as a complete nutritional breakdown. Use this information to help prepare satisfying, well-balanced meals.

In transforming and creating our recipes, we keep in mind that foods have their own built-in flavors. We use spices to enhance, not hide, flavors. We have attempted to bring out the best in food by eliminating excess sugar, salt, and fats, and replacing them with unique, flavorful combinations of extracts and spices. Our goal is to make foods taste so good that this "enlightened" way of eating can easily become a way of life.

What Is a Balanced Diet?

The meaning of "balanced diet" has changed over the years, and is currently defined as a diet that is low in fat and high in fiber. Health professionals feel that our diet should be rich in carbohydrates, such as whole grain breads, grains, dried peas and beans, fruits, vegetables, and pasta. These should be the focus of the meal, with lean meat, poultry, fish, and lowfat or nonfat dairy products playing smaller roles.

Many health professionals recommend that we get less than 30 percent of our total daily calories from fat. Of the total number, most should come from unsaturated fat. To figure your daily fat allowance, multiply your daily calorie intake by .30 (to find 30 percent of calories). Then divide your answer by 9 for the number of fat grams allowed each day.

Example: 1500 calories × .30 = 450 ÷ 9 = 50 grams of fat daily

Remember that the allowance is figured by the day, not by the individual food, so if you eat a little more fat in one meal, compensate by eating less fat at other meals. Ideally, the formula is used to evaluate your daily or weekly diet, rather than single foods.

In addition to lowering fat intake, studies show that eating a high-fiber diet may be our first line of defense against heart disease and several forms of cancer. Many health professionals recommend that we eat 20 to 25 grams of fiber daily. Fiber is abundant in many plant foods, including whole grains, fruits, vegetables, and dried peas and beans. (Meats contain no fiber.) These high-fiber foods are also relatively low in calories, so if you plan your diet around fresh fruits and vegetables, along with whole grains and beans, and use smaller portions of meats and dairy products, it becomes easy to eat fewer calories. Isn't it nice that most foods low in fat are high in fiber and also low in calories?

Sugar is high in calories and low in nutrients and should be used sparingly. In all of our recipes we keep use of sugar to a minimum. We found that we can greatly reduce the amount of sugar in a recipe by increasing vanilla extract to achieve delicious, sweet results. (There is controversy surrounding the safety of artificial sweeteners and we want our recipes to be as wholesome as possible so we have chosen not to use artificial sweeteners in these recipes.)

Sodium is a mineral that occurs naturally in many foods. Most sodium in the American diet comes from table salt and sodium added to processed foods and beverages. Some sodium is essential to health, but the recommendation from many health professionals is to limit daily sodium intake to 2,400 to 3,000 milligrams, about 1 to 1$^{1}/_{2}$ teaspoons of salt per day. In our recipes we use herbs and spices in place of most of the salt and recommend tasting the finished product and adding salt if necessary. We also choose low-sodium or salt-free canned foods whenever available and recommend rinsing canned beans to remove excess salt.

Can Food *Really* Be Both Lean *and* Luscious?

Having grown up in typical American homes, we always thought that meats had to be "smothered" with sauce or gravy in order to taste good. We thought that desserts had to be laden with butter and sugar if they were to have any flavor at all. And, like so many people, we thought that lowfat meant low flavor. Faced with the awesome responsibility of changing our own and our family's eating habits, we were determined to keep the flavor while eliminating fat and calories. The good news is that it works. Over the years we have found 3 basic ways to accomplish this goal:

1. Choose healthful cooking methods. Eliminate deep-frying and sautéing in lots of butter and oil. More healthful cooking methods include steaming, broiling, grilling, poaching, and stir-frying.
2. Rely on herbs, spices, and extracts for flavor. Experiment with the vast selection of flavors that will enhance food without adding fat.
3. Substitute high-fat ingredients with their lowfat counterparts.

Following are some basic substitutions to guide you.

BASIC SUBSTITUTIONS

Instead of:	Use:
Whole eggs	Two egg whites in place of each egg, or egg substitute
Whole milk	Skim milk
Cream	Evaporated skim milk or plain nonfat yogurt
Sour cream	Fat-free sour cream or plain nonfat yogurt
Ice cream	Reduced-fat ice cream, or frozen yogurt, or ice milk
Whipped cream (as a dessert topping)	Vanilla nonfat yogurt
Cream cheese	Fat-free cream cheese
Cheese	Reduced-fat or fat-free cheese
Mayonnaise	Reduced-calorie mayonnaise
Butter	Margarine that lists a liquid oil as the first ingredient, or vegetable oil (However, all are high in fat and should be used sparingly.)
Vegetable oil	An oil with a high amount of monounsaturated fat such as olive oil or canola oil. Nonstick cooking spray for "greasing" pans
Salad dressings with lots of oil	Replace *half* the oil with water or fruit juice

Basic Substitutions, continued

Instead of:	Use:
High-fat marinades	Nonfat salad dressings
Sugar	Use *half* the amount called for (This works in most recipes, except cookies.)
White rice	Brown rice or other whole grains
All-purpose flour	Replace *half* with whole wheat flour
French fries	Baked potatoes (with a lowfat topping such as nonfat yogurt and chopped chives)
Meat in casseroles	Replace *half* with beans

Food Families

To help you to develop healthful eating habits, we have divided foods into basic food groups, or Food Families. These groupings are similar to the exchanges used by the American Dietetic Association and several major weight reduction groups, making it easy to use them in conjunction with these plans. It is our hope that these food groupings will help you to plan variable menus and to greatly simplify your portion control. If you wish to lose weight, consult your physician or other weight-control expert regarding the number of servings from each Food Family that would be best for your particular daily needs.

Each Family contains foods of comparable nutritional and calorie values. At the end of each recipe, in addition to the nutritional analysis, you will find the number of servings from each Food Family. (Example: 2 Protein Servings, 1 Fruit Serving, and so on.) If you vary your menu, but choose foods from each Family daily, you will have all the nutrients needed for a balanced diet.

Family #1: Protein

The Protein Family is made up of meats, poultry, seafood, eggs, cheese, legumes (beans), and tofu. All of these foods are valuable sources of protein, but it is important to choose wisely in this group. Select cuts of meat carefully, choosing those that are lowest in fat. Whenever possible, remove skin from poultry before cooking and choose white meat over dark. Choose lowfat or nonfat cheeses, and replace whole eggs with egg whites or liquid egg substitute. Legumes and tofu are not of animal origin and so, while high in protein, they contain no cholesterol and low amounts of saturated fat.

One serving from the Protein Family contains 60 to 70 calories.

Family #2: Breads

The Bread Family is made up of breads, crackers, cereals, grains, and starchy vegetables. Whenever possible, choose whole grains, such as brown rice and whole wheat flour, and products made from whole grains. We have included starchy vegetables (such as corn, peas, potatoes, and sweet potatoes) in this family because their carbohydrate levels are about the same as an equivalent serving of bread. The Bread Family is a good source of fiber in the diet.

One serving from the Bread Family contains 75 to 85 calories.

Family #3: Vegetables

The Vegetable Family consists of fresh, canned, or frozen vegetables, other than the starchy vegetables. This family provides valuable sources of vitamins, minerals, and fiber. Vegetables retain more nutrients when cooked only until tender-crisp, and if you leave the skin on the vegetables whenever possible.

One serving from the Vegetable Family contains 25 to 30 calories.

Family #4: Fats

The Fat Family is made up of margarine, mayonnaise, vegetable oils, and salad dressings. Many health professionals recommend using oils that are high in monounsaturated fats, such as canola or olive oil, and margarine in place of butter, since butter is high in saturated fat. When choosing margarine, select one that contains a liquid vegetable oil as the first oil listed. Whichever fats you choose, use them in very small amounts.

One serving from the Fat Family contains 40 to 45 calories.

Family #5: Fruit

The Fruit Family consists of fruits and fruit juices. This family provides valuable sources of vitamins, minerals, and fiber. Fruits may be fresh, canned, dried, or frozen. When choosing canned or frozen fruit, select fruit packed in water or unsweetened fruit juice. Whenever possible, leave the skin on fruits.

One serving from the Fruit Family contains approximately 50 calories.

Family #6: Milk

The Milk Family is made up of milk and milk products. This family is an excellent source of vitamins, minerals, protein, and calcium. To cut down on calories and fats, choose skim milk and other nonfat or lowfat dairy products.

One serving from the Milk Family contains 80 to 90 calories.

Family #7: Free Foods

The Free Food Family consists of foods that appear in our recipes but provide no nutritional value. They are used to enhance the taste. Included in this family are spices, extracts, vinegar, lemon juice, mustard, and soy sauce. We call them "free," though some of these foods are very high in sodium and it is best to choose a reduced-sodium counterpart when available, and to use them in moderation.

Each serving from the Free Food Family contains a negligible amount of calories.

Family #8: Additional Calories

The Additional Calories Family consists of foods that appear in our recipes in small amounts and do not appreciably alter the nutritional value of each dish, but do add calories. Among these foods are sugar, honey, ketchup, jams and jellies, nuts, cocoa, broth mix, cornstarch, egg whites*, and coconut.

In each recipe we have figured the Additional Calories for you. They appear at the end of each list of Food Family servings where applicable.

*For our purposes, 3 egg whites count as 1 Protein Serving. If we use less than 3 egg whites, we count them under Additional Calories.

How to Use the Nutritional Information Found in This Book

After each recipe you will find a box that contains the nutritional information for that particular recipe. For example:

Each serving provides:

200 Calories

2	Protein Servings	7 g	Protein
1	Vegetable Serving	4 g	Fat (18% of calories)
4	Additional Calories	24 g	Carbohydrate
		46 mg	Sodium
		3 mg	Cholesterol
		1 g	Fiber

If you are following a weight reduction organization diet, you can tell at a glance how many servings from each Food Family are contained in one portion. In this example, each serving contains 2 servings from the Protein Family, 1 serving from the Vegetable Family, and 4 calories from the Additional Calorie Family.

The information in the box also tells you that each serving contains 200 calories, 7 grams of protein, 4 grams of fat, 24 grams of carbohydrate, 46 milligrams of sodium, 3 milligrams of cholesterol, and 1 gram of fiber. In this particular recipe, 18 percent of the calories come from fat.

When there is a choice between two ingredients, such as "salt-free or regular tomato sauce," the analysis is based on the first one mentioned. It is important to note that the nutritional analysis may vary slightly depending on the brand of food that is used. If a recipe contains a "trace" of a particular item (less than 1/2 gram of protein, fat, or carbohydrate, or less than 1/2 milligram of sodium or cholesterol) the number will be listed as 0 or as "trace."

It is our hope that you will use this information to select recipes and balance your diet in a delicious and healthful way.

LEAN AND LUSCIOUS
FAVORITES

Appetizers, Dips, and Spreads

The selections in this chapter can be used as party foods, meal-starters, or delicious snacks. They will whet your appetite or simply offer some easy nibbles to keep on hand when the "munchies" attack.

We've kept the fat content as low as possible by using only lowfat and nonfat dairy products. Since dairy products contain no fiber, we recommend using fresh fruits and vegetables as "dippers" and whole grain, lowfat crackers or breads for spreads. Most packaged chips, often used for dipping, are usually fried and very high in fat, so try some of our delicious, homemade chips, also found in this chapter.

Many salads and fruits make ideal appetizers, so be sure to check other chapters.

Crab-Stuffed Mushrooms

This elegant dish makes a great appetizer, as well as an entrée. If you like, add 2 tablespoons of finely minced green pepper along with the onions.

Makes 12 servings (2 mushrooms each serving)

24	large mushrooms
1	tablespoon vegetable oil
2	tablespoons finely chopped onion
12	ounces crab meat
1	tablespoon Dijon mustard
1/8	teaspoon pepper
2	tablespoons lemon juice
2	teaspoons Worcestershire sauce
1	tablespoon dry sherry
1/4	cup skim milk

Topping
2	tablespoons plus 2 teaspoons reduced-calorie mayonnaise
2	tablespoons skim milk

Preheat oven to 450 degrees F.

Spray a shallow baking pan with nonstick cooking spray.

Carefully wash mushrooms and remove stems. Slice stems into thin slices.

Heat oil in a medium nonstick saucepan over medium heat. Add sliced stems along with onion. Cook, stirring frequently, until onion is tender, about 8 minutes. Remove from heat and stir in remaining in- gredients (except topping ingredients).

Pile mixture evenly into mushroom caps.

Combine topping ingredients in a small bowl or custard cup. Mix well. Spoon evenly over crab filling.

Place mushrooms in prepared pan.

Bake 15 minutes, until mushrooms are hot and lightly browned.

Each serving provides:

72 Calories

1/2	Protein Serving	7 g	Protein
1	Vegetable Serving	3 g	Fat (40% of calories)
1/2	Fat Serving	3 g	Carbohydrate
7	Additional Calories	143 mg	Sodium
		30 mg	Cholesterol
		0 g	Fiber

Marinated Mozzarella

Serve with toothpicks as an hors d'oeuvre, or as a salad on a bed of lettuce. The flavor improves with age.

Makes 16 servings

8	ounces reduced-fat mozzarella cheese, cut into 1/2-inch cubes
2	tablespoons plus 2 teaspoons vegetable oil
1/2	cup chopped green bell pepper
3	tablespoons red wine vinegar
1/2	cup water
2	teaspoons dried oregano
1/2	teaspoon dried basil
1/4	teaspoon dried thyme
1/8	teaspoon garlic powder
1/2	teaspoon sugar

Place cheese cubes in a clean 1-quart jar.

Combine remaining ingredients in a small saucepan. Bring to a boil over medium heat. Remove from heat and let cool 10 minutes.

Pour liquid over cheese into jar.

Refrigerate 1 to 2 weeks.

Each serving provides:

52 Calories

1/2	Protein Serving	4 g	Protein
1/2	Fat Serving	4 g	Fat (68% of calories)
11	Additional Calories	1 g	Carbohydrate
		74 mg	Sodium
		5 mg	Cholesterol
		0 g	Fiber

Clams Casino

Entertaining is so elegant with this delectable appetizer. If you can get some real clam shells and scrub them well, you can serve this special dish right in the shells. A variety of ceramic shells is also available in specialty shops.

Makes 8 servings

3	10-ounce cans minced clams, drained (This will yield about 16 ounces of clams.) (Reserve 1/2 cup of the clam juice.)
1/2	cup reserved clam juice
3/4	cup dry bread crumbs
2	tablespoons minced onion flakes
2	teaspoons dried parsley flakes
1/2	teaspoon dried oregano
1/4	teaspoon garlic powder
1/4	teaspoon salt
1	tablespoon plus 1 teaspoon grated Parmesan cheese
	Lemon wedges

Preheat oven to 375 degrees F.

Spray 8 clam shells (real or ceramic) with nonstick cooking spray.

In a medium bowl, combine all ingredients, except Parmesan cheese and lemon wedges. Mix well.

Divide mixture evenly and spoon into prepared shells. Sprinkle with Parmesan cheese.

Place shells on a baking sheet.

Bake 25 minutes, until hot and bubbly.

Serve with lemon wedges.

Each serving provides:

134 Calories

1	Protein Serving	16 g	Protein
1/2	Bread Serving	2 g	Fat (16% of calories)
6	Additional Calories	11 g	Carbohydrate
		266 mg	Sodium
		39 mg	Cholesterol
		0 g	Fiber

Tomato Party Puffs

Harry suggested this appetizer and we just love it. We've also made it using a few asparagus tips in place of each tomato slice. Yum.

Makes 4 servings (4 pieces each serving)

16   slices party rye bread (1/4-ounce slices)
4   small tomatoes, sliced 1/4 inch thick (Or, cut 2 large tomatoes into quarters, then slice. The idea is to end up with tomato slices about the same size as the bread.)
2   egg whites
1/4   teaspoon cream of tartar
2   tablespoons grated Parmesan cheese

Preheat oven to 400 degrees F.

Place bread slices on a large, ungreased baking sheet. Place a slice of tomato on each piece of bread.

Place egg whites in a medium bowl. Beat on medium speed of an electric mixer until frothy. Add cream of tartar. Beat on high speed until egg whites are stiff. Fold in Parmesan cheese gently, but thoroughly.

Place a heaping tablespoonful of egg white mixture on top of each tomato. Using a table knife, spread mixture, covering tomato and top edges of bread.

Bake 10 minutes, until nicely browned.

Serve hot.

Each serving provides:
115 Calories

1	Bread Serving	6 g	Protein
1/2	Vegetable Serving	2 g	Fat (15% of calories)
25	Additional Calories	19 g	Carbohydrate
		270 mg	Sodium
		2 mg	Cholesterol
		3 g	Fiber

Salmon Pâté

This elegant spread is delicious on crackers or on cucumber slices. For a pretty presentation, chill the pâté in a bowl that is lined with plastic wrap, then invert it onto a serving plate and peel off the plastic.

Makes 8 servings (2 tablespoons each serving)

8	ounces canned salmon, drained
2	teaspoons lemon juice
1	teaspoon dill weed
$1/2$	teaspoon dried tarragon
$1/2$	teaspoon onion powder
$1/4$	teaspoon garlic powder
$1/8$	teaspoon pepper

Combine all ingredients in a food processor. With a steel blade, process until smooth. Spoon into a bowl.

Chill several hours or overnight.

Each serving provides:

42 Calories

1	Protein Serving	
	6 g	Protein
	2 g	Fat (35% of calories)
	0 g	Carbohydrate
	139 mg	Sodium
	11 mg	Cholesterol
	0 g	Fiber

Tuna Mousse

This elegant mousse can also be made with salmon. It makes a beautiful, and very tasty, appetizer that is an ideal party centerpiece. We've also served it with crusty bread as a light lunch dish.

Makes 12 servings (2¹/₂ tablespoons each serving)

1	envelope unflavored gelatin
¹/₂	cup water
1	8-ounce can salt-free (or regular) tomato sauce
1	6¹/₂-ounce can tuna (packed in water), drained
²/₃	cup lowfat (1%) cottage cheese
2	tablespoons reduced-calorie mayonnaise
1	tablespoon sugar
¹/₄	teaspoon pepper
¹/₈	teaspoon salt
¹/₂	cup finely chopped celery
2	tablespoons finely chopped onion

Sprinkle gelatin over water in a small bowl and let soften a few minutes.

In a small saucepan, over medium heat, heat tomato sauce to boiling. Reduce heat to low and stir in gelatin mixture. Heat, stirring, for 1 minute.

In a blender container, combine tuna, cottage cheese, mayonnaise, sugar, pepper, and salt. Add tomato sauce mixture. Blend until smooth.

Stir in celery and onion.

Pour mixture into a 3-cup mold.

Chill until firm.

Unmold to serve.

Each serving provides:

48 Calories

¹/₃	Protein Serving	6 g	Protein
¹/₂	Vegetable Serving	1 g	Fat (18% of calories)
¹/₄	Fat Serving	3 g	Carbohydrate
4	Additional Calories	146 mg	Sodium
		7 mg	Cholesterol
		0 g	Fiber

Dilly Dip

This is a great dip to keep on hand for dipping veggies, or try it as a salad dressing or a baked potato topper.

Makes 8 servings (2 tablespoons each serving)

1	cup plain nonfat yogurt
1	tablespoon minced onion flakes
1	teaspoon dill weed
$1/8$	teaspoon celery seed
1	teaspoon dried chives

In a small bowl, combine all ingredients, mixing well. Chill several hours or overnight to blend flavors.

Each serving provides:

18 Calories

15	Additional Calories	2 g	Protein
		0 g	Fat (3% of calories)
		3 g	Carbohydrate
		22 mg	Sodium
		1 mg	Cholesterol
		0 g	Fiber

Dijon Dip

Mustard lovers, here it is! This unusual dip doubles as a spread for chicken or fish sandwiches.

Makes 12 servings (2 tablespoons each serving)

1/2	cup reduced-calorie mayonnaise
1/2	cup part-skim ricotta cheese
1/3	cup Dijon mustard
1	teaspoon dill weed
1/8	teaspoon garlic powder

In a small bowl, combine all ingredients, mixing well. Chill to blend flavors.

Each serving provides:

48 Calories

1	Fat Serving	1 g	Protein
10	Additional Calories	4 g	Fat (76% of calories)
		1 g	Carbohydrate
		225 mg	Sodium
		6 mg	Cholesterol
		0 g	Fiber

Party Clam Dip

A favorite party dish goes lowfat and no one will ever guess! Garnished with chopped chives, either fresh or dried, and served with vegetables or melba toast rounds, this makes a wonderful party dish.

Makes 12 servings (2 1/2 tablespoons each serving)

1 1/2	cups plain nonfat yogurt*
1	10 1/2-ounce can minced clams, drained (This will yield about 6 ounces of clams.)
1 1/2	tablespoons minced onion flakes
1 1/2	teaspoons Worcestershire sauce
1/4	teaspoon salt
1/4	teaspoon pepper
1/8	teaspoon garlic powder

In a small bowl, combine all ingredients. Mix well.
Chill several hours to blend flavors.
Serve with vegetable dippers.

*If desired, you can substitute nonfat sour cream for the yogurt.

Each serving provides:

39 Calories

1/4	Protein Serving	5 g	Protein
1/4	Milk Serving	trace	Fat (8% of calories)
4	Additional Calories	3 g	Carbohydrate
		89 mg	Sodium
		10 mg	Cholesterol
		0 g	Fiber

Hot Pizza Dip

This delicious dip is served hot and tastes just like the real thing!

Makes 8 servings (about 1/4 cup each serving)

Filling
1	cup part-skim ricotta cheese
1	cup shredded part-skim mozzarella cheese (4 ounces)
1/2	teaspoon dried oregano
1/4	teaspoon dried basil
1/2	teaspoon garlic powder

Topping
1/2	cup salt-free (or regular) tomato sauce
1/4	teaspoon dried oregano
1/4	teaspoon dried basil
3	tablespoons finely chopped onion
3	tablespoons finely chopped green pepper

Preheat oven to 375 degrees F.

Have a 9-inch pie pan ready.

Prepare filling:

In a medium bowl, combine ricotta cheese, mozzarella cheese, and spices. Mix well. Spread mixture evenly in pie pan, smoothing the top with the back of a spoon.

Prepare topping:

In a small bowl, combine tomato sauce, oregano, and basil. Mix well. Spread evenly over cheese. Sprinkle onions and green pepper evenly over sauce.

Bake, uncovered, 25 minutes.

Serve hot as a dip or spread for crackers, pita bread, bagels, or French bread.

Each serving provides:

86 Calories

1/2	Protein Serving	7 g	Protein
		5 g	Fat (50% of calories)
		4 g	Carbohydrate
		108 mg	Sodium
		18 mg	Cholesterol
		0 g	Fiber

Cottage Cheese and Olive Dip

This recipe is an adaptation of one that has been in the family for three generations. We love it with raw veggies, especially celery sticks.

Makes 6 servings (3 tablespoons each serving)

1	cup lowfat (1%) cottage cheese
2	tablespoons reduced-calorie mayonnaise
1	tablespoon horseradish mustard
1/2	teaspoon white vinegar
1	tablespoon minced onion flakes
6	small pitted black olives, finely chopped
6	small stuffed green olives, finely chopped
1/8	teaspoon pepper
	Salt

In a blender container, combine cottage cheese, mayonnaise, mustard, and vinegar. Blend until smooth. Spoon mixture into a small bowl and add remaining ingredients. Mix well.

Chill to blend flavors.

Each serving provides:

52 Calories

1/2	Protein Serving	5 g	Protein
1/2	Fat Serving	2 g	Fat (42% of calories)
8	Additional Calories	3 g	Carbohydrate
		303 mg	Sodium
		3 mg	Cholesterol
		0 g	Fiber

Mexican Pinto Spread

This spicy spread is not only delicious on crackers, but it also makes a wonderful sandwich. Either way, its flavor is enhanced by the addition of fresh, sliced tomatoes.

Makes 8 servings (3 tablespoons each serving)

1/4	cup chopped onion
2	cloves garlic, coarsely chopped
1	16-ounce can pinto beans, rinsed and drained (This will yield approximately 9 ounces of cooked beans.)
1	teaspoon vinegar
1	teaspoon chili powder
1/2	teaspoon ground cumin
1/2	teaspoon dried oregano

Place onion and garlic in a food processor. Process with a steel blade until finely chopped. Add beans, vinegar, and spices. Process until smooth. (A blender can be used, but you will need to blend the mixture in small batches and be careful not to let the mixture get soupy.)

Spoon mixture into a bowl and chill thoroughly.

Each serving provides:

36 Calories

1/2	Protein Serving	2 g	Protein
4	Additional Calories	trace	Fat (8% of calories)
		6 g	Carbohydrate
		95 mg	Sodium
		0 mg	Cholesterol
		2 g	Fiber

French Herbed Cheese Spread

If you love expensive, imported herbed cheese spreads, this one's for you. It's a hit every time.

Makes 6 servings (2 tablespoons each serving)

3/4   cup part-skim ricotta cheese
1   tablespoon dried parsley
2   tablespoons dried chives
2   teaspoons grated Parmesan cheese
1/4   teaspoon dried basil
1/4   teaspoon dried marjoram
1/8   teaspoon garlic powder
       Pepper

In a small bowl, combine all ingredients, mixing well.
Chill several hours or overnight to blend flavors.
Spread on crackers or bread.

Each serving provides:

46 Calories

1/2	Protein Serving	4 g	Protein
3	Additional Calories	3 g	Fat (51% of calories)
		2 g	Carbohydrate
		49 mg	Sodium
		10 mg	Cholesterol
		0 g	Fiber

Tortilla Chips

These crispy, crunchy chips are a quick and easy snack that the kids will love to help you make.

Makes 4 servings (6 chips each serving)

4   corn tortillas
       Nonstick cooking spray
       Garlic powder
       Ground cumin
       Salt

Preheat oven to 300 degrees F.

Spray a baking sheet with nonstick cooking spray.

Cut each tortilla into 6 pie-shaped wedges. (Kitchen shears do a great job.) Place wedges in a single layer on prepared sheet. Spray chips lightly with nonstick spray. Sprinkle evenly with spices.

Bake 12 to 15 minutes, until crisp.

Remove chips to a rack to cool. Store in an airtight container.

Each serving provides:

63 Calories

1	Bread Serving		
		1 g	Protein
		2 g	Fat (22% of calories)
		12 g	Carbohydrate
		40 mg	Sodium
		0 mg	Cholesterol
		1 g	Fiber

Bagel Crackers

These crispy crackers are best when made with large, bakery-style bagels.
For variations, try different flavored bagels, such as onion, garlic, or sesame.
For a delicious snack, enjoy them plain or spread lightly with fat-free cream
cheese or jam.

Makes 4 servings (6 crackers each serving)

1   4-ounce bagel

Preheat oven to 300 degrees F.
Spray a baking sheet with nonstick cooking spray.
Cut bagel in half lengthwise then cut each half into 4 quarters. Slice
each quarter lengthwise into 3 slices.
Place slices on prepared baking sheet.
Bake 25 minutes, or until crisp. Remove to a rack to cool.
Store in an airtight container.

Each serving provides:

80 Calories

1	Bread Serving	
	3 g	Protein
	1 g	Fat (8% of calories)
	15 g	Carbohydrate
	151 mg	Sodium
	0 mg	Cholesterol
	1 g	Fiber

Cinnamon Bread Sticks

These crispy snacks are so easy to make. Why not make a lot of them, so they'll be handy to munch. They can be used as a dipper for fruit-flavored yogurt or, if you omit the sugar and cinnamon and use garlic powder instead, they can be served alongside any savory dip.

Makes 4 servings (6 sticks each serving)

4	slices thin-sliced whole wheat bread (1/2-ounce slices)
2	teaspoons reduced-calorie margarine
1	teaspoon sugar
1/4	teaspoon ground cinnamon

Preheat oven to 300 degrees F.

Spray a baking sheet with nonstick cooking spray.

Spread margarine on one side of each bread slice, using 1/2 teaspoon for each slice.

Combine sugar and cinnamon and sprinkle evenly on bread.

Cut each slice into 6 even strips. Place strips on prepared baking sheet.

Bake 18 minutes, until crisp.

Remove strips to a rack to cool. Store in an airtight container.

Each serving provides:

50 Calories

1/2	Bread Serving	1 g	Protein
1/4	Fat Serving	2 g	Fat (30% of calories)
4	Additional Calories	8 g	Carbohydrate
		97 mg	Sodium
		0 mg	Cholesterol
		1 g	Fiber

Potato Chips

What fun! You can make your own baked potato chips!

Makes 4 servings

1   5-ounce baking potato, unpeeled
       Salt

Preheat oven to 350 degrees F.

Spray a baking sheet with nonstick cooking spray.

Using a food processor, vegetable peeler, or grater/slicer, slice potato into very thin, uniform slices.

Place slices in a single layer on prepared baking sheet. Spray slices lightly with cooking spray. Sprinkle lightly with salt.

Bake 12 to 14 minutes, until lightly browned. Remove slices to a rack to cool. (Baking time may vary according to thickness of potato slices. Potatoes need to be light brown all over, or they will be soggy when cooled.)

Enjoy right away or store in an airtight container.

Each serving provides:

30 Calories

1/4	Bread Serving	
	1 g	Protein
	1 g	Fat (15% of calories)
	6 g	Carbohydrate
	2 mg	Sodium
	0 mg	Cholesterol
	1 g	Fiber

Cinnamon Popcorn

Popcorn makes a great appetizer or snack. It's low in calories and high in protein and fiber. Unfortunately, most of the popcorn available in the grocery store (even the type for microwaves) has fat added. This nutritious popcorn is made with a hot air popper, with cinnamon added for an unusual flavor.

Makes 4 servings (1 cup each serving)

2   teaspoons sugar
1/2   teaspoon ground cinnamon
4   cups freshly popped popcorn (Use a hot air popper.)
      Nonstick cooking spray

Combine sugar and cinnamon in a small bowl or custard cup, mixing well.

Spread popcorn on a baking sheet. Spray lightly with cooking spray. Sprinkle with cinnamon and sugar.

Enjoy!

Each serving provides:

43 Calories

1/4	Bread Serving	1 g	Protein
15	Additional Calories	1 g	Fat (16% of calories)
		9 g	Carbohydrate
		0 mg	Sodium
		0 mg	Cholesterol
		1 g	Fiber

Soups

Nothing can equal the flavor and warmth of a steamy bowl of home-made soup. It can really warm your bones and cheer your feelings.

Most soups are made from stock, or broth, with several choices available. If you prefer to make a homemade stock by simmering chicken and/or vegetables in water along with herbs, it is important to chill the stock before using it in a soup so that the fat can be easily skimmed off the top. If you prefer to use canned broth, choose a low-sodium variety. Remember, you can always add salt if needed. Pack-ets of low-sodium instant broth mix can also be used, and added to the soup with the specified amount of water.

As a meal starter, or as the entrée itself, these soups will prove to be delicious and satisfying—without a lot of calories, fat, or fuss.

Creamy Carrot Soup

This unusual soup is light and creamy and tastes exquisite.

Makes 6 servings (1 cup each serving)

2	teaspoons vegetable oil
1	cup chopped onion
3	cups chopped carrots
4	cups low-sodium chicken or vegetable broth (or 4 cups water and 4 packets low-sodium instant chicken or vegetable broth mix)
2	teaspoons tomato paste
1/2	cup brown rice, uncooked (4 ounces)
1 1/2	cups evaporated skim milk
	Salt and pepper

Heat oil in a large saucepan over medium heat. Add onion and cook, stirring frequently, 5 minutes or until tender. Add small amounts of water if necessary (a few teaspoons at a time), to prevent sticking.

Add carrots, water, broth mix, tomato paste, and rice. When mixture boils, reduce heat to medium-low, cover, and simmer 40 minutes, until rice and carrots are tender.

Place soup in a blender container, reserving about 1/2 cup of the carrots and rice. Blend until smooth. Return soup to saucepan and add reserved vegetables.

Stir in milk. Heat through, but do not boil.

Add salt and pepper to taste.

Each serving provides:

188 Calories

1/2	Bread Serving	9 g	Protein
1 1/2	Vegetable Servings	3 g	Fat (16% of calories)
1/4	Fat Serving	31 g	Carbohydrate
1/2	Milk Serving	179 mg	Sodium
23	Additional Calories	5 mg	Cholesterol
		3 g	Fiber

French Onion Soup

Instead of being covered with "gobs" of cheese, this version proves to be tasty with only a sprinkling of Parmesan. It's light, simple, and very elegant. Vive la France!

Makes 4 servings (1 cup per serving)

2	teaspoons vegetable oil
2	cups thinly sliced onion
4	cups low-sodium beef broth (or 4 cups water and 4 packets low-sodium instant beef broth mix)
1/4	cup dry red wine
1	bay leaf
	Salt and pepper
2	tablespoons grated Parmesan cheese

Heat oil in a medium saucepan over medium heat. Add onion. Cook, stirring frequently, until onions are golden, separating slices into rings. Add small amounts of water if necessary (a few teaspoons at a time), to keep onions from sticking. (A nonstick saucepan is ideal for making this soup.)

Add broth, wine, and bay leaf. Bring soup to a boil. Reduce heat to medium-low, cover, and simmer 20 minutes, stirring occasionally. Add salt and pepper to taste.

Remove and discard bay leaf.

Spoon soup into serving bowls and sprinkle each serving with Parmesan cheese, using 1 1/2 teaspoons for each serving.

Each serving provides:

90 Calories

1	Vegetable Serving	5 g	Protein
1/2	Fat Serving	3 g	Fat (34% of calories)
48	Additional Calories	9 g	Carbohydrate
		678 mg	Sodium
		2 mg	Cholesterol
		1 g	Fiber

Split Pea Soup

Hot, hearty, and full of protein, this soup is perfect on a cold winter's night. Add a salad and a slice of crusty whole grain bread and your meal is complete.

Makes 6 servings (1 cup each serving)

2	teaspoons vegetable oil
1	cup chopped onion
1/2	cup chopped celery
1/2	cup chopped carrots
2	cloves garlic, crushed
1	cup split peas, uncooked (6 ounces)
6	cups water
1/2	teaspoon dried thyme
1	bay leaf
	Salt and pepper

Heat oil in a large saucepan over medium heat. Add onion, celery, carrots, and garlic. Cook, stirring frequently, until vegetables are tender, about 8 minutes.

Add split peas, water, thyme, and bay leaf.

When mixture boils, reduce heat to medium-low, cover, and simmer 1 1/2 to 2 hours, until peas are very soft. Stir occasionally while cooking.

Add salt and pepper to taste.

Each serving provides:

128 Calories

1 1/4	Protein Servings	7 g	Protein
3/4	Vegetable Serving	2 g	Fat (13% of calories)
1/4	Fat Serving	21 g	Carbohydrate
10	Additional Calories	17 mg	Sodium
		0 mg	Cholesterol
		2 g	Fiber

Old World Cabbage Soup

This delectable soup tastes just like Mom's, but takes half the time to prepare.
It tastes best when reheated, so we always plan to make it a day ahead.

Makes 8 servings (1¼ cups each serving)

2   16-ounce cans salt-free (or regular) tomatoes, chopped and
       undrained
4   cups thinly shredded cabbage
1/2   cup finely chopped onion
1/3   cup lemon juice
1   cup low-sodium chicken or vegetable broth (or 1 cup of
       water and 1 packet low-sodium instant chicken or vegetable
       broth mix)
2   teaspoons sugar
       Salt and pepper

   Combine all ingredients in a large saucepan. Bring to a boil over
medium heat. Reduce heat to medium-low, cover, and simmer 40
minutes, or until cabbage is tender.
   Add additional lemon juice or sugar to taste.

Each serving provides:

44 Calories

2	Vegetable Servings	2 g	Protein
7	Additional Calories	trace	Fat (7% of calories)
		9 g	Carbohydrate
		93 mg	Sodium
		0 mg	Cholesterol
		2 g	Fiber

Leftover Bean Soup

This soup provides an excellent use for leftover beans, or, for a quick, nutritious meal, just open a can of beans and you're halfway there. Even a mixture of different types of beans will work well.

Makes 4 servings (1 cup each serving)

1	19-ounce can kidney, pinto, or Great Northern beans, rinsed and drained (This will yield approximately 12 ounces of beans.)
2	cups evaporated skim milk
$1/2$	teaspoon dried basil
$1/8$	teaspoon garlic powder
$1/8$	teaspoon dried thyme
	Salt and pepper

In a blender container, combine all ingredients, except salt and pepper. Blend until smooth.

Pour mixture into a small saucepan. Heat, stirring frequently, until soup is hot, but do not boil. Add water if desired, for a thinner consistency.

Add salt and pepper to taste.

Each serving provides:

200 Calories

$1^1/2$	Protein Servings	17 g	Protein
1	Milk Serving	1 g	Fat (5% of calories)
		31 g	Carbohydrate
		323 mg	Sodium
		5 mg	Cholesterol
		6 g	Fiber

Creamy Potato Soup

Served hot on a chilly day, or served cold on a hot day, this versatile soup is a real taste treat. It has a thick, creamy texture that tastes a lot like real cream.

Makes 4 servings (1 cup each serving)

2	cups evaporated skim milk
1	pound cooked potatoes, peeled, and diced (You can either bake, boil, or microwave the potatoes.)
2	tablespoons minced onion flakes
2	packets low-sodium instant chicken or vegetable broth mix
1/4	teaspoon celery salt
2	teaspoons margarine
	Freshly ground black pepper
1	teaspoon dried chives

In a medium saucepan, combine milk, potatoes, onion flakes, broth mix, and celery salt. Cook on low heat, stirring frequently, until mixture is hot. Do not boil.

Remove soup from heat and stir in margarine.

Spoon into serving bowls and sprinkle with pepper and dried chives.

Each serving provides:

220 Calories

1	Bread Serving	12 g	Protein
1/2	Fat Serving	2 g	Fat (9% of calories)
1	Milk Serving	39 g	Carbohydrate
5	Additional Calories	216 mg	Sodium
		5 mg	Cholesterol
		2 g	Fiber

Spiced Tomato Soup

Make lots of this delicately spiced soup in the summer when fresh tomatoes are plentiful. Freeze it and you can enjoy it all year long.

Makes 6 servings (1 cup each serving)

8	cups chopped, peeled tomatoes
1/2	cup chopped onion
1	heaping tablespoon mixed pickling spices
1	tablespoon sugar
3	tablespoons all-purpose flour
1	tablespoon soft, tub-style (not diet) margarine
	Salt and pepper

In a blender container, combine tomatoes and onion. Blend until smooth. Pour through a strainer into a medium saucepan.

Place pickling spices in a tea strainer or tie into a piece of cheese-cloth, making a little "package." Add to saucepan, along with sugar.

In a small bowl, stir flour into a small amount of soup mixture until blended. Add to the soup, along with margarine. Cook, uncovered, over low heat 30 minutes, stirring frequently.

Add salt and pepper to taste.

Remove and discard spices.

Each serving provides:

95 Calories

2³/4	Vegetable Servings	3 g	Protein
1/2	Fat Serving	3 g	Fat (24% of calories)
23	Additional Calories	17 g	Carbohydrate
		48 mg	Sodium
		0 mg	Cholesterol
		3 g	Fiber

Creamy Vegetable Chowder

This rich, flavorful soup is really a meal-in-one.

Makes 4 servings (1¼ cups each serving)

2	teaspoons vegetable oil
¼	cup chopped onion
¼	cup chopped green bell pepper
¼	cup chopped celery
¼	cup chopped carrots
2	cloves garlic, minced
1	16-ounce can salt-free (or regular) tomatoes, undrained
⅔	cup lowfat (1%) cottage cheese
½	cup water
½	teaspoon dried oregano
¼	teaspoon dried basil
⅛	teaspoon dried thyme
1	cup cooked brown rice
	Salt and pepper

Heat oil in a medium saucepan over medium heat. Add onion, bell pepper, celery, carrots, and garlic. Cook, stirring frequently, until vegetables are lightly browned. Add small amounts of water (a tablespoon or two at a time), if necessary, to prevent sticking.

In a blender container, combine tomatoes, cottage cheese, water, and spices. Blend until smooth. Add to vegetable mixture.

Stir in rice.

Reduce heat to medium-low. Cook, stirring, until heated through. Do not boil.

Add salt and pepper to taste.

Each serving provides:

137 Calories

½	Protein Serving	7 g	Protein	
½	Bread Serving	3 g	Fat (22% of calories)	
1½	Vegetable Servings	20 g	Carbohydrate	
1½	Fat Servings	181 mg	Sodium	
		2 mg	Cholesterol	
		2 g	Fiber	

Egg White Drop Soup

This is our low-cholesterol version of the Chinese favorite.

Makes 4 servings (1 cup each serving)

4   cups low-sodium chicken or vegetable broth (or 4 cups of
     water and 4 packets low-sodium instant chicken or vegetable
     broth mix)
3   egg whites
2   tablespoons thinly sliced green onion (green part only)

Place broth in a medium saucepan over medium heat. Bring
to a boil.

Place egg whites in a bowl and beat with a fork until slightly
frothy.

Gradually drizzle egg whites into boiling broth, stirring briskly in
a circular motion.

Spoon soup into individual bowls. Garnish with green onion.

Each serving provides:

44 Calories

1/4	Protein Serving	6 g	Protein
10	Additional Calories	1 g	Fat (31% of calories)
		2 g	Carbohydrate
		147 mg	Sodium
		4 mg	Cholesterol
		0 g	Fiber

Creamy Cauliflower Soup

The subtle blend of basil and tarragon gives this creamy soup a truly elegant flavor.

Makes 6 servings (1 cup each serving)

1	tablespoon vegetable oil
4	cups chopped cauliflower (^{1}/4- to ^{1}/2-inch pieces)
1	cup chopped onion
1	cup chopped celery
2^1/2	cups water
2	packets reduced-sodium instant chicken or vegetable broth mix
1	small bay leaf
^{1}/4	teaspoon salt
^{1}/8	teaspoon pepper
^{1}/8	teaspoon dried basil
^{1}/8	teaspoon dried tarragon
1^1/2	cups evaporated skim milk

Heat oil in a large saucepan over medium heat. Add cauliflower, onion, and celery. Cook 15 minutes, stirring frequently. Add small amounts of water, a little at a time, if necessary to keep vegetables from sticking. (This is in addition to the water called for.)

Add remaining ingredients, except milk. Bring mixture to a boil, cover, reduce heat to low, and simmer 20 minutes, or until vegetables are very tender. Remove and discard bay leaf.

Place about ^{2}/3 of the vegetables in a blender container. Blend until smooth, adding a little of the soup liquid if necessary. Return blended mixture to saucepan.

Add milk and heat through. (Do not boil.)

Each serving provides:

105 Calories

2	Vegetable Servings	7 g	Protein
^{1}/2	Fat Serving	3 g	Fat (21% of calories)
^{1}/2	Milk Serving	15 g	Carbohydrate
		478 mg	Sodium
		3 mg	Cholesterol
		2 g	Fiber

Millet Butternut Soup

As warm and soothing as a soup can be, this one combines the sweetness of butternut squash with a perfect blend of spices. Look for vegetable broth mix and millet in your favorite health food store.

Makes 8 servings (1 cup each serving)

2	teaspoons vegetable oil
3	cloves garlic, coarsely chopped
2	cups chopped onion
4	cups butternut squash, peeled, cut into $1/2$-inch cubes
5	cups water
4	packets reduced-sodium instant chicken or vegetable broth mix
$1/2$	teaspoon dried thyme
$1/4$	teaspoon dried tarragon
1	bay leaf
	Salt and pepper
$1/2$	cup millet, uncooked (3 ounces)

Heat oil in a large saucepan over medium heat. Add garlic and onion. Cook 5 minutes, stirring frequently. Add small amounts of water if necessary to prevent sticking.

Add remaining ingredients, except millet. Bring to a boil. Add millet, cover, reduce heat to low, and simmer 40 minutes, or until squash is tender.

Remove and discard bay leaf before serving.

Each serving provides:

107 Calories

$1 1/2$	Bread Servings	2 g	Protein
$1/2$	Vegetable Serving	2 g	Fat (14% of calories)
$1/4$	Fat Serving	21 g	Carbohydrate
		435 mg	Sodium
		0 mg	Cholesterol
		3 g	Fiber

Curried Lima Soup

Serve a salad and some whole grain crackers with this rich, high-protein soup for a complete and nutritious lunch.

Makes 4 servings (1 cup each serving)

1	10-ounce package frozen baby lima beans, thawed
2	cups water
2	packets reduced-sodium instant chicken or vegetable broth mix
2	teaspoons margarine
1	tablespoon minced onion flakes
1	teaspoon curry powder
1	bay leaf
1/2	cup evaporated skim milk
	Salt and pepper
1	tablespoon dried chives

In a medium saucepan, combine beans, water, broth mix, margarine, onion flakes, curry powder, and bay leaf. Bring to a boil over medium heat. Reduce heat to medium-low, cover, and simmer 20 minutes, or until beans are tender.

Remove and discard bay leaf.

Place soup in a blender container. Blend until smooth. Return soup to saucepan.

Stir in milk. Heat through, but do not boil.

Add salt and pepper to taste.

Spoon soup into individual serving bowls. Garnish with chives.

Each serving provides:

148 Calories

1	Bread Serving	8 g	Protein
1/2	Fat Serving	2 g	Fat (14% of calories)
1/4	Milk Serving	24 g	Carbohydrate
5	Additional Calories	526 mg	Sodium
		1 mg	Cholesterol
		4 g	Fiber

Gazpacho

Gazpacho is a spicy Spanish soup that is served cold. This cooling summer treat tastes best when made with fresh, vine-ripened tomatoes.

Makes 8 servings (3/4 cup each serving)

4	cups tomato juice
2	medium cucumbers, peeled and seeded
1/2	cup finely chopped onion
2	tablespoons red wine vinegar
2	teaspoons olive oil
1/4	teaspoon Worcestershire sauce
1	teaspoon dried basil
1	teaspoon dried parsley flakes
1/8	teaspoon garlic powder
1	cup finely chopped green bell pepper
1	cup finely chopped tomato
2	green onions, chopped (green and white parts)
	Salt and pepper
	Bottled hot sauce

In a blender container, combine tomato juice, cucumber, onion, vinegar, oil, Worcestershire, and spices. Blend until smooth.

Chill mixture several hours to blend flavors. Also chill chopped green pepper, tomato, and green onion.

Before serving, add salt, pepper, and hot sauce to taste.

Spoon cold soup into individual serving bowls. Sprinkle chilled, chopped green pepper, tomato, and green onion on top.

Each serving provides:

53 Calories

2 1/4	Vegetable Servings	2 g	Protein
1/4	Fat Serving	1 g	Fat (20% of calories)
		10 g	Carbohydrate
		449 mg	Sodium
		0 mg	Cholesterol
		2 g	Fiber

Convenience Vegetable Soup

This soup is aptly named because every ingredient comes from either a pack-age or a jar, so there's no chopping. Just dump everything in the pot and amaze your family and friends with a truly delectable soup.

Makes 10 servings (1½ cups each serving)

1	10-ounce package frozen cut green beans
1	10-ounce package frozen peas and carrots
1	10-ounce package frozen lima beans
1	10-ounce package frozen corn
1	10-ounce package frozen chopped spinach
2	16-ounce cans tomatoes
1	16-ounce can kidney beans, rinsed and drained (This will yield 10 ounces of beans.)
1	8-ounce can tomato sauce
1	tablespoon minced onion flakes
1	bay leaf
3/4	teaspoon dried thyme
2	teaspoons dried basil
1	teaspoon dried oregano
1/2	teaspoon garlic powder
5	cups water
1	cup (4½ ounces) orzo, or any type of very small pasta
	Salt and pepper

In a large soup pot, combine all ingredients, except pasta, salt, and pepper. Bring to a boil over medium heat, stirring occasionally. Use a spoon to break up large clumps of frozen vegetables and also to cut up the tomatoes. Cover, reduce heat to medium-low and simmer 45 minutes, or until vegetables are tender.

Add pasta, cover and cook 10 to 15 more minutes, until pasta is tender.

Add salt and pepper to taste.

Remove and discard bay leaf before serving.

Each serving provides:		
195 Calories		
1/2	Protein Serving	10 g	Protein
1 1/2	Bread Servings	1 g	Fat (6% of calories)
2 1/2	Vegetable Servings	39 g	Carbohydrate
8	Additional Calories	406 mg	Sodium
		0 mg	Cholesterol
		6 g	Fiber

Chicken Corn Soup

A take-off on a traditional Pennsylvania Dutch recipe, this thick, hearty soup provides a terrific use for leftover chicken.

Makes 4 servings (1 cup each serving)

1	16-ounce can cream-style corn
1¹/₂	cups water
1	packet low-sodium instant chicken or vegetable broth mix
1	cup cooked medium (yolk-free) noodles
4	ounces cooked chicken, cubed, skin discarded (1 cup)
	Salt and pepper

Combine all ingredients in a medium saucepan. Heat over medium-low heat, stirring frequently, until soup boils.

Each serving provides:

176 Calories

1	Protein Serving	12 g	Protein
1¹/₂	Bread Servings	3 g	Fat (13% of calories)
3	Additional Calories	29 g	Carbohydrate
		565 mg	Sodium
		25 mg	Cholesterol
		2 g	Fiber

Manhattan Clam Chowder

With its exquisite blend of flavors, you'll see why this thick, chunky chowder is so popular.

Makes 6 servings (1⅓ cups each serving)

2	teaspoons vegetable oil
1	cup sliced onion
1	cup diced carrots
1	cup diced celery
1	16-ounce can salt-free (or regular) tomatoes, chopped and drained (Reserve liquid.)
1	large cooked potato (12 ounces), diced (You can either bake, boil, or microwave the potato.)
4	whole black peppercorns
1	bay leaf
1	tablespoon dried parsley flakes
1½	teaspoons dried thyme
¼	teaspoon dried basil
1	10½-ounce can clams, drained (Reserve liquid.) (This will yield approximately 6 ounces of clams.)
	Salt

Heat oil in a saucepan over medium heat. Add onion, carrots, and celery. Cook 5 minutes, stirring frequently. Add small amounts of water as necessary (about a tablespoon at a time) to prevent sticking.

Add tomatoes, potato, and spices.

In a 1-quart bowl or jar, combine reserved tomato liquid and clam liquid. Add water to make 1 quart. Pour liquid over vegetables and bring to a boil. Cover, reduce heat to medium-low, and simmer 45 minutes.

Add clams. Simmer, covered, 15 minutes more.

Remove and discard bay leaf before serving. Add salt to taste.

Each serving provides:

139 Calories

½	Protein Serving	9 g	Protein
½	Bread Serving	2 g	Fat (15% of calories)
1¾	Vegetable Servings	21 g	Carbohydrate
¼	Fat Serving	67 mg	Sodium
3	Additional Calories	17 mg	Cholesterol
		3 g	Fiber

Sherried Mushroom Soup

If your supermarket has different varieties of fresh mushrooms, you can make an exotic-tasting soup. The splash of sherry at the end adds a wonderful, delicate flavor that really enhances this woodland vegetable.

Makes 6 servings (1 cup each serving)

2	teaspoons vegetable oil
1	pound fresh mushrooms, sliced
2	cups thinly sliced carrots
1/2	cup chopped onion
5	cups low-sodium chicken or vegetable broth (or 5 cups of water and 5 packets low-sodium instant chicken or vegetable broth mix)
1/2	teaspoon dried thyme
1/8	teaspoon pepper
2	tablespoons dry sherry
	Salt

Heat oil in a large saucepan over medium heat. Add mushrooms, carrots, and onion. Cook, stirring frequently, 5 minutes. Add small amounts of water if necessary (about a tablespoon at a time), to prevent sticking.

Add broth, thyme, and pepper. When mixture boils, reduce heat to medium-low, cover, and simmer 45 minutes, or until vegetables are tender.

Remove from heat and stir in sherry and salt to taste.

Each serving provides:

77 Calories

1 1/2	Vegetable Servings	4 g	Protein
1/4	Fat Serving	2 g	Fat (26% of calories)
21	Additional Calories	9 g	Carbohydrate
		483 mg	Sodium
		0 mg	Cholesterol
		2 g	Fiber

Salads and Salad Dressings

Salads are so versatile. A salad can be an appetizer, side dish, snack, main course, or even dessert. Made with fruits and vegetables, salads are valuable sources of vitamins, minerals, and fiber.

To reduce the amount of fat in salad dressings, we recommend using nonfat yogurt in place of sour cream and replacing part of the oil with fruit juice or water. The oils that we use in our recipes are monounsaturated oils such as canola oil or olive oil. When mayonnaise is used, we specify reduced-calorie mayonnaise, which has been whipped with water to reduce the fat and calories.

Remember that the word "salad" doesn't necessarily mean that a dish is automatically low in calories or fat. In fact, salads that are loaded with creamy, oily dressings can contain more fat and calories that a piece of cake or pie. It's important to practice portion control and not smother your salads with dressing.

Sesame, Broccoli, and Cauliflower Salad

The sesame oil gives this salad a wonderful flavor that will spark up any meal. Try this delicious oil in other salads, too, but go easy so the flavor will not be overpowering.

Makes 8 servings

1	10-ounce package frozen broccoli flowerets
1	10-ounce package frozen cauliflower
1	tablespoon plus 1 teaspoon reduced-sodium (or regular) soy sauce
1	tablespoon vegetable oil
2	teaspoons sesame oil
2	teaspoons red wine vinegar
1	tablespoon sesame seeds, lightly toasted
2	teaspoons sugar
	Salt and pepper

Cook vegetables according to package directions, until just crisp-tender. Drain.

In a small bowl, combine remaining ingredients. Drizzle over vegetables. Toss to coat evenly.

Chill several hours to blend flavors. Stir occasionally while chilling.

Each serving provides:

56 Calories

1	Vegetable Serving	2 g	Protein
1/2	Fat Serving	4 g	Fat (54% of calories)
15	Additional Calories	5 g	Carbohydrate
		122 mg	Sodium
		0 mg	Cholesterol
		2 g	Fiber

Mustard Potato Salad

The coarse, grainy mustard gives this old favorite a new and tangy twist.

Makes 4 servings

15	ounces red potatoes
1	tablespoon plus 1 teaspoon reduced-calorie mayonnaise
1	tablespoon red wine vinegar
2	teaspoons coarse, grainy mustard
2	teaspoons dried chives
2	teaspoons dried parsley
1/8	teaspoon pepper
	Salt

Place potatoes in two inches of boiling water in a medium saucepan. Cover and cook over medium heat 10 to 15 minutes, or until potatoes are tender. Do not let them get mushy.

Drain potatoes and let them sit until cool enough to handle. Cut potatoes into 1-inch chunks. Place in a large bowl.

In a small bowl, combine remaining ingredients, mixing well. Spoon over potatoes. Toss until well blended.

Chill.

Each serving provides:

103 Calories

3/4	Bread Serving	2 g	Protein
1/2	Fat Serving	2 g	Fat (14% of calories)
		20 g	Carbohydrate
		95 mg	Sodium
		2 mg	Cholesterol
		2 g	Fiber

Marinated Vegetable Salad

A colorful and tasty addition to any meal, this has become a family favorite in our house. If you like, eliminate 1 cup of the cauliflower and add 1 cup of broccoli in its place.

Makes 6 servings

2	cups cauliflower, cut into small flowerets
1	cup carrots, cut into 1/2-inch slices
1	cup celery, cut into 1-inch slices
1	medium, green bell pepper, cut into 1/2-inch strips
1	cup small mushrooms (or larger mushrooms cut into quarters)
1/2	cup chopped red onion
10	small stuffed green olives, cut in half crosswise
1/2	cup water
1/4	cup vinegar
2	tablespoons vegetable oil
2	tablespoons plus 2 teaspoons sugar
11/2	teaspoons dried oregano
3/4	teaspoon salt
1/2	teaspoon pepper
1/4	teaspoon garlic powder

Combine all ingredients in a large nonstick skillet. Bring to a boil over medium heat, stirring occasionally.

Reduce heat to medium-low, cover, and simmer 5 minutes, or until vegetables are barely tender-crisp.

Place salad in a bowl and chill overnight.

Each serving provides:

102 Calories

2 1/4	Vegetable Servings	2 g	Protein
1	Fat Serving	5 g	Fat (44% of calories)
28	Additional Calories	14 g	Carbohydrate
		419 mg	Sodium
		0 mg	Cholesterol
		2 g	Fiber

Confetti Pasta Salad

Pretty and colorful as well as tasty, this salad is a perfect addition to your next cookout.

Makes 4 servings

2	cups cooked elbow macaroni
1/2	cup thinly sliced celery
1/4	cup finely chopped green bell pepper
1/4	cup finely chopped carrots
2	tablespoons finely chopped onion
1	tablespoon chopped pimiento
1/4	cup reduced-calorie mayonnaise
1	teaspoon sugar
1/2	teaspoon dill weed
1/8	teaspoon dry mustard
	Salt and pepper

In a large bowl, combine macaroni, celery, bell pepper, carrots, onion, and pimiento.

In a small bowl, combine remaining ingredients, mixing well. Add to macaroni. Toss until well mixed.

Chill thoroughly.

Each serving provides:

153 Calories

1	Bread Serving	4 g	Protein
1/2	Vegetable Serving	5 g	Fat (27% of calories)
1 1/2	Fat Servings	24 g	Carbohydrate
4	Additional Calories	98 mg	Sodium
		5 mg	Cholesterol
		2 g	Fiber

Best Coleslaw

An old family standby for years, no backyard cookout is ever complete without it.

Makes 8 servings

1	medium cabbage, thinly shredded (4 cups)
1	medium carrot, grated
3	tablespoons sugar
1	teaspoon celery seed
1	teaspoon salt
1/2	cup reduced-calorie mayonnaise
3	tablespoons plain nonfat yogurt
2	tablespoons vinegar
	Freshly ground black pepper

Place cabbage and carrots in a large bowl. Sprinkle sugar, celery seed, and salt on top. Let stand for 5 minutes.

In a small bowl, combine mayonnaise, yogurt, and vinegar, mixing well. Spoon over cabbage. Toss to blend.

Add pepper to taste.

Chill several hours or overnight. Mix occasionally while chilling.

Each serving provides:

78 Calories

1 1/4	Vegetable Servings	1 g	Protein
1 1/2	Fat Servings	4 g	Fat (47% of calories)
21	Additional Calories	10 g	Carbohydrate
		372 mg	Sodium
		5 mg	Cholesterol
		1 g	Fiber

Gourmet Zucchini Salad

This salad is simple, yet tastes so elegant. It's at home with a family dinner or at a fancy dinner party.

Makes 4 servings

1¹/₂	cups zucchini, unpeeled, cut into ¹/₈-inch slices
¹/₂	cup thinly sliced celery
¹/₄	cup thinly sliced onion
¹/₄	cup thinly sliced green bell pepper
¹/₄	cup red wine vinegar
2	tablespoons sugar
1	tablespoon plus 1¹/₂ teaspoons vegetable oil
2	tablespoons water
¹/₂	teaspoon dried basil
¹/₄	teaspoon salt
¹/₈	teaspoon pepper

Combine vegetables in a shallow bowl.

Combine remaining ingredients in a small bowl, mixing well. Pour over vegetables.

Chill overnight to blend flavors. Stir several times while chilling.

Each serving provides:

87 Calories

1¹/₄	Vegetable Servings	1 g	Protein
1	Fat Serving	5 g	Fat (52% of calories)
29	Additional Calories	10 g	Carbohydrate
		150 mg	Sodium
		0 mg	Cholesterol
		1 g	Fiber

Dilled Carrots

These carrots will delight the pickle lovers in your family.

Makes 6 servings

1	pound carrots, cut into 4-inch julienne strips
1	cup vinegar
1	cup water
2	tablespoons sugar
2	teaspoons salt
1¹/₂	teaspoons dill seed
³/₄	teaspoon whole mustard seed
1	large clove garlic, cut in half lengthwise

Cook carrots, covered, in 1 inch of boiling water, 3 to 4 minutes, until just tender-crisp. Drain. Place carrots in a bowl or jar.

In a small saucepan, combine remaining ingredients. Bring to a boil over medium heat. Reduce heat to low and simmer 5 minutes. Pour mixture over carrots.

Cover and refrigerate for 5 to 7 days. Stir occasionally while chilling.

Each serving provides:

58 Calories

³/₄	Vegetable Serving	1 g	Protein
16	Additional Calories	trace	Fat (5% of calories)
		15 g	Carbohydrate
		761 mg	Sodium
		0 mg	Cholesterol
		2 g	Fiber

Szechuan Noodle Salad

This tangy, cold noodle salad is one of our tried and true favorite Asian specialties. We serve it as a side dish with dinner or with a tossed salad for a delicious and filling lunch.

Makes 4 servings

3	cups cooked thin noodles or spaghetti (We prefer the thin whole wheat noodles found in health food stores or specialty stores.)
1/4	cup thinly sliced green onions (green part only)
2	teaspoons toasted sesame seeds*
1/3	cup pineapple juice
2	tablespoons vinegar
2	tablespoons reduced-sodium (or regular) soy sauce
2	teaspoons sesame oil
2	teaspoons vegetable oil
1/8	teaspoon ground ginger
1/8	teaspoon pepper
1/8	teaspoon garlic powder
1	teaspoon sugar
	Few drops bottled hot pepper sauce (optional)

In a large bowl, combine noodles, green onions, and sesame seeds.

In a small bowl, combine remaining ingredients. Add to noodles, mixing well.

Chill several hours or overnight, stirring several times.

Stir before serving.

*To toast sesame seeds, place them in a single layer on a baking sheet or piece of aluminum foil in a 350-degree F oven. Cook until lightly toasted, about 5 minutes.

Each serving provides:

220 Calories

1 1/2	Bread Servings	6 g	Protein
1	Fat Serving	6 g	Fat (25% of calories)
1/4	Fruit Serving	35 g	Carbohydrate
14	Additional Calories	303 mg	Sodium
		0 mg	Cholesterol
		2 g	Fiber

Chunky Tomato Salad

For the best salad, we like to use fresh summer tomatoes that are ripe yet still fairly firm.

Makes 4 servings

2	cups fresh tomatoes, cut into $1/2$-inch chunks
1	cup sliced mushrooms
$1/4$	cup thinly sliced green onions (green part only)
1	tablespoon vegetable oil
1	tablespoon vinegar
1	tablespoon water
1	teaspoon dried basil
$1/2$	teaspoon sugar
$1/8$	teaspoon dried oregano
$1/8$	teaspoon garlic powder
	Salt and pepper

In a medium bowl, combine tomatoes, mushrooms, and green onions.

In a small bowl, combine remaining ingredients. Add to tomato mixture. Toss gently, until spices are evenly distributed.

Chill several hours or overnight.

Each serving provides:

57 Calories

$1^1/2$	Vegetable Servings	1 g	Protein
$3/4$	Fat Serving	4 g	Fat (54% of calories)
2	Additional Calories	6 g	Carbohydrate
		9 mg	Sodium
		0 mg	Cholesterol
		1 g	Fiber

Basil Bean Salad

Spicy and delicious, the flavor of this salad is reminiscent of the popular Italian pasta with pesto sauce.

Makes 4 servings

1	10-ounce package frozen cut green beans
1/2	cup very thinly sliced onion
3	tablespoons water
2	tablespoons red wine vinegar
1	tablespoon olive oil
1	tablespoon grated Parmesan cheese
1	teaspoon dried basil
1/8	teaspoon garlic powder
1/8	teaspoon pepper
	Salt

Cook beans according to package directions, cooking until just tender-crisp. Drain.

Combine beans and onions in a large bowl.

Combine remaining ingredients and pour over beans. Toss until well blended.

Chill several hours or overnight, stirring occasionally.

Each serving provides:

69 Calories

1 1/4	Vegetable Servings	2 g	Protein
3/4	Fat Serving	4 g	Fat (47% of calories)
8	Additional Calories	8 g	Carbohydrate
		26 mg	Sodium
		1 mg	Cholesterol
		2 g	Fiber

Mediterranean Bread Salad

This is our tangy, tasty answer to what to do with leftover bread. Served on a bed of lettuce, it's a truly economical side dish.

Makes 6 servings

3	cups leftover whole wheat or rye bread, cubed (6 ounces)
1¹/₂	cups chopped tomatoes, ¹/₂-inch pieces
1	cup chopped cucumber, ¹/₂-inch pieces (Peel cucumbers if they have been waxed and discard seeds if they are very large.)
¹/₂	cup chopped red onion
2	tablespoons vegetable oil
3	tablespoons lemon juice
3	tablespoons water
2	teaspoons dried parsley flakes
¹/₈	teaspoon salt
¹/₄	teaspoon pepper
¹/₄	teaspoon dried dill weed

Preheat oven to 350 degrees F.

Spread bread cubes on a baking sheet and bake until dry, about 10 minutes. Set aside to cool.

In a large bowl, combine remaining ingredients. Mix well. Add bread cubes. Toss until well mixed.

Chill several hours or overnight, mixing several times.

Stir before serving.

Each serving provides:

129 Calories

1	Bread Serving	3 g	Protein
1	Vegetable Serving	6 g	Fat (39% of calories)
1	Fat Serving	17 g	Carbohydrate
		203 mg	Sodium
		0 mg	Cholesterol
		3 g	Fiber

Pickled Onions

This old family favorite is slightly sweet, slightly tangy, and just plain deli-cious. It takes a while to prepare, but is definitely worth the effort.

Makes 16 servings

8	cups small white pickling onions, peeled
9	cups water
1/3	cup salt
2	cups white vinegar
2	tablespoons sugar
2	tablespoons horseradish
1¹/2	tablespoons whole allspice
1¹/2	tablespoons whole mustard seed
1¹/2	tablespoons whole peppercorns

Place peeled onions in a large bowl.

Bring 3 cups of the water to a boil. Dissolve salt in the water and pour over onions. Cover and let stand 24 hours. Drain.

Cover onions with 3 more cups of boiling water. Let stand 10 minutes. Drain.

Place onions in two 1-quart jars.

In a medium saucepan, combine remaining 3 cups of water with remaining ingredients. Bring to a boil over medium heat. Boil 3 minutes. With a slotted spoon, remove allspice and peppercorns.

Pour liquid over onions in jars. Cover and chill 1 to 2 weeks.

Each serving provides:

52 Calories

1	Vegetable Serving	1 g	Protein
6	Additional Calories	trace	Fat (6% of calories)
		12 g	Carbohydrate
		424 mg	Sodium
		0 mg	Cholesterol
		0 g	Fiber

Carrot and Orange Salad

This delicious combination of carrots and oranges has a lively tropical flavor that you're sure to love. Serve it on a bed of lettuce with a scoop of lowfat cottage cheese for a cool, light summer lunch.

Makes 4 servings

3	cups finely shredded carrots
2	small oranges, peeled and sectioned (Discard white membranes.)
1/4	cup raisins
1/2	cup nonfat vanilla yogurt
1	tablespoon honey
1/2	teaspoon vanilla extract
1/2	teaspoon coconut extract

In a large bowl, combine carrots, orange sections, and raisins.

In a small bowl, combine remaining ingredients, mixing well. Spoon over carrot mixture. Toss to combine.

Chill to blend flavors.

Each serving provides:

132 Calories

1 1/2	Vegetable Servings	3 g	Protein
1	Fruit Serving	trace	Fat (2% of calories)
1/4	Milk Serving	31 g	Carbohydrate
15	Additional Calories	50 mg	Sodium
		1 mg	Cholesterol
		4 g	Fiber

Caribbean Rice and Fruit Salad

This elegant lowfat rice salad is reminiscent of a tropical isle. Serve it as an appetizer, a dessert, or as a brand-new breakfast idea. It's a great way to use up that leftover rice.

Makes 4 servings

1	cup plain nonfat yogurt
3	tablespoons sugar
1	teaspoon vanilla extract
1/4	teaspoon coconut extract
1	cup cooked brown rice
1	medium ripe banana, sliced
1	small orange, peeled and sectioned (Discard white membranes.)
1/2	cup canned crushed pineapple, packed in juice, drained (Reserve juice.)
2	tablespoons reserved juice from pineapple

In a large bowl, combine yogurt, sugar, and extracts. Mix well.
Add remaining ingredients. Toss until well blended.
Chill.
Toss before serving.

Each serving provides:

184 Calories

1/2	Bread Serving	5 g	Protein
1	Fruit Serving	1 g	Fat (4% of calories)
1/4	Milk Serving	40 g	Carbohydrate
44	Additional Calories	46 mg	Sodium
		1 mg	Cholesterol
		2 g	Fiber

Cucumber and Onion Salad

This salad makes an excellent side dish for light summer meals and cook-outs. It's also a great addition to a tossed salad and even tastes delicious on sandwiches.

Makes 4 servings

1¹/₂	cups cucumber, peeled, sliced paper-thin
¹/₂	cup onion, sliced paper-thin
¹/₃	cup vinegar
¹/₃	cup water
¹/₃	cup sugar
¹/₄	teaspoon salt
	Dash pepper

Layer cucumber and onion in a jar or bowl. Combine remaining ingredients and pour over vegetables.

Chill overnight, stirring several times.

Each serving provides:

81 Calories

1	Vegetable Serving	1 g	Protein
64	Additional Calories	trace	Fat (1% of calories)
		21 g	Carbohydrate
		137 mg	Sodium
		0 mg	Cholesterol
		1 g	Fiber

Strawberry–Apple Mold

Quick, easy, and unusually tasty, this salad's flavor boost comes from the cinnamon.

Makes 4 servings (1/2 cup each serving)

1	package strawberry-flavored gelatin
1/4	teaspoon ground cinnamon
2	small apples, unpeeled, coarsely shredded

Prepare gelatin according to package directions. Stir in cinnamon.
Chill until slightly thickened. Stir in apples.
Pour mixture into a small bowl.
Chill until firm.

Each serving provides:

112 Calories

1/2	Fruit Serving	2 g	Protein
8	Additional Calories	trace	Fat (1% of calories)
		27 g	Carbohydrate
		54 mg	Sodium
		0 mg	Cholesterol
		1 g	Fiber

Orange, Pineapple, and Carrot Mold

This quick, easy salad can also double as a refreshing dessert.

Makes 4 servings (1/2 cup each serving)

1   package orange-flavored gelatin
1   cup coarsely shredded carrots
1   cup canned crushed pineapple, packed in juice, drained

Prepare gelatin according to package directions. Chill until slightly thickened.

Stir carrots and pineapple into gelatin. Pour into a small bowl or mold. Chill until firm.

Each serving provides:

57 Calories

1/2	Vegetable Serving	2 g	Protein
1/2	Fruit Serving	trace	Fat (8% of calories)
8	Additional Calories	13 g	Carbohydrate
		64 mg	Sodium
		0 mg	Cholesterol
		1 g	Fiber

Zesty Tomato Dressing

Zesty and delicious, tomato lovers will adore this one.

Makes 8 servings (2 tablespoons each serving)

1	8-ounce can salt-free (or regular) tomato sauce
2	tablespoons red wine vinegar
1	teaspoon Worcestershire sauce
$1/2$	teaspoon dill weed
$1/2$	teaspoon dried oregano
$1/2$	teaspoon dried basil
$1/2$	teaspoon onion powder
$1/8$	teaspoon pepper

Combine all ingredients in a small bowl or jar. Beat with a fork or wire whisk until smooth.

Chill to blend flavors.

Whisk before serving.

Each serving provides:

12 Calories

6	Additional Calories	0 g	Protein
		trace	Fat (8% of calories)
		3 g	Carbohydrate
		13 mg	Sodium
		0 mg	Cholesterol
		0 g	Fiber

French Honey Mustard

This versatile, tangy dressing is a great flavor-enhancer for sandwiches as well as salads.

Makes 6 servings (2 tablespoons each serving)

1/2   cup Dijon mustard
1/4   cup honey

Combine mustard and honey in a small bowl. Mix well. Chill several hours to blend flavors.

Each serving provides:

63 Calories

40	Additional Calories		
		0 g	Protein
		0 g	Fat
		12 g	Carbohydrate
		481 mg	Sodium
		0 mg	Cholesterol
		0 g	Fiber

Cheesy Thousand Island Dressing

Lowfat cottage cheese replaces mayonnaise in this creamy version of an all-time favorite dressing. It also makes a delicious spread for a sliced turkey and tomato sandwich.

Makes 12 servings (2 tablespoons each serving)

1	cup lowfat (1%) cottage cheese
1/4	cup ketchup
1	tablespoon vegetable oil
1	teaspoon paprika
1/4	teaspoon salt
1/8	teaspoon pepper
2	tablespoons finely minced celery
2	tablespoons finely minced green pepper
2	tablespoons finely minced onion
1	tablespoon sweet pickle relish

In a blender container, combine cottage cheese, ketchup, oil, paprika, salt, and pepper. Blend until smooth.

Stir in remaining ingredients.

Chill several hours to blend flavors.

Each serving provides:

33 Calories

1/4	Protein Serving	2 g	Protein
1/4	Fat Serving	1 g	Fat (37% of calories)
6	Additional Calories	3 g	Carbohydrate
		192 mg	Sodium
		1 mg	Cholesterol
		0 g	Fiber

Cranberry Vinaigrette

This quick dressing is mellow, smooth, and fruity. You can add a sprinkling of your favorite herbs if you like, or enjoy it as is.

Makes 8 servings (2 tablespoons each serving)

2/3   cup cranberry juice or cocktail
3   tablespoons vegetable oil
2   tablespoons red wine vinegar

Combine all ingredients in a small bowl or jar. Mix and chill. Stir before using.

Each serving provides:

58 Calories

1	Fat Serving	0 g	Protein
1/4	Fruit Serving	5 g	Fat (78% of calories)
5	Additional Calories	3 g	Carbohydrate
		1 mg	Sodium
		0 mg	Cholesterol
		0 g	Fiber

Creamy Orange Dressing

Spoon this delectable dressing over fresh fruit and create an appetizer or a light dessert with a delicious difference.

Makes 8 servings (2½ tablespoons each serving)

1	cup plain nonfat yogurt
1/4	cup frozen orange juice concentrate, thawed

In a small bowl, combine yogurt and juice concentrate. Mix well. Chill several hours.

Each serving provides:

30 Calories

1/4	Fruit Serving	2 g	Protein
15	Additional Calories	trace	Fat (2% of calories)
		6 g	Carbohydrate
		22 mg	Sodium
		1 mg	Cholesterol
		0 g	Fiber

Poultry

The versatility of chicken and turkey have made them universal favorites, with almost every culture having its own traditional favorites.

When buying chicken, the white meat is your best bet because it is lower in fat than dark meat. One very important tip in cooking chicken is to remove the skin before cooking. Because the skin itself has a very high fat content, leaving it on can add as many as 6 to 8 grams of fat per serving. Turkey cutlets are one of our quick-cooking favorites, and ground turkey is versatile for use in meat loaves and casseroles. When buying ground turkey read the label carefully, as some brands contain a high percentage of skin.

Our easy-to-prepare poultry recipes will show you that the variations are endless.

We choose our cooking methods carefully, baking and broiling, rather than frying, and use lots of herbs and spices, rather than high-fat sauces, to enliven our dishes.

Chicken in Wine Sauce

This has long been one of our favorite party dishes. It tastes best when made a day ahead and reheated, making it an easy dish for entertaining. It's delicious over couscous.

Makes 4 servings

1	cup rosé wine
3	tablespoons reduced-sodium soy sauce
2	tablespoons water
3	cloves garlic, crushed
1	tablespoon firmly packed brown sugar
1	teaspoon ground ginger
1/2	teaspoon dried oregano
1	pound boneless, skinless chicken breasts

Combine all ingredients except chicken in a shallow casserole, mixing well. Add chicken.

Marinate in the refrigerator several hours.*

Preheat oven to 375 degrees F.

Bake, covered, 1 hour.

*If chicken is to be served the following day, marinating is not necessary. Just bake and refrigerate. Reheat before serving.

Each serving provides:

192 Calories

3	Protein Servings	27 g	Protein
62	Additional Calories	1 g	Fat (9% of calories)
		6 g	Carbohydrate
		529 mg	Sodium
		66 mg	Cholesterol
		0 g	Fiber

Elegant Stuffed Chicken Breasts

*The name says it all! The results are so elegant that no one will believe how
easy they are to prepare.*

Makes 4 servings

1	pound boneless, skinless chicken breasts
2	teaspoons vegetable oil
2	cups chopped mushrooms
1/2	cup chopped onion
1	cup coarsely shredded zucchini, unpeeled
3	tablespoons dry bread crumbs
1	egg white
1/4	teaspoon ground nutmeg
1/8	teaspoon garlic powder
	Salt and pepper
	Paprika
	Parsley flakes

Preheat oven to 350 degrees F.

Place each chicken breast between 2 sheets of wax paper and flatten chicken with a mallet until 1/4 inch thick.

Heat oil in a medium nonstick skillet over medium heat. Add mushrooms and onion and cook until tender, stirring frequently, about 10 minutes. Remove from heat.

Stir zucchini, bread crumbs, egg white, nutmeg, garlic powder, salt, and pepper into mushroom mixture. Divide mixture evenly onto the center of each chicken breast. Fold up the edges to enclose the filling, making nice round "packages" and place, smooth side up, in a shallow baking pan.

Sprinkle each breast liberally with paprika and parsley flakes.

Cover pan tightly with aluminum foil and bake 40 minutes.

Each serving provides:
191 Calories

3	Protein Servings	29 g	Protein
1/4	Bread Serving	4 g	Fat (20% of calories)
1 3/4	Vegetable Servings	8 g	Carbohydrate
1/2	Fat Serving	134 mg	Sodium
5	Additional Calories	66 mg	Cholesterol
		1 g	Fiber

Golden Crowned Chicken

Apples and carrots make this an outstanding flavor treat as well as a colorful and attractive way to prepare chicken.

Makes 4 servings

1	pound boneless, skinless chicken breasts
2	small Golden Delicious apples, peeled, cut into 1-inch chunks
1	16-ounce can carrots, drained, cut into 1/2-inch chunks (or 2 cups fresh carrots, steamed)
1	packet reduced-sodium instant chicken broth mix
1	tablespoon plus 1 teaspoon honey
1/4	cup plus 2 tablespoons dry bread crumbs
1	tablespoon plus 1 teaspoon reduced-calorie margarine

Preheat oven to 350 degrees F.

Spray a 1-quart shallow casserole with nonstick cooking spray. Place chicken in prepared pan.

In a small bowl, combine apples and carrots. Stir in broth mix and honey. Spoon carrot mixture evenly over chicken. Sprinkle with crumbs. Dot with margarine.

Cover tightly and bake 30 minutes.

Uncover and continue to bake 30 minutes more.

Each serving provides:

252 Calories

3	Protein Servings	28 g	Protein
1/2	Bread Serving	4 g	Fat (15% of calories)
1	Vegetable Serving	25 g	Carbohydrate
1/2	Fat Serving	388 mg	Sodium
1/2	Fruit Serving	66 mg	Cholesterol
23	Additional Calories	2 g	Fiber

Chicken with White Wine and Tomatoes

We like this dish best when it's made a day ahead and reheated. The flavors really blend well.

Makes 6 servings

2	teaspoons olive oil
2	teaspoons lemon juice
2	cups sliced mushrooms
1	cup thinly sliced onion
3	cloves garlic, minced
1¹/₂	pounds boneless, skinless chicken parts
1	16-ounce can salt-free (or regular) tomatoes, chopped, undrained
1¹/₂	cups water
¹/₂	cup dry white wine
¹/₄	cup tomato paste
1	packet low-sodium instant chicken or vegetable broth mix
1	bay leaf
¹/₄	teaspoon dried thyme
¹/₄	teaspoon pepper

Heat oil in a large saucepan over medium heat. Add lemon juice, mushrooms, onion, and garlic. Cook, stirring frequently, until tender, about 8 minutes.

Add chicken.

Combine remaining ingredients and pour over chicken.

When mixture boils, cover, reduce heat to medium-low, and simmer 1¹/₄ hours, or until chicken is tender. Stir occasionally while cooking.

Remove and discard bay leaf before serving.

Each serving provides:

195 Calories

3	Protein Servings	26 g	Protein
2	Vegetable Servings	5 g	Fat (25% of calories)
¹/₄	Fat Serving	10 g	Carbohydrate
22	Additional Calories	330 mg	Sodium
		79 mg	Cholesterol
		2 g	Fiber

Chicken Cacciatore

There are many versions of this popular Italian dish. However, we're particularly partial to this one. Serve it over noodles, add a green vegetable, and you have a dinner to make you proud.

Makes 4 servings

2	teaspoons olive oil
1	cup sliced onion
2	cloves garlic, finely chopped
1	16-ounce can salt-free (or regular) tomatoes, chopped, undrained
1	8-ounce can salt-free (or regular) tomato sauce
1	teaspoon dried oregano
$1/2$	teaspoon celery seed
$1/4$	teaspoon salt
$1/4$	teaspoon pepper
1	bay leaf
1	pound boneless, skinless chicken breasts, cut into quarters
$1/4$	cup dry white wine

Heat oil in a large saucepan over medium heat. Add onion and garlic. Cook, stirring frequently, until onion is tender, about 10 minutes. Add small amounts of water as necessary, about a tablespoon at a time, to prevent sticking.

Add tomatoes, tomato sauce, and spices, stirring to blend.

Add chicken. Cover, reduce heat to medium-low, and simmer 1 hour, stirring occasionally.

Add wine. Cook, uncovered, 15 minutes.

Remove and discard bay leaf before serving.

Each serving provides:

218 Calories

3	Protein Servings	29 g	Protein
$2^1/2$	Vegetable Servings	4 g	Fat (19% of calories)
$1/2$	Fat Serving	14 g	Carbohydrate
13	Additional Calories	239 mg	Sodium
		66 mg	Cholesterol
		2 g	Fiber

Spanish Chicken

For a delicious and colorful accompaniment, cook brown rice or cracked wheat in chicken or vegetable broth with a pinch of saffron.

Makes 4 servings

2	teaspoons vegetable oil
1/2	cup chopped onion
1/2	cup chopped green bell pepper
1/2	cup chopped carrots
1/2	cup chopped celery
4	cloves garlic, minced
1	16-ounce can salt-free (or regular) tomatoes, chopped and drained (Reserve juice.)
1	pound boneless, skinless chicken breasts
1/4	cup water
1	packet low-sodium instant chicken broth mix
1/2	teaspoon chili powder
	Pinch saffron

Preheat oven to 350 degrees F.

Spray a shallow baking dish with nonstick cooking spray.

Heat oil in a large nonstick skillet over medium heat. Add onion, green pepper, carrots, celery, and garlic. Cook 10 minutes, stirring frequently. Add small amounts of water if necessary (about a tablespoon at a time), to prevent sticking.

Remove skillet from heat and stir in tomatoes.

Place chicken in prepared baking dish.

Combine remaining ingredients with reserved tomato juice, mixing well. Pour over chicken.

Cover tightly and bake 1 hour.

Each serving provides:

198 Calories

3	Protein Servings	28 g	Protein
2	Vegetable Servings	4 g	Fat (20% of calories)
1/2	Fat Serving	11 g	Carbohydrate
3	Additional Calories	326 mg	Sodium
		66 mg	Cholesterol
		2 g	Fiber

Honey Crunch Chicken

We found that "painting" the chicken with reduced-calorie mayonnaise seals in the moistness, and the cereal on the outside adds a wonderful crunch. You'll choose this one time and again.

Makes 4 servings

1	pound boneless, skinless chicken breasts
2	tablespoons plus 2 teaspoons reduced-calorie mayonnaise
1½	ounces Grape Nuts cereal, crushed (¹/₃ cup)
1	tablespoon plus 1 teaspoon honey

Preheat oven to 375 degrees F.

Spray a 1-quart baking pan with nonstick cooking spray.

Rinse chicken and pat dry. Place in prepared pan. Using a pastry brush, spread mayonnaise over both sides of the chicken.

Sprinkle cereal evenly over top side of chicken. Drizzle evenly with honey.

Let chicken stand at room temperature for 10 minutes.

Bake, uncovered, 45 minutes

Each serving provides:

212 Calories

3	Protein Servings	27 g	Protein
¹/₂	Bread Serving	5 g	Fat (19% of calories)
1	Fat Serving	15 g	Carbohydrate
20	Additional Calories	192 mg	Sodium
		69 mg	Cholesterol
		1 g	Fiber

Hawaiian Pineapple Chicken

Served with brown rice and steamed snow peas, this is a real tropical winner.

Makes 4 servings

1	pound boneless, skinless chicken breasts
1	16-ounce can pineapple chunks or tidbits, packed in juice, drained (Reserve juice.)
	Reserved pineapple juice plus enough water to equal 1 cup liquid
1	packet low-sodium instant chicken broth mix
3	tablespoons reduced-sodium soy sauce
1	teaspoon ground ginger
1/2	teaspoon garlic powder

Preheat oven to 350 degrees F.
Place chicken in a baking dish. Top with pineapple chunks.
Combine remaining ingredients and pour over chicken.
Bake, covered, 1 hour.

Each serving provides:

207 Calories

3	Protein Servings	27 g	Protein
1	Fruit Serving	2 g	Fat (7% of calories)
3	Additional Calories	20 g	Carbohydrate
		740 mg	Sodium
		66 mg	Cholesterol
		1 g	Fiber

Spice-Glazed Chicken

This recipe has been a family favorite for years. When you try it you'll see why.

Makes 4 servings

1	pound boneless, skinless chicken breasts
1/3	cup ketchup
1/3	cup water
2	tablespoons plus 2 teaspoons sugar
2	tablespoons vinegar
1	tablespoon vegetable oil
1	teaspoon Worcestershire sauce
3/4	teaspoon dry mustard
1	bay leaf
1	cup thinly sliced onion, separated into rings after measuring

Preheat oven to 350 degrees F.

Spray a 1-quart baking pan with nonstick cooking spray.

Place chicken in prepared pan.

In a small saucepan, combine remaining ingredients. Bring to a boil over medium heat, then reduce heat to medium-low and simmer 2 minutes, stirring frequently.

Baste chicken with a little of the sauce, leaving the onions in the saucepan.

Bake chicken, uncovered, 1 hour, basting frequently with the sauce. During the last 20 minutes of baking, arrange onion rings over chicken.

Remove and discard bay leaf.

Serve any remaining sauce with the cooked chicken.

Each serving provides:

233 Calories

3	Protein Servings	27 g	Protein
1/2	Vegetable Serving	5 g	Fat (21% of calories)
3/4	Fat Serving	18 g	Carbohydrate
52	Additional Calories	327 mg	Sodium
		66 mg	Cholesterol
		1 g	Fiber

Easy Chicken Barbecue

Served over rice or noodles, or on a bun, this is a quick and tasty way to use up leftovers.

Make 4 servings

2	teaspoons vegetable oil
1/2	cup chopped onion
1/2	cup chopped green bell pepper
2	cloves garlic, minced
1	8-ounce can salt-free (or regular) tomato sauce
1/4	cup water
1	tablespoon firmly packed brown sugar
1	tablespoon sweet pickle relish
1	teaspoon Worcestershire sauce
1/2	teaspoon dry mustard
12	ounces cooked skinless white meat chicken, shredded (3 cups)

Heat oil in a large nonstick skillet over medium heat. Add onion, green pepper, and garlic. Cook, stirring frequently, until tender, about 8 minutes. Add small amounts of water if necessary (about a table-spoon at a time) to prevent sticking.

Add remaining ingredients, except chicken, mixing well. Reduce heat to medium-low.

Stir in chicken. Cover and cook until hot and bubbly.

Each serving provides:

214 Calories

3	Protein Servings	28 g	Protein
1 1/2	Vegetable Servings	6 g	Fat (24% of calories)
1/2	Fat Serving	12 g	Carbohydrate
16	Additional Calories	119 mg	Sodium
		72 mg	Cholesterol
		1 g	Fiber

Chicken Chow Mein

This tastes so authentic! All you need is rice and our Egg White Drop Soup on page 31 for a complete Chinese dinner.

Makes 4 servings

2	teaspoons vegetable oil
1	teaspoon sesame oil
4	cups sliced onion
1	cup sliced celery
1/4	cup carrots, cut into matchstick-size pieces
3/4	cup drained, canned sliced water chestnuts
1	16-ounce can bean sprouts, drained
8	ounces cooked, cubed white meat chicken, skin removed (2 cups)
1	cup water
2	packets low-sodium instant chicken broth mix
2	tablespoons reduced-sodium soy sauce
2	tablespoons cornstarch
1	teaspoon sugar

Heat both oils in a large nonstick saucepan over medium heat. Add onions, celery, carrots, and water chestnuts. Add about 2 tablespoons of water, cover, and cook 5 minutes, stirring occasionally. Add a little more water, if necessary, to prevent sticking.

Stir in bean sprouts and chicken.

In a small bowl, combine water, broth mix, soy sauce, cornstarch, and sugar, stirring to dissolve cornstarch. Add to saucepan. Cook, stirring, 1 minute, until mixture thickens slightly and is hot and bubbly.

Each serving provides:

248 Calories

2	Protein Servings	21 g	Protein
1/4	Bread Serving	6 g	Fat (21% of calories)
3 3/4	Vegetable Servings	28 g	Carbohydrate
3/4	Fat Serving	838 mg	Sodium
24	Additional Calories	48 mg	Cholesterol
		5 g	Fiber

Oven-Fried Turkey Cutlets

One of our family's favorites, these breaded cutlets can be served as is or topped with spaghetti sauce. They also make great sandwiches—hot or cold.

Makes 4 servings

1	pound turkey breast cutlets
2	tablespoons lemon juice
3/4	cup dry bread crumbs
2	tablespoons grated Parmesan cheese
2	teaspoons dried oregano
1/2	teaspoon poultry seasoning
1/4	teaspoon salt
1/4	teaspoon pepper
1/4	teaspoon garlic powder
	Nonstick cooking spray

Preheat oven to 350 degrees F.

Spray a shallow baking pan with nonstick cooking spray.

Place turkey cutlets in a medium bowl. Cover with water. Add lemon juice.

In a shallow bowl, combine remaining ingredients. Mix well.

One at a time, take cutlets from water and dip into crumbs, turning to coat both sides of cutlets. Place in prepared pan.

Spray each cutlet lightly and evenly with cooking spray.

Bake, uncovered, 30 minutes, or until lightly browned.

Each serving provides:

231 Calories

3	Protein Servings	32 g	Protein
1	Bread Serving	4 g	Fat (16% of calories)
15	Additional Calories	16 g	Carbohydrate
		414 mg	Sodium
		72 mg	Cholesterol
		1 g	Fiber

Asian Turkey Patties

The delicious taste of this dish comes from the sesame oil, which has a unique flavor all its own. Use it sparingly, or the flavor becomes too overpowering.

Makes 4 servings

2	teaspoons vegetable oil
1	teaspoon sesame oil
2	cups sliced onion
1	cup sliced mushrooms
1	pound lean ground turkey
2	tablespoons grated onion
1	tablespoon reduced-sodium soy sauce
2	cloves garlic, crushed
1	packet low-sodium instant chicken or beef broth mix
1/4	teaspoon ground ginger

Heat both oils in a large nonstick skillet over medium heat. Add sliced onion and mushrooms. Cook, stirring frequently, until tender, about 8 minutes. Add small amounts of water as necessary (about a tablespoon at a time), to prevent sticking.

While onions are cooking, combine turkey with remaining ingredients, mixing well. Shape into 4 patties. Place patties in pan with onions and cook, turning several times, until patties are done and are nicely browned on both sides. (If onions are browning too quickly, pile them on top of the patties to keep them hot, but off the surface of the skillet.)

Each serving provides:

237 Calories

3	Protein Servings	21 g	Protein
1 1/2	Vegetable Servings	12 g	Fat (46% of calories)
3/4	Fat Serving	10 g	Carbohydrate
3	Additional Calories	475 mg	Sodium
		83 mg	Cholesterol
		2 g	Fiber

Mock-Sausage and Peppers

By refrigerating the turkey with the herbs and allowing the flavors to marry, these delicious patties taste just like the Italian specialty. Serve with pasta or on a crusty roll, topped with pasta sauce.

Makes 4 servings

1	teaspoon vegetable oil
1/2	cup finely minced green bell pepper
1/2	cup finely minced onion
1	pound lean ground turkey
1/2	teaspoon fennel seeds, crushed*
1/4	teaspoon ground sage
1/4	teaspoon dried thyme
1/4	teaspoon dried marjoram
1/4	teaspoon salt
1/4	teaspoon pepper
1/8	teaspoon ground savory

Heat oil in a small nonstick skillet over medium heat. Add green pepper and onion. Cook, stirring frequently, until tender, about 8 minutes. Add small amounts of water as necessary, about a tablespoon at a time, to prevent sticking.

In a large bowl, combine turkey with peppers and onions. Add remaining ingredients and mix well. Refrigerate mixture for 1 to 5 hours to blend flavors.

Shape mixture into 8 thin patties.

Spray a large nonstick griddle or skillet with nonstick cooking spray. Preheat over medium heat.

Place patties on griddle. Cook until patties are done and are lightly browned on both sides. Turn patties several times while cooking.

*To crush seeds, place between 2 pieces of wax paper and crush with a rolling pin or mallet.

Each serving provides:

186 Calories

3	Protein Servings	20 g	Protein
1/2	Vegetable Serving	10 g	Fat (49% of calories)
1/4	Fat Serving	3 g	Carbohydrate
		243 mg	Sodium
		83 mg	Cholesterol
		1 g	Fiber

Barbecue Turkey Loaf

Adding brown sugar and vinegar to the tomato sauce gives this moist loaf a wonderful barbecue flavor. It's delicious with our Oven-Baked French "Fries" on page 236 and a pile of steamed mixed vegetables.

Makes 6 servings

1¹/₂	pounds lean ground turkey
1	8-ounce can salt-free (or regular) tomato sauce
1	cup finely chopped onion
	Salt
¹/₄	teaspoon pepper
¹/₄	teaspoon garlic powder
2	teaspoons Worcestershire sauce
2	tablespoons firmly packed brown sugar
2	tablespoons prepared yellow mustard
1	tablespoon vinegar

Preheat oven to 350 degrees F.

In a large bowl, combine turkey, ³/₄ cup of the tomato sauce, onion, salt, pepper, garlic powder, and Worcestershire sauce. Mix well. Shape mixture into a loaf and place on a rack in a shallow baking pan.

Bake, uncovered, 20 minutes.

Combine remaining tomato sauce, brown sugar, mustard, and vinegar. Pour over loaf.

Bake, uncovered, 40 minutes longer.

Each serving provides:

208 Calories

3	Protein Servings	21 g	Protein
1	Vegetable Serving	9 g	Fat (39% of calories)
16	Additional Calories	10 g	Carbohydrate
		201 mg	Sodium
		83 mg	Cholesterol
		1 g	Fiber

Herbed Turkey Roll

This rolled "roast" is simple enough for a family dinner, yet elegant enough for a fancy dinner party. And, if there's any left over, it makes great sandwiches.

Makes 12 servings

1	3-pound skinless, boneless turkey breast
1/2	teaspoon dried rosemary, crumbled
1/2	teaspoon dried thyme
1/2	teaspoon dried oregano
1/2	teaspoon garlic powder
1/4	teaspoon dried basil
1/4	teaspoon onion powder
	Salt and pepper

Using a sharp knife, make a lengthwise slit in one side of the turkey breast, as if creating a pocket. Do not cut all the way through. Open at the pocket and lay flat.

Place turkey between 2 sheets of wax paper and flatten with a mallet to about 1 1/2 inches thick. Combine spices and sprinkle evenly over turkey.

Starting at one end, roll turkey like a jelly roll. Tie with a cord in 3 or 4 places.

Wrap turkey securely in aluminum foil and place in a shallow baking pan.

Bake 2 hours, or until meat is no longer pink.

Slice crosswise to serve.

Each serving provides:

127 Calories

3	Protein Servings	28 g	Protein
		1 g	Fat (6% of calories)
		0 g	Carbohydrate
		56 mg	Sodium
		70 mg	Cholesterol
		0 g	Fiber

Franks in Pungent Sauce

You really have to try this one to believe it! Serve it over rice for an easy, delicious, and inexpensive meal.

Makes 4 servings

2	teaspoons vegetable oil
12	ounces fat-free turkey frankfurters (or lowfat franks up to 2 grams of fat per ounce), diced into $1/4$-inch pieces
2	cups carrots, diced into $1/4$-inch pieces
2	cups green bell pepper, diced into $1/4$-inch pieces
3	tablespoons reduced-sodium soy sauce
3	tablespoons firmly packed brown sugar
2	tablespoons water

Heat oil in a large nonstick skillet over medium heat. Add frankfurters and cook, stirring, until lightly browned.

Stir in carrots. Cover and cook 2 minutes.

Stir in green pepper, soy sauce, brown sugar, and water. Cover and cook 3 minutes.

Each serving provides:

171 Calories

3	Protein Servings	14 g	Protein
2	Vegetable Servings	2 g	Fat (13% of calories)
1	Fat Serving	23 g	Carbohydrate
36	Additional Calories	1,257 mg	Sodium
		26 mg	Cholesterol
		3 g	Fiber

Fish and Seafood

Many varieties of fish and seafood are low in fat and fit nicely into a healthful diet. Often, if dishes are high in fat, it is not the seafood that is the culprit, but the way in which it is prepared. So, for our sauces we are careful to choose ingredients such as lemon juice, broth, and vegetables, along with a delectable array of spices. Now you can have all of the flavor without the fat.

Seafood contains no fiber. Therefore we recommend adding a whole grain, such as brown rice or barley, to every seafood meal. If you serve a salad and a steamed vegetable in addition, you have a beautifully balanced, and filling, meal.

Our selection of seafood dishes will definitely please your taste buds and delight your family and friends.

Caribbean Fish

The unique blend of flavors is reminiscent of the exotic tastes of the Caribbean. It's delicate and complex, all at the same time.

Makes 4 servings

1¹/₄	pounds flounder, sole, or orange roughy fillets
1	6-ounce can tomato paste
¹/₂	cup water
1¹/₂	tablespoons lime juice
1¹/₂	teaspoons coconut extract
¹/₂	teaspoon dried oregano
¹/₂	teaspoon onion powder
¹/₄	teaspoon garlic powder
¹/₄	teaspoon salt
¹/₄	teaspoon pepper
1	bay leaf, crumbled

Preheat oven to 375 degrees F.

Spray a 7 × 11-inch baking pan with nonstick cooking spray.

Place fish fillets in prepared pan.

In a small bowl, combine remaining ingredients, mixing well. Spoon evenly over fish.

Bake, uncovered, 20 minutes, or until fish flakes easily when tested with a fork.

Each serving provides:

175 Calories

2	Protein Servings	28 g	Protein
1¹/₂	Vegetable Servings	3 g	Fat (13% of calories)
		10 g	Carbohydrate
		587 mg	Sodium
		68 mg	Cholesterol
		2 g	Fiber

Thyme for Fish

If crispier fish is desired, after baking, place fish under the broiler for a few minutes.

Makes 4 servings

1¹/₄	pounds flounder or sole fillets
2	tablespoons reduced-calorie mayonnaise
¹/₂	teaspoon dried thyme
¹/₈	teaspoon grated lemon peel
	Salt and pepper
2	tablespoons dry bread crumbs (or wheat germ)

Preheat oven to 375 degrees F.

Place fish in a shallow baking pan sprayed with nonstick cooking spray.

Combine mayonnaise, thyme, lemon peel, salt, and pepper. Spread mixture evenly over fillets.

Sprinkle with bread crumbs.

Bake, uncovered, 20 minutes, or until fish flakes easily when tested with a fork.

Each serving provides:

165 Calories

2	Protein Servings	27 g	Protein
³/₄	Fat Serving	4 g	Fat (24% of calories)
15	Additional Calories	3 g	Carbohydrate
		185 mg	Sodium
		71 mg	Cholesterol
		0 g	Fiber

Baked Herbed Fish

You may want to make extra sauce and serve it over rice as a flavorful accompaniment to this dish.

Makes 4 servings

1¹/₄	pounds thickly cut, boneless fish steaks, such as haddock
1	8-ounce can salt-free (or regular) tomato sauce
¹/₂	cup finely chopped onion
2	cloves garlic, crushed
¹/₄	teaspoon dried thyme
¹/₄	teaspoon dried basil
¹/₈	teaspoon pepper
¹/₄	teaspoon salt

Preheat oven to 375 degrees F.

Place fish in a shallow baking pan sprayed with a nonstick cooking spray.

In a small bowl, combine remaining ingredients, mixing well. Spread evenly over fish.

Bake, uncovered, 20 minutes, or until fish flakes easily when tested with a fork.

Each serving provides:

156 Calories

2	Protein Servings	28 g	Protein
1¹/₄	Vegetable Servings	2 g	Fat (9% of calories)
		7 g	Carbohydrate
		245 mg	Sodium
		81 mg	Cholesterol
		1 g	Fiber

Lemony Stuffed Fish

We used to make this luscious dish with butter and serve it at all of our dinner parties. Now we use reduced-calorie margarine instead, along with some butter flavor and, even though we've trimmed the fat, the result is still a wonderful party dish. (Look for butter flavor with the extracts in most large grocery stores.)

Makes 4 servings

1/4	cup reduced-calorie margarine
1/2	cup finely chopped onion
1/2	cup finely chopped celery
1/2	cup plain nonfat yogurt
2	tablespoons lemon juice
1	tablespoon grated fresh lemon peel
1	teaspoon imitation butter flavor
1	teaspoon paprika (plus a sprinkle)
1	teaspoon dill weed
1/4	teaspoon salt
4	slices whole wheat bread (1-ounce slices), cubed
1 1/4	pounds flounder fillets

Preheat oven to 375 degrees F.

Spray a 1-quart baking dish with nonstick cooking spray.

Melt margarine in a small nonstick skillet over medium heat. Add onion and celery and cook, stirring frequently, until tender, about 5 minutes. Transfer to a small bowl.

Stir in yogurt, lemon juice, lemon peel, butter flavor, paprika, dill weed, and salt. Add bread cubes, mixing well.

Place half of the fillets in prepared pan. Spoon stuffing evenly over fish. Top with remaining fillets. Press fish down firmly onto stuffing. Sprinkle with paprika.

Bake, uncovered, 30 minutes, or until fish flakes easily when tested with a fork.

Each serving provides:

282 Calories

2	Protein Servings	32 g	Protein
1	Bread Serving	9 g	Fat (28% of calories)
1/2	Vegetable Serving	19 g	Carbohydrate
1 1/2	Fat Servings	573 mg	Sodium
15	Additional Calories	69 mg	Cholesterol
		3 g	Fiber

Fish and Peppers

In this colorful dish, a delicious blend of herbs are combined with the green peppers and tomato sauce to create a dish fit for a king.

Makes 4 servings

2	teaspoons vegetable oil
2	cups chopped green bell pepper
1/2	cup chopped onion
1	clove garlic, minced
1	8-ounce can salt-free (or regular) tomato sauce
2	teaspoons Worcestershire sauce
1	tablespoon firmly packed brown sugar
	Salt and pepper
1¹/4	pounds scrod or orange roughy fillets

Preheat oven to 375 degrees F.

Spray a 7 × 11-inch baking dish with nonstick cooking spray.

Heat oil in a large nonstick skillet over medium heat. Add green pepper, onion, and garlic. Cook, stirring frequently, until tender, about 10 minutes. Add small amounts of water if necessary (about a tablespoon at a time), to prevent sticking.

Stir in remaining ingredients, except fish.

Place fish in prepared baking dish. Spoon sauce evenly over fish.

Bake, uncovered, 20 minutes, or until fish flakes easily when tested with a fork.

Each serving provides:

196 Calories

2	Protein Servings	27 g	Protein
2¹/4	Vegetable Servings	4 g	Fat (18% of calories)
1/2	Fat Serving	13 g	Carbohydrate
12	Additional Calories	120 mg	Sodium
		61 mg	Cholesterol
		2 g	Fiber

Cod à l'Orange

This recipe is also delicious with chicken in place of the fish.

Makes 4 servings

1¹/₄	pounds cod or orange roughy fillets
¹/₂	cup frozen orange juice concentrate, thawed
2	teaspoons sherry extract
3	tablespoons reduced-sodium soy sauce
¹/₈	teaspoon garlic powder
2	teaspoons vegetable oil
3	tablespoons dry bread crumbs (or wheat germ)

Place fish in a shallow baking pan.

Combine remaining ingredients, except bread crumbs. Pour over fish. Marinate in the refrigerator for several hours, turning fish occasionally.

When ready to cook, let fish stand at room temperature for 15 minutes.

Preheat oven to 375 degrees F.

Sprinkle bread crumbs evenly over fish.

Bake, uncovered, 25 minutes, or until fish flakes easily when tested with a fork.

Each serving provides:

227 Calories

2	Protein Servings	27 g	Protein
¹/₄	Bread Serving	4 g	Fat (15% of calories)
¹/₂	Fat Serving	19 g	Carbohydrate
1	Fruit Serving	571 mg	Sodium
		61 mg	Cholesterol
		0 g	Fiber

Parmesan Fish

This delicious dish is elegant enough for your most discriminating guests.

Makes 4 servings

1¹/₄	pounds scrod or orange roughy fillets
2	tablespoons reduced-calorie mayonnaise
2	teaspoons Worcestershire sauce
1	tablespoon minced onion flakes
1	teaspoon Dijon mustard
1	teaspoon sherry extract
3	tablespoons grated Parmesan cheese (1 ounce)

Preheat oven to 375 degrees F.

Place fish in a shallow baking pan sprayed with a nonstick cooking spray.

Combine remaining ingredients, except Parmesan cheese. Spread mixture evenly over fillets.

Sprinkle with Parmesan cheese.

Bake, uncovered, 20 minutes, or until fish flakes easily when tested with a fork.

Each serving provides:

180 Calories

2	Protein Servings	28 g	Protein
³/₄	Fat Serving	5 g	Fat (28% of calories)
23	Additional Calories	2 g	Carbohydrate
		307 mg	Sodium
		69 mg	Cholesterol
		0 g	Fiber

Salmon Salad

For a delicious change-of-pace from tuna salad, try this with lettuce and tomato in a pita bread or piled on a toasted English muffin.

Makes 4 servings

1	14³/₄-ounce can salmon, drained and flaked (12 ounces when drained)
1	tablespoon lemon juice
2	teaspoons Dijon mustard
2	tablespoons reduced-calorie mayonnaise
¹/₄	cup finely chopped onion
¹/₄	cup finely chopped celery
¹/₄	teaspoon dill weed
	Salt and pepper

In a small bowl, combine all ingredients, mixing well.
Chill several hours to blend flavors.

Each serving provides:

149 Calories

3	Protein Servings	18 g	Protein
¹/₄	Vegetable Serving	7 g	Fat (43% of calories)
³/₄	Fat Serving	2 g	Carbohydrate
		523 mg	Sodium
		36 mg	Cholesterol
		0 g	Fiber

"Pretend" Salmon Salad

Less expensive than salmon, haddock fillets make a wonderful cold salad that will please even the most discriminating gourmet. Make this dish up to a day ahead and chill it thoroughly to blend the wonderful flavors.

Makes 4 servings

1¹/₄	pounds haddock fillets
2	tablespoons lemon juice
¹/₂	cup plain nonfat yogurt
¹/₄	cup chili sauce
2	tablespoons reduced-calorie mayonnaise
¹/₂	cup finely chopped celery
2	tablespoons finely chopped onion
1	teaspoon sugar
¹/₄	teaspoon celery salt
¹/₈	teaspoon pepper

Preheat oven to 375 degrees F.

Place fish in a shallow pan sprayed with nonstick cooking spray.
Bake 20 minutes, or until fish flakes easily when tested with a fork.
Cool for 15 minutes, then flake fish into a large bowl.
Combine remaining ingredients in a small bowl and mix well.
Spoon over fish and blend well with a fork.

Chill several hours or overnight to blend flavors.

Each serving provides:

187 Calories

2	Protein Servings	29 g	Protein
¹/₄	Vegetable Serving	3 g	Fat (16% of calories)
³/₄	Fat Serving	9 g	Carbohydrate
9	Additional Calories	441 mg	Sodium
		84 mg	Cholesterol
		0 g	Fiber

Salmon–Potato Patties

Ever wonder what to do with leftover mashed potatoes?

Makes 4 servings (2 patties each serving)

1	14³/₄-ounce can salmon, drained and flaked (12 ounces)
12	ounces cooked potatoes, peeled, cooked,* and mashed
¹/₄	cup liquid egg substitute
2	tablespoons grated onion
1	tablespoon lemon juice
1	teaspoon Worcestershire sauce
3	tablespoons grated Parmesan cheese (1 ounce)
¹/₂	teaspoon grated fresh lemon peel
	Salt and pepper

In a large bowl, combine all ingredients, mixing well. Shape into 8 patties.

Spray a nonstick griddle or skillet with nonstick cooking spray. Heat over medium heat.

Cook patties until lightly browned on both sides, turning carefully.

*If you don't have leftover potatoes available, then bake the potatoes in a 350-degree F oven for about 1 hour, or microwave for about 8 minutes, until very tender.

Each serving provides:

239 Calories

3¹/₂	Protein Servings	24 g	Protein
³/₄	Bread Serving	7 g	Fat (27% of calories)
5	Additional Calories	19 g	Carbohydrate
		590 mg	Sodium
		38 mg	Cholesterol
		1 g	Fiber

Tuna–Vegetable Pie

Easy and delicious, this unique casserole has an Italian flavor that goes well with a side dish of noodles and a tossed green salad.

Makes 6 servings

2	6¹/₂-ounce cans tuna (packed in water), drained and flaked
¹/₄	cup liquid egg substitute
3	tablespoons grated Parmesan cheese (1 ounce)
1	8-ounce can salt-free (or regular) tomato sauce
¹/₂	teaspoon dried oregano
¹/₂	teaspoon dried basil
¹/₄	teaspoon garlic powder
2	tablespoons dry bread crumbs or wheat germ
¹/₂	cup finely chopped green bell pepper
¹/₄	cup finely chopped onion
¹/₂	cup finely chopped zucchini, unpeeled
1	4-ounce can mushroom pieces, drained

Preheat oven to 350 degrees F.

Spray a 9-inch pie pan with nonstick cooking spray.

In a large bowl, combine all ingredients. Mix well. Spoon mixture into prepared pan. Press down gently with a fork.

Bake, uncovered, 40 minutes, until lightly browned.

Cut into wedges to serve.

Each serving provides:

109 Calories

1	Protein Serving	15 g	Protein
1¹/₄	Vegetable Servings	2 g	Fat (17% of calories)
13	Additional Calories	7 g	Carbohydrate
		311 mg	Sodium
		20 mg	Cholesterol
		1 g	Fiber

Tuna Noodle Casserole

This homestyle casserole has been a family favorite for years. Although the ingredients have changed (lowfat dairy products in place of the original sour cream), this is still the best tuna casserole we ever tasted.

Makes 6 servings

6	ounces medium yolk-free noodles, uncooked
1	cup lowfat (1%) cottage cheese
3/4	cup plain nonfat yogurt
1	tablespoon all-purpose flour
2	teaspoons Worcestershire sauce
1/4	teaspoon salt
1/8	teaspoon pepper
1/8	teaspoon garlic powder
1/2	cup frozen peas
1/4	cup finely minced onion
1	8-ounce can mushroom pieces, drained
2	6 1/2-ounce cans tuna (packed in water), drained and flaked (8 ounces)
3	tablespoons grated Parmesan cheese

Preheat oven to 350 degrees F.

Spray an 8-inch square baking pan with nonstick cooking spray.

Cook noodles according to package directions. Drain.

In a large bowl, combine cottage cheese, yogurt, flour, Worcestershire sauce, salt, pepper, and garlic powder. Mix well. Stir in peas, onion, mushrooms, tuna, and cooked noodles. Spoon into prepared baking pan.

Sprinkle Parmesan cheese evenly over casserole.

Bake, uncovered, 30 minutes, or until hot.

Each serving provides:

250 Calories

1	Protein Serving	29 g	Protein
1 1/2	Bread Servings	2 g	Fat (9% of calories)
1/2	Vegetable Serving	28 g	Carbohydrate
45	Additional Calories	632 mg	Sodium
		27 mg	Cholesterol
		2 g	Fiber

Crab and Cheddar Casserole

This has been one of our favorite special occasion dishes for years, with the splash of sherry adding a richness and elegance that will win you rave reviews. It can also be made with flaked fish in place of the crab.

Makes 4 servings

3	tablespoons all-purpose flour
2/3	cup nonfat dry milk
1/4	teaspoon dry mustard
1/8	teaspoon salt
1/8	teaspoon pepper
1	cup water
3	ounces shredded reduced-fat Cheddar cheese (3/4 cup)
2	tablespoons sherry
12	ounces crab meat (1 1/2 cups)

Preheat oven to 350 degrees F.

Spray a 1-quart casserole with nonstick cooking spray.

In a small saucepan, combine flour, dry milk, mustard, salt, and pepper. Mix well. Gradually add water, stirring briskly to avoid lumps. Heat over medium heat, stirring constantly, until mixture thickens. Remove from heat.

Stir cheese and sherry into milk mixture, mixing until cheese is completely melted. Stir in crab meat. Place in prepared casserole.

Bake, uncovered, 20 minutes.

Each serving provides:

223 Calories

2 1/2	Protein Servings	29 g	Protein
1/4	Bread Serving	6 g	Fat (24% of calories)
1/2	Milk Serving	11 g	Carbohydrate
6	Additional Calories	535 mg	Sodium
		102 mg	Cholesterol
		0 g	Fiber

Shrimp Teriyaki

These shrimp are also delicious on an outdoor grill. If you thread them on a skewer, they won't fall through the openings in the rack.

Makes 4 servings

3	tablespoons reduced-sodium soy sauce
1	tablespoon water
1	tablespoon sesame oil
2	tablespoons dry sherry
1/4	teaspoon garlic powder
1/4	teaspoon ground ginger
2	teaspoons honey
1 1/4	pounds cleaned raw shrimp

Combine all ingredients, except shrimp, in a shallow bowl. Add shrimp and marinate in the refrigerator for several hours, turning shrimp occasionally.

Preheat broiler.

Remove shrimp from marinade and place on a broiler pan. Broil 6 inches from heat for 8 to 10 minutes, turning occasionally, until shrimp are done.

Each serving provides:

180 Calories

2	Protein Servings	29 g	Protein
3/4	Fat Serving	4 g	Fat (22% of calories)
16	Additional Calories	4 g	Carbohydrate
		435 mg	Sodium
		216 mg	Cholesterol
		0 g	Fiber

Shrimp and Water Chestnuts

Over cooked rice or thin noodles, this makes a very tasty treat.

Makes 4 servings

1¹/₄	pounds cleaned raw shrimp
2	cups sliced mushrooms
6	ounces canned water chestnuts, drained, thinly sliced
¹/₂	cup chopped onion
2	cloves garlic, minced
1	cup water
2	tablespoons cornstarch
2	tablespoons dry sherry
1	tablespoon reduced-sodium soy sauce
1	teaspoon sugar
1	packet low-sodium instant chicken or vegetable broth mix
1	tablespoon plus 1 teaspoon vegetable oil

Combine shrimp, mushrooms, water chestnuts, onion, and garlic in a large bowl.

In a small bowl, combine water, cornstarch, sherry, soy sauce, sugar, and broth mix. Stir to dissolve cornstarch.

Heat oil in a large nonstick skillet over medium-high heat. (Or a wok may be used.) Add shrimp mixture and cook until shrimp is done, about 5 minutes, stirring frequently. Lower heat to medium.

Pour broth mixture over shrimp. Cook, stirring, until mixture thickens, about 3 minutes.

Each serving provides:

257 Calories

2	Protein Servings	30 g	Protein
¹/₄	Bread Serving	7 g	Fat (26% of calories)
1¹/₄	Vegetable Servings	14 g	Carbohydrate
1	Fat Serving	581 mg	Sodium
38	Additional Calories	216 mg	Cholesterol
		2 g	Fiber

Easiest Shrimp Salad

Served on a bed of lettuce and garnished with sliced tomatoes and cucumbers, this salad makes a wonderful, tasty lunch or light supper.

Makes 4 servings

12	ounces cooked, peeled shrimp, cut into 1-inch pieces
1/4	cup reduced-calorie mayonnaise
2	tablespoons ketchup
1	tablespoon grated onion
1	teaspoon lemon juice
	Dash garlic powder
	Salt and pepper

In a medium bowl, combine all ingredients and mix well.
Chill several hours to blend flavors.

Each serving provides:

134 Calories

1 1/2	Protein Servings	18 g	Protein
1 1/2	Fat Servings	5 g	Fat (34% of calories)
8	Additional Calories	3 g	Carbohydrate
		361 mg	Sodium
		171 mg	Cholesterol
		0 g	Fiber

Barbecued Shrimp

An attractive way to serve these is to place all 4 skewers of shrimp on a large platter of cooked rice.

Makes 4 servings

1   8-ounce can salt-free (or regular) tomato sauce
1/2   cup chopped onion
1/4   cup lemon juice
1   tablespoon plus 1 teaspoon firmly packed brown sugar
1   tablespoon vegetable oil
2   teaspoons Worcestershire sauce
1   tablespoon prepared mustard
1/8   teaspoon garlic powder
        Salt and pepper
1   cup canned pineapple chunks (unsweetened), drained
        (Reserve juice.)
1/4   cup reserved juice from pineapple
1 1/4   pounds cleaned raw shrimp
1   large green bell pepper, cut into 1-inch squares

In a small saucepan, combine tomato sauce, onion, lemon juice, brown sugar, oil, Worcestershire sauce, mustard, garlic powder, salt, pepper, and juice from pineapple.

Bring to a boil over medium heat. Reduce heat to low, cover, and simmer 15 minutes.

Pour sauce over shrimp in a shallow bowl and marinate in the refrigerator for several hours, turning shrimp occasionally.

Remove shrimp from marinade. Alternately thread shrimp, pineapple, and green pepper on 4 skewers. Place on broiler pan or barbecue grill.

Broil or grill for 8 to 18 minutes, turning occasionally, until shrimp are done.

While shrimp is broiling, bring marinade to a boil in a small saucepan. Simmer 2 minutes.

Serve marinade over shrimp.

Each serving provides:

278 Calories

2	Protein Servings	31 g	Protein
2	Vegetable Servings	6 g	Fat (21% of calories)
3/4	Fat Serving	25 g	Carbohydrate
1/2	Fruit Serving	305 mg	Sodium
16	Additional Calories	216 mg	Cholesterol
		2 g	Fiber

Bengal Seafood Salad

This unusual salad has an exotic flavor and a wonderful blend of textures. It's lovely served on a bed of lettuce, accompanied by sliced, fresh pineapple and tomatoes.

Makes 6 servings

12	ounces crab meat (1¹/₂ cups)
4	ounces cooked, peeled shrimp, cut into 1-inch pieces
1	cup thinly sliced celery
¹/₄	cup finely chopped onion
3	ounces sliced water chestnuts
1	cup canned crushed pineapple (packed in juice), undrained
¹/₄	cup raisins
2	tablespoons sunflower seeds (raw or dry roasted)
³/₄	cup plain nonfat yogurt
3	tablespoons reduced-calorie mayonnaise
3	tablespoons lemon juice
1	teaspoon coconut extract
2	teaspoons curry powder, or more to taste

In a large bowl, combine crab meat, shrimp, celery, onion, water chestnuts, pineapple, raisins, and sunflower seeds. Mix well.

In a small bowl, combine remaining ingredients. Add to crab mixture and mix well.

Chill several hours to blend flavors.

Each serving provides:

198 Calories

1¹/₄	Protein Servings	19 g	Protein
¹/₂	Vegetable Serving	5 g	Fat (22% of calories)
³/₄	Fat Serving	20 g	Carbohydrate
¹/₂	Fruit Serving	285 mg	Sodium
55	Additional Calories	97 mg	Cholesterol
		1 g	Fiber

Beef, Pork, and Lamb

There's no need to give up meat altogether when planning a healthful diet. Most health professionals recommend instead that you limit the amount of meat you consume. Select the cuts of meat carefully, choosing the leanest cuts. Extra-lean ground beef, flank steak, and pork tenderloin are among the leanest choices. Also, trim away all visible fat before cooking.

Meat contains no fiber, so serve it with ample portions of whole grains and vegetables. To reduce your overall fat intake, use smaller portions of meat and larger portions of grains and vegetables.

In the following recipes, we've lowered fat content and increased flavor by emphasizing the use of herbs and spices. We know these dishes will delight the entire family.

Teriyaki Flank Steak

This is one of our very favorite dishes for cookouts. We usually serve it with a tossed salad, a rice dish, and a pile of steamed fresh green beans.

Makes 6 servings

1	1¹/₂ -pound flank steak
¹/₄	cup reduced-sodium soy sauce
¹/₄	cup dry sherry
¹/₄	teaspoon garlic powder
¹/₄	teaspoon ground ginger

Score meat diagonally on both sides, making several cuts about ¹/₄ inch deep. Place meat in a shallow bowl or baking dish.

Combine remaining ingredients and pour over meat. Marinate in the refrigerator 4 to 5 hours, turning meat over several times.

Preheat broiler.

Place meat on a broiler rack and broil until done to taste. Turn meat several times while cooking and baste with marinade.

To slice, tilt knife blade slightly and slice meat, across the grain, into paper-thin slices.

Each serving provides:

198 Calories

3	Protein Servings	24 g	Protein
8	Additional Calories	9 g	Fat (43% of calories)
		2 g	Carbohydrate
		471 mg	Sodium
		57 mg	Cholesterol
		0 g	Fiber

Steak-Kabobs

From summer cookouts to elegant dinner parties, this one can't miss.

Makes 6 servings

1¹/₂	pounds boneless beef top sirloin steaks, cut into 1-inch cubes, all visible fat removed
¹/₄	cup reduced-sodium soy sauce
1¹/₂	cups canned pineapple chunks, packed in juice, drained (Reserve juice.)
2	tablespoons pineapple juice
2	tablespoons dry sherry
2	tablespoons firmly packed brown sugar
1	teaspoon onion powder
¹/₂	teaspoon ground ginger
¹/₄	teaspoon garlic powder
1	large green bell pepper, cut into 1-inch squares

Place meat in a shallow pan.

In a small bowl, combine soy sauce, pineapple juice, sherry, brown sugar, onion powder, ginger, and garlic powder. Pour over meat. Marinate in the refrigerator for several hours, turning meat occasionally. Drain, reserving marinade.

Alternately thread the meat, green pepper, and pineapple on 6 skewers. Place on a broiler rack or outdoor grill. Broil 5 inches from heat for about 10 minutes, or until done to taste, turning skewers to brown on both sides. Baste with marinade while cooking.

Each serving provides:

241 Calories

3	Protein Servings	27 g	Protein
¹/₂	Vegetable Serving	6 g	Fat (24% of calories)
¹/₂	Fruit Serving	17 g	Carbohydrate
20	Additional Calories	460 mg	Sodium
		76 mg	Cholesterol
		1 g	Fiber

Chinese Pepper Steak

A favorite in Chinese restaurants, this delectable dish is usually served over rice. The meat is best when sliced very thin, which is easier to do if it is partially frozen.

Makes 6 servings

2	teaspoons vegetable oil
1¹/₄	pounds boneless beef top round steak, sliced across the grain into very thin strips
¹/₂	cup chopped onion
3	cloves garlic, finely chopped
1	packet low-sodium instant beef flavored broth mix
1¹/₄	cups water
1	16-ounce can salt-free (or regular) tomatoes, chopped, drained
2	large green bell peppers, sliced vertically into ¹/₂-inch strips
1	tablespoon plus 1 teaspoon cornstarch dissolved in ¹/₄ cup water
2	tablespoons reduced-sodium (or regular) soy sauce
¹/₈	teaspoon pepper

Heat oil in a large nonstick skillet over medium-high heat. Add beef. Cook until browned, then remove beef from skillet and place in a covered bowl to keep warm.

Add onion and garlic to skillet. Cook, stirring frequently, about 3 minutes, until onion starts to brown. Return meat to skillet. Add broth mix, water, tomatoes, and green pepper. Reduce heat to medium, cover skillet, and simmer 5 minutes, stirring occasionally.

Combine cornstarch mixture, soy sauce, and pepper. Add to skillet. Reduce heat to medium-low and cook, stirring, until mixture has thickened slightly and is hot and bubbly, about 3 minutes.

Each serving provides:

177 Calories

2¹/₂	Protein Servings	23 g	Protein
1¹/₂	Vegetable Servings	5 g	Fat (25% of calories)
¹/₄	Fat Serving	10 g	Carbohydrate
12	Additional Calories	261 mg	Sodium
		54 mg	Cholesterol
		1 g	Fiber

Sukiyaki

This delectable Japanese recipe also works well with chicken, shrimp, or tofu in place of the beef.

Makes 6 servings

2	teaspoons vegetable oil
1¹/₂	pounds boneless beef top sirloin steak, sliced paper-thin, all visible fat removed
2	cups sliced onions
1	cup sliced celery
1	cup sliced mushrooms
2	cups fresh bean sprouts
¹/₂	cup canned bamboo shoots, drained
¹/₂	cup canned sliced water chestnuts, drained
¹/₂	cup water
¹/₄	cup reduced-sodium soy sauce
2	tablespoons dry sherry
2	tablespoons sugar
1	packet low-sodium instant beef broth mix
¹/₄	teaspoon pepper
3	cups raw spinach leaves, stems removed
1	cup thinly sliced green onion (green and white parts)

Heat oil in a large nonstick skillet over medium heat. Add beef. Cook until browned, then remove beef from skillet and place in a covered bowl to keep warm.

Add onions, celery, and mushrooms. Cook, stirring frequently, 5 minutes. Add bean sprouts, bamboo shoots, and water chestnuts. Cook, stirring frequently, until onions and celery are tender-crisp.

In a small bowl, combine water, soy sauce, sherry, sugar, broth mix, and pepper. Pour over vegetables.

Return meat to skillet, along with spinach and green onions. Cook, tossing frequently, until mixture is heated through.

Each serving provides:

250 Calories

3	Protein Servings	28 g	Protein
3 1/2	Vegetable Servings	7 g	Fat (25% of calories)
1/4	Fat Serving	18 g	Carbohydrate
34	Additional Calories	516 mg	Sodium
		69 mg	Cholesterol
		4 g	Fiber

Chili Meat Loaf

Chili powder and garlic add a wonderful zip to this easy dish. Serve it with a baked potato topped with nonfat sour cream and salsa, add a tossed salad, and dinner is complete. The leftovers make great sandwiches.

Makes 6 servings

1	pound lean ground beef (10% fat)
3	slices whole wheat bread (1-ounce slices), crumbled
1	cup salsa (hot or mild)
1	egg white
2	tablespoons grated onion
1	tablespoon prepared yellow mustard
1	teaspoon chili powder (or more to taste)
1/2	teaspoon dry mustard
1/4	teaspoon garlic powder

Preheat oven to 350 degrees F.

In a large bowl, combine beef with remaining ingredients, mixing well. Shape mixture into a loaf. Place on a rack in a shallow baking pan.

Bake, uncovered, 1 hour.

Each serving provides:

176 Calories

2	Protein Servings	18 g	Protein
1/2	Bread Serving	9 g	Fat (46% of calories)
3/4	Vegetable Serving	10 g	Carbohydrate
3	Additional Calories	602 mg	Sodium
		47 mg	Cholesterol
		1 g	Fiber

French Meat Loaf

Sweet French dressing gives new life to this traditional dish. Add a baked potato and a steamed green vegetable and your meal is complete.

Makes 6 servings

1	pound lean ground beef (10% fat)
1	egg white
1/2	cup finely chopped onion
1/4	cup finely chopped green bell pepper
1/2	cup reduced-fat French dressing (Choose the dark-colored sweet and spicy kind.)
3	tablespoons dry bread crumbs or wheat germ
	Salt and pepper

Preheat oven to 350 degrees F.

In a large bowl, combine beef with remaining ingredients, mixing well. Shape mixture into a loaf. Place the loaf on a rack in a shallow baking pan.

Bake, uncovered, 1 hour.

Each serving provides:

176 Calories

2	Protein Servings	17 g	Protein
1/4	Vegetable Serving	9 g	Fat (46% of calories)
52	Additional Calories	8 g	Carbohydrate
		253 mg	Sodium
		47 mg	Cholesterol
		0 g	Fiber

Pepper Burgers

Red and green peppers are colorful and tasty in these easy burgers

Makes 6 servings

1	8-ounce can salt-free (or regular) tomato sauce
1	teaspoon dried oregano
1	teaspoon dried basil
1/4	teaspoon garlic powder
1/4	teaspoon dry mustard
	Salt and pepper
3/4	pound lean ground beef (10% fat)
1	egg white
1/2	cup finely chopped red bell pepper
1/2	cup finely chopped green bell pepper
3	tablespoons dry bread crumbs (or wheat germ)

In a small bowl, combine tomato sauce, oregano, basil, garlic powder, mustard, salt, and pepper.

In a large bowl, combine beef, egg white, bell peppers, bread crumbs, and half of the sauce mixture. Mix well. Shape into 4 burgers.

Spray a large nonstick skillet or griddle with nonstick cooking spray. Heat over medium heat.

Place burgers in skillet. Cook until burgers are done and are nicely browned on both sides. Turn burgers several times while cooking.

Spoon remaining sauce over burgers. Cover skillet and continue cooking until sauce is heated through.

Each serving provides:

134 Calories

1 1/2	Protein Servings	13 g	Protein
1	Vegetable Serving	6 g	Fat (41% of calories)
18	Additional Calories	7 g	Carbohydrate
		88 mg	Sodium
		35 mg	Cholesterol
		1 g	Fiber

Grilled Ham Steak

The smoky ham flavor is a perfect match for the sweet preserves in this easy meal. Use any flavor preserves you like and, whether made in the broiler or on the outside grill, it's sure to be a hit.

Makes 6 servings

$1/2$	cup canned crushed pineapple (packed in juice), drained
$1/4$	cup fruit-only spread (Choose any flavor. Our favorites are peach, apricot, or raspberry.)
1	tablespoon lemon juice
2	teaspoons dry mustard
1	teaspoon grated fresh orange peel
$1/2$	teaspoon cornstarch
1	1-pound slice boneless ham, cut $1^1/2$ inches thick, trimmed of all visible fat

In a small saucepan, combine all ingredients, except ham. Bring to a boil over medium heat, stirring constantly. Continue to cook, stirring, 2 minutes. Remove from heat.

Broil ham to desired doneness on both sides. Spread preserves over top. Return to broiler until hot and bubbly.

Each serving provides:

144 Calories

2	Protein Servings	15 g	Protein
$3/4$	Fruit Serving	4 g	Fat (25% of calories)
6	Additional Calories	12 g	Carbohydrate
		1082 mg	Sodium
		36 mg	Cholesterol
		0 g	Fiber

Ham Barbecue on a Bun

This is a perfect Sunday football supper. Add a bowl of soup and a salad and enjoy the game.

Makes 6 sandwiches

1	teaspoon vegetable oil
1	cup chopped onions
3	cloves garlic, finely chopped
1	8-ounce can salt-free (or regular) tomato sauce
1/4	cup vinegar
1	tablespoon plus 1 teaspoon lemon juice
2	tablespoons prepared yellow mustard
2	tablespoons firmly packed brown sugar
1	teaspoon Worcestershire sauce
	Dash hot pepper sauce
1	pound cooked boneless ham, sliced paper-thin, all visible fat removed
6	2-ounce hamburger buns

Heat oil in a large nonstick skillet over medium heat. Add onion and garlic. Cook, stirring frequently, until onion is tender, about 5 minutes.

Add remaining ingredients, except ham and buns. Reduce heat to medium-low and cook, stirring frequently, 5 minutes. Add ham and heat through.

Serve on buns.

Each serving provides:

328 Calories

2¹/₂	Protein Servings	22 g	Protein
2	Bread Servings	8 g	Fat (23% of calories)
1	Vegetable Serving	41 g	Carbohydrate
33	Additional Calories	1315 mg	Sodium
		40 mg	Cholesterol
		2 g	Fiber

Dijon Pork Steaks

*This unusual marinade combines soy sauce and Dijon mustard with tangy,
delicious results. The marinade also works well with chicken.*

Makes 4 servings

1	pound boneless center-cut loin pork chops, trimmed of all visible fat
1/4	cup dry white wine
3	tablespoons reduced-sodium soy sauce
2	tablespoons dry sherry
1	tablespoon Dijon mustard
1/4	teaspoon garlic powder

Place pork chops in a shallow bowl. Combine remaining ingredients and pour over chops. Marinate in the refrigerator several hours
or overnight, turning chops occasionally.

Preheat broiler or grill.

Place chops on a broiler pan or barbecue rack, reserving marinade.
Broil, turning several times and basting with marinade, until chops
are lightly browned and cooked through.

Each serving provides:

203 Calories

3	Protein Servings	26 g	Protein
19	Additional Calories	7 g	Fat (36% of calories)
		2 g	Carbohydrate
		592 mg	Sodium
		70 mg	Cholesterol
		0 g	Fiber

Orange Baked Pork Chops

Sweet sauces like this one seem to bring out the flavor of pork. For an elegant touch, serve these chops over cooked brown rice, garnished with fresh orange sections.

Makes 4 servings

1	pound boneless center-cut loin pork chops, trimmed of all visible fat
1/2	cup orange juice
1	tablespoon grated onion
1	tablespoon reduced-sodium soy sauce
1	tablespoon honey
1/2	teaspoon grated fresh orange peel
1/4	teaspoon dry mustard
1/8	teaspoon dried thyme

Place pork chops in a shallow pan.

Combine remaining ingredients and pour over chops. Marinate in the refrigerator several hours or overnight, turning chops occasionally.

Preheat broiler or grill.

Place chops on a broiler pan or barbecue rack, reserving marinade. Broil, turning several times and basting with marinade, until chops are lightly browned and cooked through.

Each serving provides:

206 Calories

3	Protein Servings	26 g	Protein
1/4	Fruit Serving	7 g	Fat (31% of calories)
15	Additional Calories	8 g	Carbohydrate
		202 mg	Sodium
		70 mg	Cholesterol
		0 g	Fiber

Dill Roasted Pork

Roast pork is a simple and delicious favorite all over the country. The addition of dill to this one makes a nice accent.

Makes 4 servings

1	1-pound boneless lean pork tenderloin, trimmed of all visible fat
1/2	teaspoon garlic powder
1/4	teaspoon dill weed
	Salt and pepper

Preheat oven to 325 degrees F.

Place roast on a rack in a shallow baking pan. Sprinkle evenly with spices.

Bake, uncovered, 45 minutes to 1 hour, or until meat is done.

Each serving provides:

141 Calories

3	Protein Servings	24 g	Protein
		4 g	Fat (27% of calories)
		0 g	Carbohydrate
		48 mg	Sodium
		67 mg	Cholesterol
		0 g	Fiber

Marinated Lamb Roast

Since a leg of lamb can be boned and grilled, cookouts have become a lot more exciting. Put some potatoes on the grill, add a tossed salad, and what a feast!

Makes 10 servings

1	6-pound leg of lamb
1/4	cup dry white wine
3	tablespoons lemon juice
3/4	teaspoon garlic powder
1/2	teaspoon dried rosemary, crumbled
1/2	teaspoon dried oregano
1/4	teaspoon dried thyme

Have the butcher remove the bone from the lamb and open the meat lengthwise so it can be spread on the grill.

Place meat in a large plastic bag and set in a large pan.

Combine remaining ingredients and pour over meat. Marinate in the refrigerator several hours or overnight, turning bag over several times.

Grill 5 inches from heat, turning frequently and basting with marinade, until done to taste. (Allow about 1 hour for medium.)

Remove all visible fat before slicing. Serve 3 ounces of sliced lamb per portion, reserving remaining lamb for another time.

Each serving provides:

165 Calories

3	Protein Servings	24 g	Protein
5	Additional Calories	7 g	Fat (38% of calories)
		1 g	Carbohydrate
		59 mg	Sodium
		76 mg	Cholesterol
		0 g	Fiber

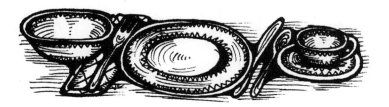

Roast Leg of Lamb

The rosemary adds a touch of distinction to this delicious dish. It's a favorite company dish and goes well with mashed potatoes, steamed broccoli, and a tossed salad. Add a light fruit dessert and you have a lowfat meal fit for royalty.

Makes 10 servings

1	6-pound leg of lamb
6	large cloves garlic, cut in half lengthwise
2	teaspoons seasoned salt
1	teaspoon dried rosemary, crumbled
1	teaspoon dried thyme
1/2	teaspoon onion powder
1/4	teaspoon pepper
1/4	teaspoon garlic powder

Preheat oven to 450 degrees F.

Place lamb on a rack in a shallow roasting pan.

With a sharp knife, make twelve 1-inch deep cuts in lamb. Place a garlic half in each cut.

Combine seasonings and rub into meat, covering entire surface.

Place pan in oven. Reduce heat to 325 degrees F.

Roast 2 to 2 1/2 hours, or until done to taste.

Remove all visible fat before slicing. Serve 3 ounces of sliced lamb per portion, reserving remaining lamb for another time.

Each serving provides:

167 Calories

3	Protein Servings	
	24 g	Protein
	7 g	Fat (37% of calories)
	1 g	Carbohydrate
	99 mg	Sodium
	76 mg	Cholesterol
	0 g	Fiber

Beans and Tofu

The beans in this section are actually legumes, which are the seeds from certain pod-bearing plants. Among the most popular types of legumes are kidney beans, pinto beans, chick peas or garbanzo beans, Great Northern beans, black beans, split peas, and lentils. Legumes are extremely versatile. They can be used to replace all or part of the meat in stews and add fiber and texture to soups. Besides being low in fat and high in fiber, legumes contain iron, B vitamins, and minerals.

Tofu is a product that is made from soy beans in much the same way that cheese is made from milk. Available in the produce section of most large grocery stores, tofu is high in protein, low in saturated fat, and contains no cholesterol. Its very mild flavor is a definite advantage, allowing the tofu to blend easily with other ingredients and take on the flavor of whatever it is combined with.

In this section we offer delicious, creative recipes that will add variety to your meals, along with a refreshing change of pace.

Italian Beans and Cheese

This is one of our favorite bean recipes. We make it into a hearty meal by spooning the tasty beans over brown rice or a split baked potato.

Makes 6 servings

2	teaspoons vegetable oil
1/2	cup chopped onion
1/2	cup chopped green bell pepper
1	16-ounce can salt-free (or regular) tomatoes, chopped, undrained
1	16-ounce can kidney beans, rinsed and drained (This will yield approximately 10 ounces of beans.)
1	teaspoon dried oregano
1	teaspoon dry mustard
1/2	teaspoon dried basil
1/4	teaspoon garlic powder
1/8	teaspoon dried thyme
2	ounces shredded reduced-fat Cheddar cheese (1/2 cup)
2	ounces shredded part-skim mozzarella cheese (1/2 cup)

Heat oil in a large nonstick skillet over medium heat. Add onion and green pepper. Cook, stirring frequently, until tender, about 5 minutes. Add small amounts of water if necessary, about a table-spoon at a time, to prevent sticking.

Add tomatoes, beans, and spices. Cook, stirring frequently, until mixture is hot and bubbly.

Remove from heat and sprinkle cheese evenly over bean mixture. Cover pan and let cheese melt (about 5 minutes).

Each serving provides:

145 Calories

1 1/2	Protein Servings	10 g	Protein
1	Vegetable Serving	5 g	Fat (33% of calories)
1/4	Fat Serving	14 g	Carbohydrate
17	Additional Calories	226 mg	Sodium
		12 mg	Cholesterol
		4 g	Fiber

Mushroom Bean Loaf Supreme

And supreme it is! This meatless loaf has the texture of a fine pâté. Serve it hot for dinner and serve the leftovers, hot or cold, in a sandwich or on crackers as an appetizer.

Makes 6 servings

1	16-ounce can pinto beans, rinsed and drained (This will yield approximately 9 ounces of beans.)
$3/4$	cup liquid egg substitute
2	slices whole wheat bread (1-ounce slices), crumbled
2	teaspoons vegetable oil
2	packets low-sodium instant chicken broth mix
1	tablespoon grated onion
$1/4$	teaspoon garlic powder
	Salt and pepper
1	8-ounce can mushroom pieces, drained

Preheat oven to 350 degrees F.

Spray a 4 × 8-inch loaf pan with nonstick cooking spray.

In a blender container, combine all ingredients, except mushrooms. Blend until smooth. Stir in mushrooms.

Spoon mixture into prepared pan.

Bake 50 to 55 minutes, until set and lightly browned.

Let loaf stand for 5 minutes, then invert onto a serving plate.

Each serving provides:

105 Calories

$1^1/4$	Protein Servings	7 g	Protein
$1/4$	Bread Serving	3 g	Fat (21% of calories)
$1/4$	Vegetable Serving	14 g	Carbohydrate
$1/4$	Fat Serving	311 mg	Sodium
13	Additional Calories	0 mg	Cholesterol
		3 g	Fiber

Delhi Beans and Apples

Serve this unusual, slightly sweet, fruit and vegetable combo over brown rice for a delicious meal, Indian style.

Makes 4 servings

2	teaspoons vegetable oil
1/2	cup chopped onions
2	small Golden Delicious apples, peeled, chopped into 1/2-inch pieces
1	16-ounce can kidney beans, rinsed and drained (This will yield 10 ounces of beans.)
1	16-ounce can stewed tomatoes
2	tablespoons honey
1	teaspoon curry powder
1	tablespoon cornstarch
1	tablespoon water

Preheat oven to 350 degrees F.

Spray a 1 1/2-quart baking dish with nonstick cooking spray.

Heat oil in a large nonstick skillet over medium heat. Add onions and cook 5 minutes, stirring frequently. Add apples and continue to cook 5 more minutes, stirring frequently.

Remove skillet from heat and add remaining ingredients, dissolving cornstarch in the 1 tablespoon of water first. Mix well. Spoon into prepared baking dish.

Cover and bake 40 minutes.

Each serving provides:

212 Calories

1 1/4	Protein Servings	8 g	Protein
1 1/4	Vegetable Servings	4 g	Fat (14% of calories)
1/2	Fat Serving	41 g	Carbohydrate
1/2	Fruit Serving	436 mg	Sodium
30	Additional Calories	0 mg	Cholesterol
		9 g	Fiber

Cajun Bean Pot

*Add as little or as much hot sauce as you like in this easy dish for a crowd.
It's perfect over rice or with a chunk of crusty bread for a football Sunday.*

Makes 8 servings

2	teaspoons olive oil
1	cup chopped onion
1	cup chopped green bell pepper
$^1/_2$	cup chopped celery
3	cloves garlic, finely chopped
3	16-ounce cans kidney beans, rinsed and drained (Or use a mixture of 3 different kinds of beans.) (This will yield approximately 30 ounces of beans.)
1	16-ounce can stewed tomatoes, undrained
1	6-ounce can tomato paste
$1^1/_4$	cups water
1	teaspoon Worcestershire sauce
$^1/_2$	teaspoon dried oregano
$^1/_4$	teaspoon dried thyme
$^1/_8$	to $^1/_4$ teaspoon bottled hot sauce
2	bay leaves

Heat oil in a large saucepan over medium heat. Add onion, green pepper, celery, and garlic. Cook, stirring frequently, until tender, about 10 minutes. Add small amounts of water as necessary, about a tablespoon at a time, to prevent sticking.

Add remaining ingredients, mixing well. When mixture boils, reduce heat to medium-low, cover, and simmer 30 minutes.

Remove and discard bay leaves before serving.

Each serving provides:

178 Calories

$1^3/_4$	Protein Servings	11 g	Protein
2	Vegetable Servings	2 g	Fat (12% of calories)
$^1/_4$	Fat Serving	30 g	Carbohydrate
8	Additional Calories	541 mg	Sodium
		0 mg	Cholesterol
		10 g	Fiber

Refried Beans

Homemade refried beans are delicious on tacos, on crackers, or stuffed into pita bread. Top with shredded lettuce and chopped tomato and they're ready to enjoy in no time.

Makes 4 servings

2	teaspoons vegetable oil
1	cup finely chopped onion
3	cloves garlic, finely minced
1	16-ounce can pinto beans, rinsed and drained (This will yield approximately 9 ounces of beans.)
1/2	teaspoon dried oregano
1/2	teaspoon ground cumin
	Salt and pepper

Heat oil in a large nonstick skillet over medium heat. Add onion and garlic. Cook, stirring frequently, until onion is tender and begins to brown, about 5 minutes.

While onion is cooking, place beans in a large bowl and mash with a fork or potato masher. Add to skillet, along with spices.

Heat through, stirring frequently.

Each serving provides:

104 Calories

1	Protein Serving	5 g	Protein
1/2	Vegetable Serving	3 g	Fat (25% of calories)
1/2	Fat Serving	15 g	Carbohydrate
10	Additional Calories	189 mg	Sodium
		0 mg	Cholesterol
		4 g	Fiber

Kidney Beans Provençal

Simple and straightforward, this dish can be thrown together in no time. It can be served as an entrée or side dish, alone or over noodles or rice.

Makes 4 servings

2	teaspoons olive oil
2	cloves garlic, minced
1/2	cup chopped onion
1	cup chopped mushrooms
1	16-ounce can salt-free (or regular) tomatoes, chopped, drained (Reserve liquid.)
1	tablespoon cornstarch
1	teaspoon dried basil
1	teaspoon dried oregano
1	19-ounce can white kidney beans, rinsed and drained (This will yield approximately 12 ounces of beans.)
1	tablespoon imitation bacon bits
1	tablespoon Italian seasoned bread crumbs
1	teaspoon grated Parmesan cheese

Preheat oven to 350 degrees F.

Spray a 1-quart casserole with nonstick cooking spray.

Heat oil in a large nonstick skillet over medium heat. Add garlic, onion, and mushrooms. Cook, stirring frequently, until vegetables are tender, 8 to 10 minutes. Add tomatoes.

Place reserved tomato liquid in a small bowl and add cornstarch, stirring until dissolved. Add to skillet along with basil and oregano. Cook, stirring, until mixture comes to a boil. Remove skillet from heat and stir in beans and bacon bits.

Spoon mixture into prepared casserole. Combine bread crumbs and Parmesan cheese and sprinkle evenly over the top.

Bake, uncovered, 30 minutes.

Each serving provides:

183 Calories

1 1/2	Protein Servings	10 g	Protein
1 3/4	Vegetable Servings	4 g	Fat (20% of calories)
1/2	Fat Serving	28 g	Carbohydrate
25	Additional Calories	295 mg	Sodium
		0 mg	Cholesterol
		7 g	Fiber

Butter Bean and Cheese Squares

The blend of onions, garlic, and Cheddar cheese make this a dish your family and guests will love. Don't let the name fool you. Butter beans contain no butter!

Makes 6 servings

15	ounces potatoes, unpeeled, coarsely shredded
1/3	cup nonfat dry milk
1	16-ounce can butter beans, rinsed and drained (This will yield approximately 10 ounces of beans.)
3	ounces shredded reduced-fat Cheddar cheese (3/4 cup)
3/4	cup liquid egg substitute
2/3	cup lowfat (1%) cottage cheese
1	tablespoon all-purpose flour
1	tablespoon minced onion flakes
1	tablespoon dried parsley flakes
1/4	teaspoon garlic powder
	Salt and pepper

Preheat oven to 350 degrees F.

Spray an 8-inch square baking pan with nonstick cooking spray.

Place potatoes in prepared pan. Press them lightly in place.

Sprinkle dry milk evenly over potatoes. Top with beans.

In a large bowl, combine remaining ingredients, mixing well. (Mixture will be lumpy.) Spoon mixture over beans.

Bake, uncovered, 35 minutes, until set and lightly browned.

Each serving provides:

193 Calories

2¹/4	Protein Servings	16 g	Protein
1/2	Bread Serving	3 g	Fat (15% of calories)
25	Additional Calories	25 g	Carbohydrate
		400 mg	Sodium
		12 mg	Cholesterol
		1 g	Fiber

Turkish Stew

For a real authentic touch, serve this uniquely spiced stew over cooked cous-cous, add a tossed salad, and pass a basket of pita bread.

Makes 6 servings

18	ounces sweet potatoes, peeled, cut into 1-inch chunks
2$^1/_2$	cups butternut squash, peeled, cut into 1-inch chunks (About a 1$^1/_4$ pound squash)
1$^1/_2$	cups carrots, cut into $^1/_2$-inch slices
1$^1/_2$	cups chopped onion
1	16-ounce can chick peas, rinsed and drained (This will yield approximately 10 ounces of chick peas.)
1$^2/_3$	cups water
1$^1/_2$	teaspoons chili powder
1$^1/_2$	teaspoons ground coriander
$^1/_4$	teaspoon ground nutmeg
$^1/_{16}$	teaspoon saffron
$^1/_{16}$	teaspoon ground cloves

Combine all ingredients in a large saucepan. Bring to a boil over medium heat. Reduce heat to low, cover, and simmer 1 hour, or until vegetables are tender. Stir occasionally while cooking.

Each serving provides:

187 Calories

$^1/_2$	Protein Serving	6 g	Protein
2	Bread Servings	2 g	Fat (8% of calories)
1	Vegetable Serving	39 g	Carbohydrate
12	Additional Calories	122 mg	Sodium
		0 mg	Cholesterol
		7 g	Fiber

Bean and Cheese Quesadillas

These are the Mexican answer to a quick meal. If you like, place a teaspoonful of chopped tomato, green onion, or green chilies on top of the cheese before you fold the tortillas. Served with salsa, this makes a great appetizer or lunch.

Makes 4 servings

4   6-inch flour tortillas
1/2   cup canned fat-free refried beans (Available in the Mexican
        food section of most large grocery stores.)
2   ounces shredded reduced-fat Cheddar or Monterey Jack cheese
        (1/2 cup)
        Salsa (optional)

Preheat a large nonstick griddle over medium heat. Spray with a nonstick cooking spray.

Place tortillas on a flat surface. Place 2 tablespoons of beans on each tortilla and spread it evenly, covering just half of each tortilla. Divide cheese evenly and place on top of the beans. Add chopped green onion, and other vegetables, if desired. Fold tortillas in half and press down gently. Heat tortillas, flipping them back and forth, until cheese is melted and tortillas are hot and crispy on both sides.

Serve right away, topped with salsa, if you like.

Each serving provides:

134 Calories

1	Protein Serving	8 g	Protein
1	Bread Serving	4 g	Fat (29% of calories)
28	Additional Calories	16 g	Carbohydrate
		306 mg	Sodium
		10 mg	Cholesterol
		2 g	Fiber

Pineapple–Black Bean Salad

*As cool and colorful as Caribbean breezes, this refreshing bean salad can be
served on a bed of lettuce or piled into a pita for a delicious sandwich.*

Makes 4 servings

1	16-ounce can black beans, rinsed and drained (This will yield approximately 10 ounces of beans.)
1	8-ounce can pineapple tidbits (packed in juice), drained (Reserve juice.)
1/4	cup pineapple juice
1/2	cup finely chopped red bell pepper
1/2	cup thinly sliced green onion (green and white parts)
2	teaspoons vinegar
1/2	teaspoon ground cumin
1/4	teaspoon salt
	Pepper
1	jalapeño pepper, finely chopped, seeds and inner membranes discarded (optional)

Combine all ingredients in a medium bowl. Mix well.
Chill thoroughly.
Mix before serving.

Each serving provides:

105 Calories

1 1/4	Protein Servings	5 g	Protein
1/2	Vegetable Serving	1 g	Fat (5% of calories)
1/2	Fruit Serving	21 g	Carbohydrate
		321 mg	Sodium
		0 mg	Cholesterol
		4 g	Fiber

Black Bean Casserole Olé

Picture a thick cornmeal pudding. Now picture that pudding chock full of black beans, chilies, tomatoes, corn, and spices. Now try it. You'll love it.

Makes 6 servings

1	tablespoon olive oil
1	cup chopped onion
3/4	cup plus 2 tablespoons yellow cornmeal (4¹/2 ounces)
2	teaspoons chili powder
1¹/4	cups skim milk
1	16-ounce can black beans, rinsed and drained (This will yield 10 ounces of beans.)
1	16-ounce can corn, drained
1	16-ounce can stewed tomatoes
1	4-ounce can chopped green chilies (mild or hot), drained
1/4	cup shredded reduced-fat Cheddar cheese (1 ounce)

Preheat oven to 350 degrees F.

Spray an 8-inch square baking pan with nonstick cooking spray.

In a large bowl, combine all ingredients, except cheese. Mix well. Place in prepared pan. Sprinkle with cheese.

Bake, uncovered, 45 minutes.

Each serving provides:

256 Calories

1	Protein Serving	11 g	Protein
1¹/2	Bread Servings	5 g	Fat (16% of calories)
1	Vegetable Serving	45 g	Carbohydrate
1/2	Fat Serving	629 mg	Sodium
30	Additional Calories	4 mg	Cholesterol
		7 g	Fiber

Bean Gravy

What a wonderful idea—a gravy made from protein instead of fat! We like to serve this thick, tasty treat over rice, pasta, or baked potatoes. It's so versatile.

Makes 4 servings

1	16-ounce can kidney or pinto beans, rinsed and drained (This will yield approximately 10 ounces of cooked beans.)
1/2	cup water
1	packet low-sodium instant chicken or vegetable broth mix
1	teaspoon minced onion flakes
	Pepper

Combine all ingredients in a blender container. Blend until smooth.

Spoon mixture into a small saucepan. Heat, stirring frequently, over medium-low heat, until hot and bubbly. Add water if a thinner consistency is desired.

Each serving provides:

88 Calories

1 1/4	Protein Servings	6 g	Protein
3	Additional Calories	1 g	Fat (7% of calories)
		14 g	Carbohydrate
		362 mg	Sodium
		0 mg	Cholesterol
		5 g	Fiber

Chili Con Tofu

Served over brown rice or a baked potato, this flavorful dish is nutritious and very filling.

Makes 4 servings

8	ounces medium or firm tofu, sliced and drained well between towels
2	ounces shredded reduced-fat Cheddar cheese ($1/2$ cup)
1	ounce shredded part-skim mozzarella cheese ($1/4$ cup)
1	8-ounce can salt-free (or regular) tomato sauce
2	tablespoons grated onion
$3/4$	teaspoon ground cumin
$1/2$	teaspoon chili powder, or more to taste
$1/2$	teaspoon dried oregano
$1/4$	teaspoon garlic powder
1	4-ounce can mushroom pieces, drained
1	16-ounce can kidney beans rinsed and drained (This will yield approximately 10 ounces of beans.)

In a large bowl, combine all ingredients, except mushrooms and beans. Mash with a fork or potato masher until well blended. Stir in mushrooms and beans.

Spray a large nonstick skillet with nonstick cooking spray. Add tofu mixture. Cook, stirring frequently, until mixture is hot and bubbly.

Each serving provides:

214 Calories

$3^1/4$	Protein Servings	18 g	Protein
$1^1/4$	Vegetable Servings	7 g	Fat (30% of calories)
		21 g	Carbohydrate
		376 mg	Sodium
		14 mg	Cholesterol
		7 g	Fiber

Sweet and Spicy Tofu and Vegetables

This unusual stir-fry makes a superb dish that's easy and inexpensive.

Makes 4 servings

1	pound medium or firm tofu, sliced 1/4 inch thick, then cut into 1/2-inch strips
1/4	cup lowfat French dressing (Choose the dark-colored, sweet and spicy variety.)
2	tablespoons water
1	tablespoon reduced-sodium soy sauce
2	teaspoons lemon juice
1/4	teaspoon garlic powder
2	teaspoons vegetable oil
1	cup onion, sliced vertically into thin strips
1	cup thinly sliced zucchini, unpeeled
1	cup broccoli, cut into small flowerets
1	cup sliced mushrooms

Spray a large nonstick skillet with nonstick cooking spray. Heat over medium heat.

Add tofu to skillet. Cook, turning carefully, until tofu is lightly browned on both sides. Place tofu in a bowl and cover to keep warm.

Combine dressing, water, soy sauce, lemon juice, and garlic powder. Mix well and set aside.

Heat oil in skillet. Add onion. Cook 5 minutes, stirring frequently. Add remaining vegetables. Cook, stirring frequently, until vegetables are tender-crisp.

Return tofu to skillet, along with dressing mixture. Mix well. Cook, stirring, until heated through.

Each serving provides:

158 Calories

2	Protein Servings	11 g	Protein
2	Vegetable Servings	8 g	Fat (44% of calories)
1/2	Fat Serving	12 g	Carbohydrate
25	Additional Calories	287 mg	Sodium
		0 mg	Cholesterol
		3 g	Fiber

Tofu–Rice Patties with Sweet and Sour Sauce

This "action-packed" version of egg foo yung is high in both protein and flavor.

Makes 4 servings

Sauce

1¹/₂	cups water
2	tablespoons cornstarch
1	tablespoon plus 1 teaspoon fruit-only apricot preserves
1	tablespoon dry sherry
2	packets low-sodium instant chicken broth mix

Patties

1	pound medium tofu, sliced and drained well between towels
1	cup liquid egg substitute
2	tablespoons reduced-sodium soy sauce
2	tablespoons all-purpose flour
2	teaspoons baking powder
¹/₄	teaspoon garlic powder
¹/₄	teaspoon ground ginger
2	cups cooked brown rice

Combine sauce ingredients in a small saucepan. Stir to dissolve cornstarch. Cook, stirring constantly, until mixture boils. Continue to cook, stirring, 1 minute. Cover tightly and set aside.

In a large bowl, combine all patty ingredients, except rice. Mash with a fork or potato masher until well blended. Stir in rice.

Spray a large nonstick skillet or griddle with nonstick cooking spray. Heat over medium heat.

Drop tofu mixture into skillet, using about ¹/₃ cup of mixture for each patty. When bottoms of patties are lightly browned, turn carefully and brown the other sides.

Serve patties topped with sauce.

Each serving provides:			
289 Calories			
2¹/₄	Protein Servings	19 g	Protein
1	Bread Serving	7 g	Fat (20% of calories)
¹/₄	Fruit Serving	39 g	Carbohydrate
48	Additional Calories	1088 mg	Sodium
		0 mg	Cholesterol
		3 g	Fiber

Tofu Fajitas

Serve these juicy fajitas plain or topped with salsa.

Makes 6 servings

1	pound firm tofu, cut into matchstick-size pieces
1¹/₂	cups onion, thinly sliced
1¹/₂	cups green pepper, thinly sliced
1	4-ounce can chopped green chilies
¹/₂	cup orange juice
1	tablespoon olive oil
2	tablespoons vinegar
3	cloves garlic, finely chopped
1	teaspoon ground cumin
1	teaspoon ground coriander
1	teaspoon dried oregano
6	6-inch flour tortillas

Place tofu, onions, and green pepper in a 9 × 13-inch baking pan.

In a small bowl, combine remaining ingredients, except tortillas, mixing well. Pour over tofu mixture. Cover pan and refrigerate 4 or 5 hours, gently stirring tofu mixture occasionally.

To cook:

Wrap tortillas tightly in aluminum foil and heat in a 350-degree F oven for 10 minutes.

Heat a large nonstick skillet over medium-high heat. Drain tofu mixture (reserve marinade) and place in skillet. Cook, stirring gently, until vegetables are slightly tender.

Add marinade, a little at a time, to keep mixture from sticking. (If you prefer a juicy fajita filling, add all of the marinade.)

To serve:

Spoon tofu filling into the center of heated tortillas, roll, and enjoy.

Each serving provides:

236 Calories

³/₄	Protein Serving	15 g	Protein
1	Bread Serving	11 g	Fat (38% of calories)
1	Vegetable Serving	24 g	Carbohydrate
¹/₂	Fat Serving	225 mg	Sodium
22	Additional Calories	0 mg	Cholesterol
		2 g	Fiber

Tofu Creole

Over a mound of steaming brown rice, this makes an unforgettable lunch or dinner.

Makes 4 servings

2	teaspoons vegetable oil
1	cup chopped green bell pepper
1/2	cup chopped onion
3	cloves garlic, finely chopped
1	8-ounce can salt-free (or regular) tomato sauce
2	tablespoons water
1	pound medium or firm tofu, cut into 1/2-inch cubes, drained well between towels
1/2	teaspoon dried oregano
1/2	teaspoon dried basil
1	tablespoon grated Parmesan cheese

Heat oil in a large nonstick skillet over medium heat. Add green pepper, onion, and garlic. Cook, stirring frequently, until tender. Add small amounts of water if necessary, about a tablespoon at a time, to prevent sticking.

Add tomato sauce, water, tofu, and spices. Reduce heat to medium-low, cover, and simmer 10 minutes.

Spoon mixture into a serving bowl and sprinkle with Parmesan cheese.

Each serving provides:

151 Calories

2	Protein Servings	11 g	Protein
1 3/4	Vegetable Servings	8 g	Fat (46% of calories)
1/2	Fat Serving	11 g	Carbohydrate
8	Additional Calories	45 mg	Sodium
		1 mg	Cholesterol
		3 g	Fiber

Tropical Tofu Fritters

Everyone loves pancakes, and in these little gems, the protein, fruit, and milk are rolled into one. What a nutritious breakfast.

Makes 4 servings

8	ounces medium tofu, sliced and drained well between towels
2/3	cup nonfat dry milk
1/2	cup liquid egg substitute
1/4	cup plus 2 tablespoons all-purpose flour
3	tablespoons sugar
1	teaspoon baking powder
2	teaspoons vegetable oil
2	teaspoons vanilla extract
1/2	teaspoon coconut extract
1	medium, ripe banana, sliced
1	cup canned crushed pineapple, packed in juice, drained

In a blender container, combine all ingredients, except pineapple. Blend until smooth. Pour mixture into a small bowl and stir in pineapple.

Spray a large nonstick skillet or griddle with nonstick cooking spray. Heat over medium heat.

Drop batter into skillet, using about 2 tablespoons of batter for each fritter. Turn fritters carefully, browning evenly on both sides. Makes 20 four-inch fritters.

Each serving provides:

271 Calories

1	Protein Serving	13 g	Protein
1/2	Bread Serving	6 g	Fat (18% of calories)
1/2	Fat Serving	43 g	Carbohydrate
1	Fruit Serving	240 mg	Sodium
1/2	Milk Serving	2 mg	Cholesterol
46	Additional Calories	2 g	Fiber

Italian Tofu Squares

One of our favorite tofu recipes, this dish makes a delicious dinner and is also great for brunch.

Makes 6 servings

1	pound medium tofu, sliced and drained well between towels
1	cup liquid egg substitute
1	cup lowfat (1%) cottage cheese
3	tablespoons grated Parmesan cheese (1 ounce), divided in half
2	tablespoons minced onion flakes
1	tablespoon all-purpose flour
1	tablespoon dried parsley flakes
1	teaspoon dried oregano
$1/4$	teaspoon garlic powder
$1/4$	teaspoon pepper
3	tablespoons dry bread crumbs

Sauce

1	8-ounce can salt-free (or regular) tomato sauce
$1/4$	teaspoon dried oregano
$1/4$	teaspoon dried basil
$1/8$	teaspoon garlic powder

Preheat oven to 350 degrees F.

Spray a 9-inch square baking pan with nonstick cooking spray.

In a blender container, combine tofu, egg substitute, cottage cheese, half of the Parmesan cheese, onion flakes, flour, and spices. Blend until smooth. Spoon mixture into prepared pan.

Combine bread crumbs with remaining Parmesan cheese and sprinkle evenly over the top.

Bake 35 minutes, until set and lightly browned.

While tofu is baking, combine sauce ingredients in a small saucepan and heat until bubbly.

To serve cut tofu into squares. Top each serving with sauce.

Each serving provides:

165 Calories

2	Protein Servings	18 g	Protein
3/4	Vegetable Serving	6 g	Fat (32% of calories)
37	Additional Calories	11 g	Carbohydrate
		351 mg	Sodium
		5 mg	Cholesterol
		2 g	Fiber

Tofu Raisin and Rice Patties

These sweet little patties make a great brunch dish. They taste a lot like rice pudding, and the leftovers are delicious cold.

Makes 4 servings

Sauce

1¹/₂	cups water
2	tablespoons cornstarch
1	tablespoon plus 1 teaspoon fruit-only peach or apricot preserves
1	tablespoon sugar

Patties

1	pound medium tofu, sliced and drained well between towels
1	cup liquid egg substitute
¹/₄	cup sugar
1	tablespoon vanilla extract
2	tablespoons all-purpose flour
2	teaspoons baking powder
1	teaspoon ground cinnamon
¹/₂	teaspoon lemon extract
¹/₄	cup raisins
2	cups cooked brown rice

Combine sauce ingredients in a small saucepan. Stir to dissolve cornstarch. Cook, stirring constantly, until mixture boils. Continue to cook, stirring, 1 minute. Cover tightly and set aside.

In a large bowl, combine all patty ingredients, except rice. Mash with a fork or potato masher until well blended. Stir in rice.

Spray a large nonstick skillet or griddle with nonstick cooking spray. Heat over medium heat.

Drop tofu mixture into skillet, using about 1/3 cup of mixture for each patty. When bottoms of patties are lightly browned, turn carefully and brown the other sides.

Serve patties topped with sauce.

Each serving provides:

372 Calories

2 1/4	Protein Servings	18 g	Protein
1	Bread Serving	7 g	Fat (16% of calories)
3/4	Fruit Serving	60 g	Carbohydrate
100	Additional Calories	359 mg	Sodium
		0 mg	Cholesterol
		4 g	Fiber

Marinated Tofu Kabobs

Grilled or broiled and served on a bed of brown rice, these kabobs are at home at any dinner, casual or elegant.

Makes 4 servings

8	pearl onions, peeled
8	medium mushrooms
2	cups fresh pineapple, cut into 1-inch pieces
1	16-ounce can small, whole potatoes, drained (This will yield 12 ounces of potatoes.)
1	cup green bell pepper, cut into 1-inch squares
1	pound firm tofu, cut into 1-inch cubes
8	cherry tomatoes

Marinade

$1/4$	cup reduced-sodium soy sauce
$1/4$	cup dry red wine
$1/4$	cup water
1	teaspoon sesame oil
$1/2$	teaspoon dried oregano
$1/4$	teaspoon garlic powder
$1/8$	teaspoon ground ginger

Place onions, mushrooms, pineapple, potatoes, and green pepper in a large plastic bag and set bag in a large bowl. Add tofu. Set cherry tomatoes aside.

In a small bowl, combine all marinade ingredients, mixing well. Pour over ingredients in bag. Marinate in the refrigerator 4 to 5 hours, or longer, turning bag over several times so that all ingredients are marinated.

To cook:

Thread the marinated ingredients, along with the cherry tomatoes, alternately on 4 skewers. Place on a broiler rack or outdoor grill.

Cook until edges of fruits and vegetables are crisp. Turn several times and baste with marinade while cooking.

Each serving provides:

311 Calories

2	Protein Servings	22 g	Protein
1	Bread Serving	12 g	Fat (32% of calories)
1³/₄	Vegetable Servings	34 g	Carbohydrate
¹/₄	Fat Serving	623 mg	Sodium
1	Fruit Serving	0 mg	Cholesterol
13	Additional Calories	2 g	Fiber

Tofu Stuffed Potatoes

A simple and nutritious side dish or light entrée. They reheat beautifully and prove just how versatile tofu can be.

Makes 4 servings

2	6-ounce baking potatoes, baked
8	ounces medium tofu, sliced and drained well between towels
2	ounces shredded reduced-fat Cheddar cheese ($^1/_2$ cup)
2	tablespoons skim milk
1	tablespoon plus 1 teaspoon reduced-calorie margarine
1	tablespoon minced onion flakes
$1^1/_2$	teaspoons Dijon mustard
$^1/_8$	teaspoon garlic powder
	Salt and pepper
	Paprika

Preheat oven to 375 degrees F.

Cut potatoes in half lengthwise. Carefully scoop out the pulp with a spoon, leaving a $^1/_4$-inch shell.

In a large bowl, combine potato pulp with remaining ingredients, except paprika. Mash with a fork or potato masher until well blended.

Divide mixture evenly and fill potato shells, smoothing the tops with the back of a spoon.

Sprinkle with paprika.

Place potatoes in a shallow baking pan that has been sprayed with nonstick cooking spry.

Bake 30 minutes, until lightly browned.

Each serving provides:

169 Calories

1	Protein Serving	11 g	Protein
$^1/_2$	Bread Serving	7 g	Fat (37% of calories)
$^1/_2$	Fat Serving	17 g	Carbohydrate
31	Additional Calories	213 mg	Sodium
		10 mg	Cholesterol
		2 g	Fiber

Pasta and Pasta Sauces

Everyone's favorite, pasta is a versatile food that can change dramatically, taking on a new character with the addition of each delectable sauce. Pasta is high in carbohydrates, which are our bodies' main source of fuel. In fact, athletes are now turning to pasta for meals, rather than the heavy, high-protein meals they used to eat.

We've avoided butter and cream sauces in our recipes, proving to our mothers that it isn't the pasta that adds pounds, but what we put on top of it. When noodles are called for, we always choose the yolk-free variety, thereby reducing the amount of cholesterol in the dishes. We recommend trying whole wheat pasta for a dish that's higher in carbohydrates, vitamins, minerals, and fiber.

With its variety of shapes and colors, this nutritious food can be an important part of a healthful diet.

Macaroni Verde

This easy recipe will work with any type of cooked pasta or noodles.

Makes 4 servings

2	teaspoons vegetable oil
1	10-ounce package frozen chopped spinach, thawed but not drained
2/3	cup lowfat (1%) cottage cheese
1	ounce grated Parmesan cheese (3 tablespoons)
1/2	teaspoon dried basil
1/4	teaspoon garlic powder
1/8	teaspoon pepper
3	cups cooked macaroni

In a blender container, combine all ingredients, except macaroni. Blend until smooth.

Spoon mixture into a medium saucepan. Heat over medium-low heat until mixture is hot and bubbly, stirring constantly. Remove from heat.

Add macaroni and stir until coated.

Each serving provides:

246 Calories

3/4	Protein Serving	15 g	Protein
1 1/2	Bread Servings	7 g	Fat (21% of calories)
1	Vegetable Serving	34 g	Carbohydrate
1/2	Fat Serving	339 mg	Sodium
5	Additional Calories	7 mg	Cholesterol
		3 g	Fiber

Tofu–Spinach Lasagne

No one will believe that the cheesy, herbed filling is really tofu. And you don't even cook the noodles first!

Makes 6 servings

1	8-ounce package regular or whole wheat lasagne noodles
1	32-ounce jar meatless spaghetti sauce (70 calories or less per $1/2$ cup serving)
$1^1/_2$	cups water

Filling

1	pound soft or medium tofu
1	10-ounce package frozen, chopped spinach, thawed and drained well
1	teaspoon dried oregano
$1/_2$	teaspoon dried basil
$1/_8$	teaspoon garlic powder

Preheat oven to 350 degrees F.

In a large bowl, combine sauce and water. Set aside.

Drain tofu slightly, but do not squeeze out the water. Place in a blender container and blend until smooth. Spoon into a bowl and add remaining filling ingredients, mixing well.

To assemble lasagne, spread 1 cup of the sauce in the bottom of a 9 × 13-inch lasagne pan. Top with 1/3 of the noodles, then 1/2 cup of the sauce. Next, spoon 1/2 of the tofu mixture over the noodles and top with another 1/2 cup of the sauce.

Top with another 1/3 of the noodles. Press them down firmly onto the filling. Repeat layers, adding 1/2 cup sauce, remaining tofu, 1/2 cup sauce, and remaining noodles. Again, press noodles down firmly.

Spoon remaining sauce over noodles, making sure all parts of noodles are covered with sauce.

Bake 40 minutes, covered. Uncover and continue to bake 20 more minutes.

Cut into squares to serve.

Each serving provides:		
284 Calories		
3/4	Protein Serving	13 g	Protein
13/4	Bread Servings	5 g	Fat (14% of calories)
4	Vegetable Servings	49 g	Carbohydrate
1/2	Fat Serving	844 mg	Sodium
21	Additional Calories	0 mg	Cholesterol
		2 g	Fiber

Italian Macaroni Salad

Perfect for a summer barbecue, but delicious all year round, this salad is colorful and easy. You can add any other vegetables if you like—a great way to use leftovers.

Makes 4 servings

1	10-ounce package frozen cut green beans
3	cups cooked macaroni
1	cup coarsely shredded carrots
1	cup sliced celery
1/4	cup sliced green onions (green part only)
1/2	cup fat-free Italian dressing
1/4	teaspoon dried oregano

Cook green beans according to package directions, cooking until tender-crisp. Drain.

In a large bowl, combine green beans, macaroni, carrots, celery, and onions. Toss until blended.

Add remaining ingredients and mix well.

Chill to blend flavors. Stir occasionally while chilling.

Each serving provides:

200 Calories

1 1/2	Bread Servings	7 g	Protein
2 1/4	Vegetable Servings	1 g	Fat (4% of calories)
10	Additional Calories	41 g	Carbohydrate
		330 mg	Sodium
		0 mg	Cholesterol
		4 g	Fiber

Macaroni with Cheddar and Tomatoes

An easy dinner awaits you when you alternate layers of macaroni, Cheddar cheese, and stewed tomatoes. If you like spicy food, add a finely minced jalapeño to one of the tomato layers.

Makes 4 servings

1	cup elbow macaroni, uncooked (4 ounces)
1	16-ounce can salt-free (or regular) stewed tomatoes, drained
4	ounces shredded reduced-fat Cheddar cheese (1 cup)
1	tablespoon grated Parmesan cheese
1/4	teaspoon oregano
1/4	teaspoon dried basil
1/8	teaspoon pepper
1	tablespoon all-purpose flour
1	cup evaporated skim milk
2	tablespoons dry bread crumbs
	Nonstick cooking spray

Cook macaroni according to package directions. Drain.

Preheat oven to 375 degrees F.

Spray a 1-quart casserole with nonstick cooking spray.

Place half of the macaroni in the prepared baking dish. Top with half each measure of the stewed tomatoes, Cheddar, Parmesan, oregano, basil, and pepper.

Repeat, using remaining half of the tomatoes, cheeses, and spices.

Place flour in a small bowl. Gradually add milk, stirring briskly to avoid lumps. Pour milk over casserole.

Sprinkle with bread crumbs. Spray lightly and evenly with nonstick cooking spray.

Bake, uncovered, 35 minutes, until set.

Let stand 5 minutes before serving.

Each serving provides:

295 Calories

1 1/4	Protein Servings	20 g	Protein
1 1/4	Bread Servings	7 g	Fat (20% of calories)
1	Vegetable Serving	40 g	Carbohydrate
1/2	Milk Serving	368 mg	Sodium
49	Additional Calories	24 mg	Cholesterol
		3 g	Fiber

Italian Mushroom Noodle Bake

A layer of cheese and noodles topped with a rich mushroom sauce makes this a special dish. It's our "lazy day lasagne." Look for noodles made without egg yolks or, for added flavor and fiber, try whole wheat noodles.

Makes 8 servings

Mushroom Sauce

2	teaspoons vegetable oil
1	cup chopped onion
1	cup chopped green bell pepper
3	cloves garlic, finely chopped
6	cups sliced mushrooms
1	teaspoon dried basil
1	teaspoon dried oregano
$1/4$	teaspoon dried thyme
$1/4$	teaspoon dried rosemary, crumbled
	Salt and pepper
1	16-ounce can tomatoes, undrained, chopped
1	6-ounce can tomato paste

Noodle Layer

1	ounce grated Parmesan cheese (3 tablespoons)
1	cup part-skim ricotta cheese
3	egg whites
4	cups cooked medium or thin noodles

Topping

4	ounces shredded part-skim mozzarella cheese (1 cup)

Preheat oven to 350 degrees F.

Spray a 9 × 13-inch baking pan with nonstick cooking spray.

To prepare sauce:

Heat oil in a large nonstick skillet over medium heat. Add onion, green pepper, and garlic. Cook for 5 minutes, stirring frequently. Add mushrooms and spices. Continue to cook, stirring frequently, until mushrooms are tender, about 10 minutes. Remove from heat and stir in tomatoes and tomato paste, mixing well.

To prepare noodle layer:

In a large bowl, combine Parmesan cheese, ricotta cheese, and egg whites, mixing until blended. Add noodles. Mix well.

To assemble:

Spread noodle mixture in prepared pan, pressing gently with the back of a spoon. Spoon mushroom sauce evenly over noodles.

Cover tightly and bake 40 minutes.

Uncover, sprinkle with mozzarella cheese, and return to oven for 5 minutes, until cheese is melted.

Remove from oven, let stand 5 minutes, then cut into squares to serve.

Each serving provides:

242 Calories

1¼	Protein Servings	16 g	Protein
1	Bread Serving	8 g	Fat (29% of calories)
2½	Vegetable Servings	29 g	Carbohydrate
¼	Fat Serving	459 mg	Sodium
		21 mg	Cholesterol
		3 g	Fiber

Pasta and Broccoli

This is a delicious blend of pasta, garlic, and broccoli. It makes a wonderful side dish or an unbeatable entrée.

Makes 4 servings

3   cups broccoli, cut into small flowerets
2   teaspoons vegetable oil
4   cloves garlic, minced
1   16-ounce can salt-free (or regular) tomatoes, drained slightly, chopped
3   cups cooked pasta spirals

Steam broccoli until tender-crisp, about 8 minutes.

Heat oil in a large nonstick skillet over medium heat. Add garlic and cook, stirring, until garlic begins to brown.

Add tomatoes and broccoli. Cook, stirring frequently, until hot and bubbly.

Add pasta. Toss gently until mixture is well blended and hot.

Each serving provides:

219 Calories

1¹/₂	Bread Servings	9 g	Protein
2¹/₂	Vegetable Servings	4 g	Fat (15% of calories)
¹/₂	Fat Serving	39 g	Carbohydrate
		58 mg	Sodium
		0 mg	Cholesterol
		5 g	Fiber

Italian Noodles

Top with cheese, add a green vegetable, and your dinner is complete.

Makes 6 servings

2	teaspoons olive oil
1	cup chopped onion
1	cup chopped green bell pepper
3	cloves garlic, minced
1	16-ounce can salt-free (or regular) tomatoes, drained slightly, chopped
1	4-ounce can mushroom pieces, drained
1/2	teaspoon dried basil
1/4	teaspoon dried oregano
	Pepper
3	cups cooked (yolk-free) noodles

Heat oil in a large nonstick skillet over medium heat. Add onion, green pepper, and garlic. Cook, stirring frequently, until onion begins to brown.

Add tomatoes, mushrooms, and spices to skillet. When mixture is hot and bubbly, stir in noodles. Toss until heated through.

Each serving provides:

123 Calories

1	Bread Serving	4 g	Protein
1 1/2	Vegetable Servings	2 g	Fat (16% of calories)
1/4	Fat Serving	23 g	Carbohydrate
3	Additional Calories	60 mg	Sodium
		0 mg	Cholesterol
		2 g	Fiber

Noodles with Peanut Sauce

Inspired by a love of Asian food and a love of peanut butter, this dish is a favorite in our house. It's a delicious side dish, and it can also be served as an entrée. Try it with whole wheat noodles for the best flavor.

Makes 6 servings

1	8-ounce package thin Asian whole wheat noodles (or linguine)
2	tablespoons creamy-style peanut butter (Choose one without added sugar or fat.)
2	tablespoons reduced-sodium soy sauce
1	tablespoon honey
	Dash ground ginger
	Dash garlic powder

Cook noodles according to package directions. Drain.

While noodles are cooking, place peanut butter in a small bowl. Gradually stir in soy sauce, then honey and spices, stirring until mixture is smooth.

Place drained noodles in a serving bowl. Drizzle sauce over noodles and mix well.

Serve right away.

Each serving provides:

179 Calories

1/4	Protein Serving	7 g	Protein
1 1/2	Bread Servings	3 g	Fat (15% of calories)
1/4	Fat Serving	33 g	Carbohydrate
41	Additional Calories	224 mg	Sodium
		0 mg	Cholesterol
		5 g	Fiber

Fruit and Noodle Kugel

Noodle puddings have so many variations. Some are sweet, others not so sweet. Some contain fruit, others do not. This one is sweet and filled with fruit. It can be served as a side dish, a brunch entrée, or even a delicious dessert.

Makes 8 servings

6	ounces fine noodles (yolk-free), uncooked (3 cups)
2	small, sweet apples, peeled, coarsely shredded
1	cup canned crushed pineapple (packed in juice), drained
$1/4$	cup plus 2 tablespoons raisins
$1^1/3$	cups lowfat (1%) cottage cheese
1	cup liquid egg substitute
$1/2$	cup orange juice
$1/4$	cup sugar
2	teaspoons vanilla extract
$1/2$	teaspoon ground cinnamon

Cook noodles according to package directions. Drain.

Preheat oven to 350 degrees F.

Spray an 8-inch square baking pan with nonstick cooking spray.

In a large bowl, combine cooked noodles, apples, pineapple, and raisins. Toss to combine.

In a blender container, combine remaining ingredients. Blend until smooth. Add to noodles and mix well. Spoon into prepared pan.

Bake 45 minutes, or until set.

Serve warm or cold, cut into squares.

Each serving provides:

205 Calories

1	Protein Serving	11 g	Protein
1	Bread Serving	1 g	Fat (5% of calories)
2	Fruit Servings	39 g	Carbohydrate
24	Additional Calories	209 mg	Sodium
		2 mg	Cholesterol
		2 g	Fiber

No-Bake Eggless Noodle Pudding

Unlike traditional noodle puddings that contain lots of eggs, this one is especially healthful and tasty. It can be served as a side dish, dessert, or wholesome and filling breakfast.

Makes 4 servings

2	cups skim milk
3	tablespoons sugar
1	tablespoon plus 1 teaspoon cornstarch
2	teaspoons vanilla extract
1/4	teaspoon lemon extract
1/4	teaspoon ground cinnamon
2	cups cooked (eggless) noodles (room temperature or warmer)
1/4	cup raisins

In a medium saucepan, combine milk, sugar, cornstarch, extracts, and cinnamon. Stir to dissolve cornstarch.

Heat over medium heat, stirring constantly, until mixture just starts to boil.

Stir in noodles and raisins. Cook, stirring, until mixture boils again. Continue to cook and stir 1 minute.

Pour mixture into a 1-quart shallow bowl. Press noodles down into liquid with the back of a spoon.

Cool slightly, then cover and chill.

Each serving provides:

199 Calories

1	Bread Serving	7 g	Protein
1/2	Fruit Serving	1 g	Fat (3% of calories)
1/2	Milk Serving	40 g	Carbohydrate
46	Additional Calories	70 mg	Sodium
		2 mg	Cholesterol
		1 g	Fiber

Garden Pasta Sauce

A simple package of frozen vegetables makes this one of our favorite, and most interesting, pasta sauces. This recipe makes a lot, and you'll be glad!

Makes 9 servings (1 cup each serving)

1	tablespoon olive oil
2	cups chopped onions
2	cloves garlic, finely chopped
2	16-ounce cans tomatoes, chopped, undrained
2	8-ounce cans salt-free (or regular) tomato sauce
1	6-ounce can tomato paste
1/2	teaspoon dried oregano
1/2	teaspoon dried basil
1/4	teaspoon dried thyme
1/4	teaspoon paprika
1/4	teaspoon dried rosemary, crumbled
1	teaspoon sugar
1/8	teaspoon pepper
	Salt
1	16-ounce package frozen mixed broccoli, cauliflower, and carrots (Or, try other vegetable combinations if you like.)

Heat oil in a large saucepan over medium heat. Add onions and garlic. Cook 5 minutes, stirring frequently.

Add remaining ingredients, mixing well. Bring mixture to a boil. Reduce heat to low, cover, and simmer 30 minutes, or until vegetables are tender.

Serve over your favorite type of pasta.

Each serving provides:

98 Calories

1 1/4	Protein Servings	4 g	Protein
2 3/4	Vegetable Servings	2 g	Fat (19% of calories)
15	Additional Calories	18 g	Carbohydrate
		340 mg	Sodium
		0 mg	Cholesterol
		4 g	Fiber

Pacific Pasta Sauce with Salmon

In the Pacific Northwest, where salmon is plentiful, this tender fish is added to lots of dishes—even pasta. This one starts with already prepared sauce. Choose your favorite lowfat brand and just add the rest.

Makes 6 servings (³/4 cup each serving)

1	28-ounce jar reduced-fat, meatless spaghetti sauce
1	tablespoon dried parsley flakes
1	teaspoon grated fresh lemon peel
	Pepper
1	14¹/2-ounce can salmon, drained and flaked, skin and bones discarded (12 ounces)

Combine spaghetti sauce, parsley, lemon peel, and pepper in a medium saucepan. Bring to a boil over medium heat. Reduce heat to medium-low, cover, and simmer 15 minutes. Add salmon.

Serve over pasta or noodles.

Each serving provides:

141 Calories

2	Protein Servings	16 g	Protein
1¹/2	Vegetable Servings	4 g	Fat (25% of calories)
¹/2	Fat Serving	11 g	Carbohydrate
		716 mg	Sodium
		24 mg	Cholesterol
		2 g	Fiber

Spaghetti Sauce Italiano

This recipe makes a big pot of sauce, but you'll be glad you have it. Not only is it good over pasta, but also over burgers, baked potatoes, or baked chicken or fish.

Makes 8 servings (3/4 cup each serving)

2	teaspoons olive oil
1	cup chopped onion
1	cup chopped green bell pepper
1	cup sliced mushrooms
3	cloves garlic, minced
3	8-ounce cans salt-free (or regular) tomato sauce
1	6-ounce can tomato paste
1	16-ounce can salt-free (or regular) tomatoes, drained and chopped
2	teaspoons dried oregano
1	teaspoon dried basil
1/4	teaspoon dried thyme
1	bay leaf
	Salt and pepper

Heat oil in a large saucepan. Add onion, green pepper, mushrooms, and garlic. Cook until onion and bell pepper are tender. Stir occasionally while cooking and add small amounts of water, about a tablespoon at a time, if necessary to prevent sticking.

Add tomato sauce, tomato paste, tomatoes, and spices. Reduce heat to low, cover and simmer 1 hour, stirring occasionally.

Remove and discard bay leaf before serving.

Each serving provides:

86 Calories

3 1/2	Vegetable Servings	3 g	Protein
1/4	Fat Serving	2 g	Fat (18% of calories)
		17 g	Carbohydrate
		195 mg	Sodium
		0 mg	Cholesterol
		3 g	Fiber

Sicilian Lentil Pasta Sauce

*Thick and rich with mushrooms, lentils, and spices, this sauce is high in pro-
tein and fiber as well as flavor. If you like a thick pasta sauce, this is it.*

Makes 8 servings (about 2/3 cup each serving)

2	teaspoons olive oil
1	cup chopped onions
2	cups sliced mushrooms
3	cloves garlic, finely chopped
1	cup lentils, uncooked (7¹/₂ ounces)
3	cups water
2	8-ounce cans salt-free (or regular) tomato sauce
1	6-ounce can tomato paste
1¹/₂	teaspoons sugar
¹/₂	cup water

Heat oil in a large saucepan over medium heat. Add onions, mushrooms, and garlic. Cook until tender, about 5 minutes.

Add lentils and water. Bring to a boil, stirring occasionally. Reduce
heat to low, cover, and cook 40 minutes.

Add remaining ingredients and bring to a boil. Cover and cook 20
minutes, stirring occasionally. Add more water if a thinner sauce is
desired.

Serve over pasta or rice.

Each serving provides:

154 Calories

1¹/₄	Protein Servings	10 g	Protein
1¹/₃	Vegetable Servings	2 g	Fat (10% of calories)
¹/₄	Fat Serving	27 g	Carbohydrate
3	Additional Calories	184 mg	Sodium
		0 mg	Cholesterol
		5 g	Fiber

Eggs and Cheese

Eggs and cheese are versatile, tasty, and inexpensive. There's only one problem: Both eggs and cheese are high in fat and cholesterol. Fortunately, we have found a few easy solutions.

The cholesterol in eggs is entirely in the yolk. You can use 2 egg whites to replace 1 whole egg, or use a liquid egg substitute. Either solution will work in most recipes that call for eggs. In omelets many people prefer the flavor and ease of egg substitutes to the "whiteness" of egg whites.

There are reduced-fat and fat-free versions of most cheeses. In our opinion, some fat-free cheeses lack flavor and "meltability," so our choice is usually the reduced-fat version. Some cheeses, such as feta and Parmesan, have a rich, distinctive taste that goes a long way, so simply cut back on the amount and you can still enjoy their wonderful flavors.

We've made the adjustments for you, and have combined eggs and cheese with other delicious ingredients, bringing you many scrumptious taste delights.

Eggs Suzette with Strawberry Sauce

This fancy dish turns simple egg substitute into a wonderful company breakfast.

Makes 4 servings

1	cup liquid egg substitute
2	teaspoons vanilla extract
1	tablespoon sugar
1/2	teaspoon ground cinnamon

Sauce

1/2	cup water
1	tablespoon cornstarch
2	tablespoons fruit-only strawberry spread

Spray a small nonstick skillet with nonstick cooking spray. Heat over medium heat. Combine egg substitute and vanilla, mixing well. Make 4 individual egg pancakes by cooking the egg substitute, 1/4 cup at a time, in prepared pan. Tilt the pan back and forth so the egg substitute is evenly distributed, forming a thin pancake. Cook each one until set. Do not turn.

As each pancake is finished, slide it onto a serving plate.

Combine sugar and cinnamon and sprinkle evenly over the pancakes. Fold each pancake into quarters. Cover and keep warm.

Combine sauce ingredients in a small saucepan. Stir to dissolve cornstarch. Bring to a boil over medium heat, stirring constantly. Boil 1 minute, stirring.

Serve sauce over pancakes.

Each serving provides:

79 Calories

1	Protein Serving	6 g	Protein
1/2	Fruit Serving	trace	Fat (3% of calories)
20	Additional Calories	12 g	Carbohydrate
		100 mg	Sodium
		0 mg	Cholesterol
		0 g	Fiber

Apple Strudel Omelet

Turn ordinary egg substitute into an elegant dish. For more servings, just increase the amount of each ingredient according to the number of servings you need.

Makes 1 serving

1/4	cup applesauce, unsweetened
2	teaspoons fruit-only orange marmalade
1	teaspoon sugar
1/4	teaspoon ground cinnamon
1/4	teaspoon coconut extract
1/4	cup liquid egg substitute

Topping

1	teaspoon sugar
1/4	teaspoon ground cinnamon

Combine applesauce, marmalade, sugar, cinnamon, and coconut extract in a small bowl or custard cup. Mix well and set aside.

Spray a small nonstick skillet with nonstick cooking spray. Heat over medium heat. Add egg substitute. Tilt pan back and forth so egg is evenly distributed and forms a thin pancake. When egg is set, slide it gently onto a serving plate. Do not turn.

Spread applesauce mixture evenly over egg. Roll up like a jelly roll. Combine remaining cinnamon and sugar and sprinkle over egg.

Each serving provides:

129 Calories

1	Protein Serving	6 g	Protein
1/2	Fruit Serving	1 g	Fat (7% of calories)
72	Additional Calories	24 g	Carbohydrate
		102 mg	Sodium
		0 mg	Cholesterol
		1 g	Fiber

Mexican Tomato Omelet

Tomato slices add color and flavor to this upside-down omelet. Garnish it with fresh basil, serve it with salsa, and it really reflects the Mexican love of color.

Makes 2 servings

2	teaspoons vegetable oil
1	cup liquid egg substitute
1	teaspoon dried basil
1	teaspoon ground cumin
1/4	teaspoon garlic powder
	Salt and pepper
1	tablespoon grated Parmesan cheese
1	tablespoon skim milk
1	medium, ripe tomato, sliced

Heat oil in an 8-inch nonstick skillet over medium heat.

In a medium bowl, combine egg substitute with remaining ingredients, except tomato slices. Beat with a fork or wire whisk until blended. Pour into hot skillet.

Reduce heat to medium-low, cover skillet, and cook 5 minutes. Arrange tomato slices over eggs and continue to cook, covered, 5 minutes more, or until eggs are set enough to invert without breaking.

Slide omelet out of pan onto a plate. Then, invert into pan so that tomatoes are now on the bottom. Cook, uncovered, 1 minute, or until eggs are set.

Invert onto serving plate tomato-side up.

Each serving provides:

137 Calories

2	Protein Servings	14 g	Protein
1	Vegetable Serving	6 g	Fat (38% of calories)
1	Fat Serving	7 g	Carbohydrate
18	Additional Calories	259 mg	Sodium
		2 mg	Cholesterol
		0 g	Fiber
		1g	Fiber

Pennsylvania Dutch Apple Spoon Omelet

This recipe can be increased to make as many servings as you like. It works best in small baking dishes and makes an interesting and unique brunch dish.

Makes 2 servings

1/2	cup liquid egg substitute
1/2	cup applesauce, unsweetened
1	tablespoon sugar
1	teaspoon vanilla extract
1/4	teaspoon almond extract
1/4	teaspoon ground cinnamon

Preheat oven to 350 degrees F.

Spray a small (2-cup) baking dish with nonstick cooking spray.

Combine all ingredients in a small bowl. Beat with a fork or wire whisk until blended. Pour mixture into prepared baking dish.

Bake, uncovered, 35 minutes, or until set.

Each serving provides:

92 Calories

1	Protein Serving	6 g	Protein
1/2	Fruit Serving	1 g	Fat (5% of calories)
24	Additional Calories	15 g	Carbohydrate
		102 mg	Sodium
		0 mg	Cholesterol
		1 g	Fiber

Eggs in Tomato Cups

Colorful and delicious, this dish is good for breakfast, lunch, or a light dinner.

Makes 4 servings

4	medium tomatoes (red, but not overripe)
1	cup liquid egg substitute
3	tablespoons dry bread crumbs
2	tablespoons grated Parmesan cheese
1	teaspoon dried parsley flakes
$1/4$	teaspoon dried oregano
$1/8$	teaspoon pepper
	Salt

Preheat oven to 425 degrees F.

Spray an 8-inch square baking pan with nonstick cooking spray.

Cut a thin slice from the stem end of each tomato. Scoop out tomato pulp carefully with a spoon.

Place tomatoes, cut-side-up, in a prepared pan.

Pour $1/4$ cup of egg substitute into each tomato.

In a small bowl, combine remaining ingredients, mixing well. Sprinkle evenly over tomatoes.

Bake 15 to 20 minutes, until eggs are set.

Each serving provides:

90 Calories

1	Protein Serving	9 g	Protein
$1/4$	Bread Serving	2 g	Fat (16% of calories)
2	Vegetable Servings	11 g	Carbohydrate
15	Additional Calories	202 mg	Sodium
		2 mg	Cholesterol
		2 g	Fiber

Almond Bread Puff

This sensational version of French toast is light and lots of fun to eat. The taste is great and you can vary the flavors by replacing the almond extract with any other favorite extract.

Makes 2 servings

1/4	cup liquid egg substitute
2	tablespoons skim milk
1	tablespoon sugar
2	teaspoons vanilla extract
1/2	teaspoon almond extract
2	slices whole wheat bread (1-ounce slices)
2	egg whites (Do not use egg substitute.)

Preheat oven to 350 degrees F.

Spray a 4 × 8-inch loaf pan with nonstick cooking spray.

In a small bowl, combine egg substitute, milk, half of the sugar, half of the vanilla, and half of the almond extract. Mix well and pour into prepared pan. Place bread slices in mixture, turning carefully until all of the liquid has been absorbed.

Bake 15 minutes. Remove from oven.

In a medium bowl, beat egg whites until stiff, using high speed of an electric mixer. Beat in remaining sugar and extracts. Spread over bread. Return to oven and continue to bake for 10 more minutes, or until nicely browned.

Each serving provides:

156 Calories

1/2	Protein Serving	10 g	Protein
1	Bread Serving	2 g	Fat (13% of calories)
50	Additional Calories	22 g	Carbohydrate
		262 mg	Sodium
		0 mg	Cholesterol
		2 g	Fiber

Egg Foo Yung

For an Asian treat, and a dinner the family will love, serve this dish with brown rice and steamed broccoli. Spoon a little of the sauce over the broccoli.

Makes 4 servings

Sauce
1 packet low-sodium instant chicken or vegetable broth mix
³/₄ cup water
1 tablespoon soy sauce
1 tablespoon cornstarch

Pancakes
1 cup liquid egg substitute
8 ounces cooked, cubed, skinless chicken (2 cups)
1¹/₂ cups bean sprouts, fresh or canned
¹/₂ cup sliced mushrooms
2 tablespoons sliced green onions
1 tablespoon minced onion flakes

In a small saucepan, combine sauce ingredients, stirring to dissolve cornstarch. Bring to a boil over medium heat, stirring constantly. Continue to cook 2 minutes, stirring. Cover tightly and remove from heat.

In a medium bowl, combine egg substitute with remaining ingredients. Mix well.

Spray a small nonstick skillet with nonstick cooking spray. Heat over medium heat. Pour egg mixture, 1 cup at a time, into skillet. Cook until brown on both sides, turning carefully.

Serve topped with sauce.

Each serving provides:

171 Calories

3	Protein Servings	24 g	Protein
1	Vegetable Serving	5 g	Fat (24% of calories)
10	Additional Calories	8 g	Carbohydrate
		625 mg	Sodium
		50 mg	Cholesterol
		1 g	Fiber

Italian Frittata

This easy, inexpensive dish can be served for breakfast, lunch, or dinner. It also works well with other vegetable combinations, so you can customize it to your own taste.

Makes 8 servings

2	teaspoons vegetable oil
1	cup broccoli, cut into small flowerets
1	cup zucchini, unpeeled, cut into 1-inch chunks
1	cup sliced mushrooms
1/2	cup chopped onion
1/2	cup chopped green bell pepper
1	16-ounce can salt-free (or regular) tomatoes, drained and chopped
2	cups liquid egg substitute
1	teaspoon dried oregano
1/2	teaspoon dried basil
1/8	teaspoon garlic powder
	Salt and pepper
1/2	cup plain nonfat yogurt
3	tablespoons grated Parmesan cheese (1 ounce)

Preheat oven to 375 degrees F.

Heat oil in a heavy, ovenproof skillet over medium heat. Add vegetables, including canned tomatoes. Cook, stirring frequently, until vegetables are tender, about 5 minutes.

Combine egg substitute with remaining ingredients, using only half of the Parmesan cheese. Mix well and pour over vegetables. Sprinkle with remaining Parmesan cheese. Cook for 2 minutes without stirring, then place skillet in oven.

Bake, uncovered, until edges are set and lightly browned, about 25 minutes.

Cut into pie-shaped wedges to serve.

Each serving provides:

91 Calories

1	Protein Serving	10 g	Protein
1 1/2	Vegetable Servings	3 g	Fat (24% of calories)
1/4	Fat Serving	8 g	Carbohydrate
19	Additional Calories	193 mg	Sodium
		3 mg	Cholesterol
		1 g	Fiber

Potato–Cheese Casserole

*This casserole is almost a meal in itself. Just add a steamed green vegetable
for a colorful and nutritious dinner.*

Makes 6 servings

1	cup liquid egg substitute
1 1/3	cups lowfat (1%) cottage cheese
15	ounces cooked potatoes, peeled and mashed (Bake the potatoes in a 350-degree F oven for about 1 hour, or microwave for about 8 minutes, until very tender.)
2/3	cup nonfat dry milk
1/2	cup water
2	tablespoons minced onion flakes
1	tablespoon vegetable oil
1/2	teaspoon salt
1/4	teaspoon pepper

Preheat oven to 350 degrees F.

Spray an 8-inch square baking dish with nonstick cooking spray.

Combine all ingredients in a large bowl. Beat with an electric mixer
on low speed until blended. Beat on high speed 1 minute. Add additional skim milk if mixture is too dry.

Spoon mixture into prepared baking dish.

Bake, uncovered, 45 minutes, or until set and lightly browned.

Each serving provides:

158 Calories

1 1/4	Protein Servings	14 g	Protein
1/2	Bread Serving	3 g	Fat (17% of calories)
1/2	Fat Serving	18 g	Carbohydrate
1/4	Milk Serving	497 mg	Sodium
13	Additional Calories	3 mg	Cholesterol
		1 g	Fiber

"Almost" Lasagna

In place of noodles, we've used thinly sliced zucchini. The result is colorful, delicious, and fun!

Makes 6 servings

4	cups zucchini, unpeeled, sliced crosswise into $1/8$-inch slices
$1^1/4$	cups part-skim ricotta cheese
4	ounces shredded reduced-fat mozzarella cheese (1 cup)
3	tablespoons grated Parmesan cheese (1 ounce)
1	8-ounce can salt-free (or regular) tomato sauce
1	teaspoon dried oregano
$1/2$	teaspoon dried basil
$1/8$	teaspoon garlic powder

Preheat oven to 350 degrees F.

Spray an 8-inch square baking pan with nonstick cooking spray.

Place a steamer rack in the bottom of a medium saucepan. Add enough water to come almost up to the bottom of the rack. Place saucepan over medium heat. When water boils, add zucchini, cover, and cook 5 minutes, or until zucchini is tender-crisp. Drain.

In a medium bowl, combine ricotta, mozzarella, and Parmesan cheeses, reserving 1 tablespoon of the Parmesan cheese for topping.

In a small bowl, combine tomato sauce with remaining ingredients.

Spread a thin coating of sauce in the bottom of prepared pan. Top with a layer of zucchini, using 1/3 of the zucchini. Then dot with a layer of cheese, using 1/2 of the cheese.

Add a layer of sauce, then 1/3 more zucchini, and then remaining cheese.

Top with remaining zucchini, then remaining sauce.

Press mixture down gently with the back of a spoon.

Sprinkle with remaining Parmesan cheese.

Bake, uncovered, 30 minutes.

Let stand 10 minutes before serving.

Each serving provides:

159 Calories

1 1/2	Protein Servings	14 g	Protein
2	Vegetable Servings	8 g	Fat (45% of calories)
28	Additional Calories	8 g	Carbohydrate
		262 mg	Sodium
		26 mg	Cholesterol
		1 g	Fiber

Lemon-Pepper Spinach Puff

You'll love the unusual combination of flavors in this easy, cheesy side dish.

Makes 6 servings

1	tablespoon vegetable oil
1/2	cup chopped onion
1/2	cup chopped red bell pepper
2	cloves garlic, minced
1	cup lowfat (1%) cottage cheese
3	egg whites
1	teaspoon grated fresh lemon peel
1/8	teaspoon pepper
	Dash grated nutmeg
1	10-ounce package frozen, chopped spinach, thawed and drained very well (Squeeze out water.)
1/4	teaspoon cream of tartar

Preheat oven to 350 degrees F.

Spray a 1-quart baking dish with nonstick cooking spray.

Heat oil in a small nonstick skillet over medium heat. Add onion, bell pepper, and garlic. Cook, stirring frequently, 5 to 8 minutes, until tender. Remove from heat.

In a blender container, combine cottage cheese, 1 of the egg whites, lemon peel, pepper, and nutmeg. Blend until smooth. Pour into a large bowl and stir in onion mixture and spinach. Mix well.

Place remaining 2 egg whites in a medium, deep bowl. Beat on medium speed with an electric mixer until frothy. Add cream of tartar on high speed until egg whites are stiff. Fold egg whites into spinach mixture gently but thoroughly. Spoon mixture into prepared pan.

Bake, uncovered, 40 minutes, until set and lightly browned.

Serve right away.

Each serving provides:

78 Calories

1/2	Protein Serving	8 g	Protein
1	Vegetable Serving	3 g	Fat (34% of calories)
1/2	Fat Serving	5 g	Carbohydrate
10	Additional Calories	216 mg	Sodium
		2 mg	Cholesterol
		1 g	Fiber

Cheesy Squash and Rice Casserole

This unique blend of two kinds of squash with rice and cheese makes a side dish so filling, we often eat it as our main course.

Makes 6 servings

2	teaspoons vegetable oil
2	cloves garlic, finely chopped
1	cup finely chopped onions
2	cups zucchini squash, unpeeled, sliced into $^1/_4$-inch slices ($^3/_4$ pound)
2	cups yellow summer squash, unpeeled, sliced into $^1/_4$-inch slices ($^3/_4$ pound)
$^1/_2$	cup skim milk
2	ounces shredded part-skim mozzarella cheese ($^1/_2$ cup)
1	ounce grated Parmesan cheese (3 tablespoons)
$^1/_4$	teaspoon pepper
	Salt
3	cups cooked brown rice
3	tablespoons wheat germ ($^3/_4$ ounce)

Preheat oven to 400 degrees F.

Spray an 8-inch square baking dish with nonstick cooking spray.

Heat oil in a large nonstick skillet over medium heat. Add garlic and onions. Cook 5 minutes, stirring frequently, until tender. Add squash. Cook 10 minutes, stirring frequently, until squash is slightly tender. Remove from heat and stir in remaining ingredients, except wheat germ. Mix well.

Spoon mixture into prepared baking dish. Press down firmly into pan with the back of a spoon. Sprinkle with wheat germ.

Cover and bake 25 minutes.

Each serving provides:

220 Calories

$^1/_2$	Protein Serving	10 g	Protein
1	Bread Serving	6 g	Fat (25% of calories)
1$^3/_4$	Vegetable Servings	32 g	Carbohydrate
$^1/_4$	Fat Serving	151 mg	Sodium
36	Additional Calories	10 mg	Cholesterol
		3 g	Fiber

Easy Cheesy

Yes, it's easy and it's cheesy. This quick casserole is perfect for any meal, from breakfast through dinner. You can add lots of different touches, if you wish, such as sliced green onions, sliced olives, imitation bacon bits, chopped jalapeño peppers. . . .

Makes 6 servings

1¹/₃	cups lowfat (1%) cottage cheese
4	ounces shredded reduced-fat Cheddar cheese (1 cup)
1	cup liquid egg substitute
1¹/₂	teaspoons vegetable oil
1	tablespoon all-purpose flour
1	tablespoon minced onion flakes
1	packet instant reduced-sodium chicken broth mix
¹/₈	teaspoon garlic powder

Preheat oven to 350 degrees F.

Spray an 8-inch square baking pan with nonstick cooking spray.

In a blender container, combine all ingredients. Blend until smooth. Pour into prepared pan.

Bake, uncovered, 30 minutes, or until puffy and lightly browned. Cut into squares and serve hot.

Each serving provides:

129 Calories

2	Protein Servings	17 g	Protein
¹/₄	Fat Serving	5 g	Fat (36% of calories)
20	Additional Calories	4 g	Carbohydrate
		418 mg	Sodium
		15 mg	Cholesterol
		0 g	Fiber

Cheese Pie with Potato Crust

Once you've tried this, you'll make it over and over again. It freezes well, so make an extra one!

Makes 6 servings

15	ounces potatoes, unpeeled, coarsely shredded
2/3	cup nonfat dry milk
1 1/3	cups lowfat (1%) cottage cheese
1	cup liquid egg substitute
4	ounces shredded reduced-fat Cheddar cheese (1 cup)
1	tablespoon minced onion flakes
1/8	teaspoon garlic powder
1	tablespoon all-purpose flour
1	tablespoon dried parsley flakes

Preheat oven to 350 degrees F.

Arrange shredded potato in the bottom and sides of a 10-inch pie pan that has been sprayed with a nonstick cooking spray, forming a crust.

Sprinkle dry milk evenly over potatoes.

Combine remaining ingredients in a bowl and mix with a fork or wire whisk until blended. (Mixture will be lumpy.) Spread evenly over potatoes.

Bake 35 to 40 minutes, until set.

Cool 5 minutes before serving.

Each serving provides:

197 Calories

2	Protein Servings	21 g	Protein
1/2	Bread Serving	4 g	Fat (19% of calories)
1/4	Milk Serving	19 g	Carbohydrate
16	Additional Calories	464 mg	Sodium
		17 mg	Cholesterol
		1 g	Fiber

Cheddar Bread Pudding

This is a great use for leftover bread. In fact, it works best with bread that's slightly stale. It's a delicious side dish that can double as a special brunch treat.

Makes 8 servings

4	slices whole wheat bread, cubed
2	cups skim milk
1	cup liquid egg substitute
4	ounces shredded reduced-fat Cheddar cheese (1 cup)
1	teaspoon dry mustard
1	tablespoon minced onion flakes
1/2	teaspoon sherry extract

Preheat oven to 350 degrees F.

Spread bread cubes evenly in an 8-inch square baking pan that has been sprayed with nonstick cooking spray.

In a blender container, combine remaining ingredients. Blend until smooth.

Pour egg mixture evenly over bread cubes. Let stand for 5 minutes. Bake 30 minutes, until set.

Let cool 10 minutes before serving.

Each serving provides:

115 Calories

1	Protein Serving	11 g	Protein
1/2	Bread Serving	3 g	Fat (26% of calories)
1/4	Milk Serving	10 g	Carbohydrate
10	Additional Calories	267 mg	Sodium
		11 mg	Cholesterol
		1 g	Fiber

Italian Eggplant and Cheese Casserole

Serve this easy favorite with rice or noodles and a green vegetable for a complete dinner. As an entrée for 6, or a filling side dish for 8, this one will be requested again and again.

Makes 6 servings

1	large eggplant (1¼ pounds), peeled, cut crosswise into ½-inch slices
2	cups marinara sauce (or reduced-fat, meatless spaghetti sauce)
2	cups part-skim ricotta cheese
2	ounces part-skim mozzarella cheese (½ cup)
1	tablespoon grated Parmesan cheese

Preheat broiler.

Arrange eggplant slices in a single layer on a nonstick baking sheet. Broil until lightly browned on both sides, turning slices once.

Reduce oven temperature to 375 degrees F.

Spray a 9 × 13-inch baking pan with nonstick cooking spray.

Spread a thin layer of the sauce in the bottom of prepared pan. Arrange half of the eggplant slices over the sauce. Drop ricotta cheese by spoonfuls onto eggplant. Top with ⅔ cup of sauce.

Top with remaining eggplant slices, pressing them down gently. Top with remaining sauce, then sprinkle with mozzarella and Parmesan cheese.

Bake, uncovered, 35 minutes.

Let stand 3 to 5 minutes before serving.

Each serving provides:

195 Calories

1½	Protein Servings	14 g	Protein
2¼	Vegetable Servings	9 g	Fat (40% of calories)
1	Fat Serving	16 g	Carbohydrate
22	Additional Calories	425 mg	Sodium
		32 mg	Cholesterol
		2 g	Fiber

Cheesy Peaches

A real treat when fresh summer peaches are in season, this dish makes a great lunch, served with a salad and a basket of hot rolls.

Makes 4 servings

4	medium, ripe peaches, peeled, sliced 1/4 inch thick
1/2	cup liquid egg substitute
2/3	cup lowfat (1%) cottage cheese
2/3	cup nonfat dry milk
1/3	cup water
1 1/2	teaspoons vanilla extract
1/2	teaspoon maple extract
1	teaspoon ground cinnamon
3	tablespoons sugar

Preheat oven to 350 degrees F.

Arrange peach slices in an 8-inch baking pan that has been sprayed with nonstick cooking spray.

In a blender container, combine remaining ingredients. Blend until smooth. Pour mixture evenly over peaches.

Bake 40 minutes, or until set.

Serve warm, or chill and serve cold.

Each serving provides:

185 Calories

1	Protein Serving	13 g	Protein
1	Fruit Serving	1 g	Fat (4% of calories)
1/2	Milk Serving	32 g	Carbohydrate
36	Additional Calories	267 mg	Sodium
		4 mg	Cholesterol
		2 g	Fiber

Sandwiches

In today's world, everyone seems to be in love with fast food. Those of us who want healthful foods for ourselves and our families are sometimes at a loss. What can we make that is quick and easy and, at the same time, nutritious? A sandwich is often the answer.

In this chapter you'll find sandwiches that are both easy and nutritious. Of course, you aren't limited to just the suggestions found here. Lots of delicious dishes in our other sections make great sandwich fillings. And definitely don't overlook leftovers. Last night's dinner may make a spectacular sandwich.

Mexican Salmon Pitas

If you pack your lunch, you can make this sandwich ahead of time and take the dressing along in a small container.

Makes 2 servings

Mexican Dressing
1/2   cup plain nonfat yogurt
2   tablespoons finely chopped onion
1/4   teaspoon ground cumin
1/4   teaspoon dried oregano
1/8   teaspoon garlic powder

Sandwich
4   ounces drained canned salmon, flaked (Tuna may also be used.)
1/4   cup chopped green bell pepper
1/4   cup shredded carrots
2   tablespoons finely chopped onion
1   medium tomato, chopped
2   ounces shredded reduced-fat Cheddar cheese (1/2 cup)
2   1-ounce pita breads, each split open at one end

In a small bowl, combine all dressing ingredients. Chill several hours to blend flavors.

In a medium bowl, combine remaining ingredients, except pitas. Divide mixture evenly and stuff into openings in pitas.

Spoon half of the dressing into each sandwich.

Each serving provides:

302 Calories

3	Protein Servings	28 g	Protein
1	Bread Serving	9 g	Fat (27% of calories)
1³/4	Vegetable Servings	27 g	Carbohydrate
1/4	Milk Serving	703 mg	Sodium
28	Additional Calories	43 mg	Cholesterol
		2 g	Fiber

Italian Cheese-Stuffed Pita

For cheese-lovers, this is an easy sandwich that can be varied by choosing different cheese combinations. For instance, Swiss or provolone add their own distinctive flavors.

Makes 2 servings

1/4	cup part-skim ricotta cheese
2	ounces shredded reduced-fat Cheddar cheese
1	teaspoon grated Parmesan cheese
1/2	teaspoon dried basil
1/4	teaspoon onion powder
	Dash garlic powder
	Pepper
2	1-ounce whole wheat pita breads
2	slices tomato

Preheat oven to 350 degrees F.

In a small bowl, combine cheeses with basil, onion powder, garlic powder, and pepper. Mix well.

Split open one end of each pita, forming a pocket. Place tomato slices inside pita, then divide cheese mixture and spoon into the pita.

Wrap sandwiches in foil and bake 20 minutes.

Each serving provides:

206 Calories

1 1/2	Protein Servings	16 g	Protein
1	Bread Serving	8 g	Fat (36% of calories)
1/4	Vegetable Serving	18 g	Carbohydrate
25	Additional Calories	426 mg	Sodium
		30 mg	Cholesterol
		2 g	Fiber

Crab and Cheese Meltwich

For a delicious alternative, instead of topping an English muffin, spoon this tasty crab mixture over a baked potato.

Makes 2 servings

4   ounces crab meat
2   ounces shredded reduced-fat Cheddar cheese (1/2 cup)
1   tablespoon reduced-calorie mayonnaise
1/2 teaspoon sherry extract
1   English muffin, split and lightly toasted

Combine crab meat, cheese, mayonnaise, and sherry extract in a small bowl. Mix well. Divide mixture evenly and spread on muffin halves.

Place in a broiler or toaster oven until cheese is melted and topping is hot and bubbly.

Each serving provides:

228 Calories

2	Protein Servings	23 g	Protein
1	Bread Serving	9 g	Fat (35% of calories)
3/4	Fat Serving	14 g	Carbohydrate
20	Additional Calories	551 mg	Sodium
		79 mg	Cholesterol
		1 g	Fiber

Beany Burgers

Try these moist burgers on a bun with your favorite burger "fixins" for a cholesterol-free fast food dinner you can make quickly at home.

Makes 8 servings

1	16-ounce can kidney beans, rinsed and drained (This will yield 10 ounces of beans.)
2	cups cooked brown rice
2	tablespoons ketchup
1	teaspoon dried oregano
1/2	teaspoon garlic powder
1/4	teaspoon ground sage
1/8	teaspoon dried thyme
	Salt and pepper
1/4	cup very finely chopped onions

In a large bowl, combine beans, rice, ketchup, and spices. Mash with a fork or a potato masher until beans are mashed well. (Rice will be lumpy.)

Add chopped onions and mix well.

Divide mixture evenly and form into 8 burgers, 1/2 to 3/4 inch thick. Wet your hands slightly to avoid sticking.

Spray a large nonstick griddle or skillet with nonstick cooking spray. Preheat over medium heat. Place burgers on griddle and cook until browned on both sides, turning burgers several times.

Serve hot with lettuce, tomato, relish, ketchup, or your other favorite burger toppings.

Each serving provides:

104 Calories

1/2	Protein Serving	4 g	Protein
1/2	Bread Serving	1 g	Fat (8% of calories)
13	Additional Calories	20 g	Carbohydrate
		121 mg	Sodium
		0 mg	Cholesterol
		3 g	Fiber

Italian Turkey Burgers

Served on a whole grain bun or on a bed of rice or noodles, these burgers will definitely be a hit.

Makes 4 servings

Burgers

1	pound lean ground turkey
2	tablespoons grated onion
1	teaspoon dried oregano
1/2	teaspoon dried basil
1/4	teaspoon garlic powder

Sauce

1	8-ounce can salt-free (or regular) tomato sauce
1	4-ounce can mushroom pieces, drained
1/4	teaspoon dried oregano
1/4	teaspoon dried basil
1/8	teaspoon garlic powder

In a large bowl, combine turkey with remaining burger ingredients. Mix well. Shape into 4 patties.

Spray a large nonstick griddle or skillet with nonstick cooking spray. Heat over medium heat.

Place burgers on griddle. Cook until burgers are done and are nicely browned on both sides. Turn burgers several times while cooking.

While burgers are cooking, combine sauce ingredients in a small saucepan. Cook over medium heat until hot and bubbly. Keep warm over low heat until burgers are done.

Divide sauce evenly and spoon over burgers to serve.

Each serving provides:

192 Calories

3	Protein Servings	21 g	Protein
1¼	Vegetable Servings	9 g	Fat (43% of calories)
		6 g	Carbohydrate
		185 mg	Sodium
		83 mg	Cholesterol
		1 g	Fiber

Antipasto-Stuffed Hoagies

Sliced and arranged on a platter, these sandwiches make a gorgeous appetizer. Or just munch them whole. Either way, you're in for a real treat.

Makes 6 servings

12	ounces French bread (approximately 2¹/₂ inches in diameter)
1	cup finely chopped tomatoes
¹/₄	cup finely chopped onion
¹/₄	cup finely shredded carrots
¹/₄	cup finely chopped green bell pepper
2	tablespoons reduced-calorie Italian dressing (16 calories or fewer per tablespoon)
1	tablespoon dried parsley flakes
¹/₁₆	teaspoon garlic powder
¹/₁₆	teaspoon pepper
10	small pitted black olives, sliced (3 tablespoons)
10	small stuffed green olives, sliced (3 tablespoons)
3	ounces shredded reduced-fat Cheddar cheese (³/₄ cup)

Cut bread crosswise into 4-inch sections. With a long, sharp knife, cut out the inside of each section, leaving a ¹/₂-inch shell. Crumble the insides of the bread into a large bowl.

Add remaining ingredients. Mix well. Pat mixture down firmly in bowl, cover, and chill at least 1 hour. (Meanwhile, wrap bread or place in a plastic bag to retain freshness.)

Stir vegetable mixture, then, using a teaspoon, stuff mixture tightly into hollowed-out rolls.

Wrap each roll and chill several hours or overnight.

To serve, slice each roll crosswise into 1-inch slices, or eat them as hoagies.

Each serving provides:

219 Calories

¹/₂	Protein Serving	10 g	Protein
2	Bread Servings	5 g	Fat (22% of calories)
¹/₂	Vegetable Serving	33 g	Carbohydrate
¹/₃	Fat Serving	647 mg	Sodium
5	Additional Calories	10 mg	Cholesterol
		2 g	Fiber

Cottage Cheese Dijon Sandwich

For a change-of-pace lunch, you'll love this tangy cheese blend on toasted whole wheat bread. Romaine lettuce and sliced tomatoes add even more flavor and nutrition.

Makes 2 servings

1	cup lowfat (1%) cottage cheese
1/2	medium cucumber, peeled, seeded, and finely chopped (1/2 cup)
1/4	cup shredded carrot
1/4	cup shredded zucchini, unpeeled
1	tablespoon finely minced onion
1	teaspoon Dijon mustard
1/2	teaspoon Worcestershire sauce
4	slices whole wheat bread, toasted

Combine all ingredients, except bread, in a medium bowl. Mix well. Chill several hours to blend flavors.

To serve, toast bread, divide cottage cheese mixture evenly, and spoon onto 2 slices of toast. Top with remaining toast slices.

Each serving provides:

240 Calories

1½	Protein Servings	20 g	Protein
2	Bread Servings	4 g	Fat (13% of calories)
1	Vegetable Serving	33 g	Carbohydrate
		839 mg	Sodium
		5 mg	Cholesterol
		5 g	Fiber

Marvelous Meatless Mushroom Cheeseburgers

These wonderful burgers can also be made without the cheese, but we really love the combined flavor of cheese and mushrooms. Serve on a burger bun or on a pita with your favorite burger "fixins."

Makes 4 servings

1/4	cup plus 2 tablespoons whole wheat flour
1/4	cup plus 2 tablespoons wheat germ (1 1/2 ounces)
1/2	teaspoon baking powder
1/8	teaspoon salt
1/8	teaspoon pepper
1/8	teaspoon dried oregano
1/8	teaspoon dried basil
1/8	teaspoon garlic powder
4	egg whites
1/4	cup very finely chopped onion
2	cups chopped mushrooms (about 1/4-inch pieces)
4	ounces sliced reduced-fat Cheddar, mozzarella, Swiss, or American cheese

In a medium bowl, combine flour, wheat germ, baking powder, and spices. Mix well.

In another bowl, combine egg whites, onion, and mushrooms. Add to dry mixture, mixing until all ingredients are moistened.

Shape mixture into four $3^1/_2$-inch burgers, wetting your hands slightly to prevent sticking.

Spray a large nonstick skillet or griddle with nonstick cooking spray. Heat over medium heat.

Place burgers on preheated skillet. Cook until nicely browned on both sides, turning burgers several times. When burgers are ready, top with cheese and heat just until cheese starts to melt.

Each serving provides:

191 Calories

1	Protein Serving	18 g	Protein
1	Bread Serving	7 g	Fat (31% of calories)
1	Vegetable Serving	17 g	Carbohydrate
20	Additional Calories	407 mg	Sodium
		20 mg	Cholesterol
		3 g	Fiber

French Toast Cheesewich

This sandwich version of French toast has lots of variations. For example, try adding chopped chives, imitation bacon bits, or chopped jalapeño peppers, or try different types of cheese.

Makes 2 servings

2	ounces sliced, reduced-fat Cheddar cheese
4	slices thin-sliced whole wheat bread (40 calories per slice)
$1/2$	cup liquid egg substitute
$1/4$	cup skim milk
1	tablespoon reduced-calorie margarine

Place cheese between the bread slices, making two sandwiches.

In a shallow pan, combine the egg substitute and milk, whisking to combine. Soak the sandwiches in the mixture, turning carefully to soak both sides. Add a little more milk if necessary, to moisten all of the bread.

Melt half of the margarine in a large nonstick skillet or griddle over medium heat. Place sandwiches in skillet and brown lightly on both sides, turning carefully several times.

Each serving provides:

224 Calories

2	Protein Servings	20 g	Protein
1	Bread Serving	9 g	Fat (33% of calories)
$3/4$	Fat Serving	20 g	Carbohydrate
31	Additional Calories	609 mg	Sodium
		21 mg	Cholesterol
		5 g	Fiber

Zucchini Mock Crab Cakes

You won't believe how much these vegetable patties taste like the real thing. We like to serve them Chesapeake Bay style—on crackers, spread with ketchup or tartar sauce.

Makes 4 servings

4	slices whole wheat bread (1-ounce slices), crumbled
1	tablespoon plus 1 teaspoon reduced-calorie mayonnaise
1	teaspoon baking powder
1	teaspoon seafood seasoning (such as Old Bay)
2	egg whites
2	cups finely shredded zucchini, unpeeled (Pack tightly in cup to measure.)

In a large bowl, combine all ingredients, except zucchini. Mix well.

Place zucchini in a large strainer. Press out as much liquid as possible. Add zucchini to bread mixture. Mix with a fork for several minutes, until mixture is well combined and holds together.

Spray a nonstick griddle or skillet with nonstick cooking spray. Heat over medium heat.

Divide zucchini mixture evenly into 8 portions and shape each portion into a patty. Place on prepared griddle and cook, turning several times, until patties are lightly browned on both sides.

Serve hot. (Leftovers are good hot or cold.)

Each serving provides:

108 Calories

1	Bread Serving	6 g	Protein
1	Vegetable Serving	3 g	Fat (23% of calories)
1/2	Fat Serving	17 g	Carbohydrate
10	Additional Calories	494 mg	Sodium
		2 mg	Cholesterol
		2 g	Fiber

Grilled Turkey Bagel

This popular sandwich is also delicious on a toasted English muffin. It's a great after-Thanksgiving favorite, but can be enjoyed at any time of year.

Makes 2 servings

1   tablespoon reduced-calorie mayonnaise
1   2-ounce bagel, cut in half and lightly toasted
2   teaspoons imitation bacon bits
2   ounces sliced, cooked white meat turkey
4   slices tomato
2   ounces sliced reduced-fat Cheddar cheese

Preheat oven (or toaster oven) to 375 degrees F.

Spread mayonnaise on bagel halves. Then layer bacon bits, turkey, and tomato, and top with cheese.

Place sandwiches on a baking sheet.

Bake 15 minutes, until sandwiches are hot and cheese is melted.

Each serving provides:

229 Calories

2	Protein Servings	22 g	Protein
1	Bread Serving	8 g	Fat (32% of calories)
1/2	Vegetable Serving	17 g	Carbohydrate
3/4	Fat Serving	489 mg	Sodium
30	Additional Calories	46 mg	Cholesterol
		1 g	Fiber

Bean and Cheese Wrap-Ups

This is one of our favorite hot lunches—cheese and beans in pita bread. We think you'll love it, too.

Makes 4 servings

2/3	cup cooked kidney beans (4 ounces)
4	ounces shredded part-skim mozzarella cheese (1 cup)
1	cup finely chopped tomato
1/4	cup finely chopped onions
10	small black olives, chopped (3 tablespoons)
1	tablespoon plus 1 teaspoon reduced-calorie Italian dressing (16 calories or fewer per tablespoon)
4	1-ounce pita breads

Preheat oven to 400 degrees F.

In a large bowl, combine all ingredients, except pita breads. Mix well.

Split open one end of each pita. Divide filling evenly and spoon into open end.

Wrap each sandwich tightly in a piece of aluminum foil.

Bake 15 to 20 minutes.

Serve hot.

Each serving provides:

208 Calories

1 1/2	Protein Servings	12 g	Protein
1	Bread Serving	6 g	Fat (25% of calories)
1/2	Vegetable Serving	27 g	Carbohydrate
1/4	Fat Serving	392 mg	Sodium
5	Additional Calories	16 mg	Cholesterol
		2 g	Fiber

Vegetables

Low in fat, high in fiber, and loaded with vitamins and minerals, vegetables are virtual powerhouses of nutrition. With health professionals recommending that vegetables play a major role in our daily meals, it is wise to include a wide variety of vegetables in your diet.

For the best flavor and nutritional value, cook vegetables until just tender-crisp and leave the skin on whenever possible. Fresh vegetables are best, with frozen vegetables being our second choice. Canned vegetables often contain high amounts of salt and tend to be overcooked.

Our creative vegetable dishes are good enough for company, but also easy to prepare.

Golden Carrot Loaf

This golden loaf is sweet, moist, and delicious. It provides an excellent way to get them to eat their vegetables.

Makes 6 servings

1	cup liquid egg substitute
2	tablespoons dry sherry
1	packet low-sodium instant chicken or vegetable broth mix
1/2	cup plus 1 tablespoon all-purpose flour
1	1-pound bag of carrots, grated or finely shredded (The food processor, using the steel blade, does the best job. Cut the carrots into large chunks first.)
1	small onion, grated (Or put it in the food processor with the carrots.)

Preheat oven to 350 degrees F.

Spray a 4 × 8-inch loaf pan with nonstick cooking spray.

Combine egg substitute, sherry, and broth mix in a large bowl. Stir in flour, using a wire whisk. Whisk until smooth. Add carrots and onion. Mix well.

Spoon mixture into prepared pan.

Bake, uncovered, 50 to 55 minutes, until set.

Cool in pan on a wire rack for 5 minutes, then invert onto a serving plate.

Cut into slices to serve.

Each serving provides:

110 Calories

1/2	Protein Serving	6 g	Protein
1/2	Bread Serving	trace	Fat (4% of calories)
3/4	Vegetable Serving	19 g	Carbohydrate
16	Additional Calories	95 mg	Sodium
		0 mg	Cholesterol
		3 g	Fiber

Nacho Vegetable Medley

The cumin and garlic add a delectable flavor that lovers of Mexican food will adore. This dish makes a great accompaniment to bean burritos.

Makes 4 servings

2	teaspoons vegetable oil
2	cups shredded cabbage
1	cup thinly sliced green bell pepper
1	cup chopped onions
1	cup sliced mushrooms
1/4	cup tomato paste
2	tablespoons water
3/4	teaspoon ground cumin
1/4	teaspoon garlic powder

Heat oil in a large nonstick skillet over medium heat. Add remaining ingredients.

Cover and cook over medium heat, stirring frequently, until vegetables are tender-crisp, about 15 minutes.

Each serving provides:

71 Calories

3	Vegetable Servings	2 g	Protein
1/2	Fat Serving	3 g	Fat (32% of calories)
		11 g	Carbohydrate
		139 mg	Sodium
		0 mg	Cholesterol
		3 g	Fiber

Party Vegetable Loaf

Pretty as a picture and delicious, too. Your guests will rave over this layered beauty!

Makes 8 servings

Layer 1

2	10-ounce packages frozen peas
2	teaspoons vegetable oil
2	egg whites
1/4	cup all-purpose flour
1	tablespoon minced onion flakes
1/8	teaspoon garlic powder
	Salt and pepper

Layer 2

2	10-ounce packages frozen cauliflower
2	teaspoons vegetable oil
2	egg whites
1/4	cup all-purpose flour
1	tablespoon minced onion flakes
1	teaspoon grated fresh lemon peel
1/8	teaspoon garlic powder
	Salt and pepper

Layer 3

1 1/2	1-pound packages frozen sliced carrots
2	teaspoons vegetable oil
2	egg whites
1/4	cup all-purpose flour
1	teaspoon grated fresh orange peel
	Salt and pepper

Preheat oven to 350 degrees F.

Spray a 5 × 9-inch loaf pan with nonstick cooking spray. Place a 9-inch wide piece of wax paper in the pan, lining the sides and bottom. Spray again.

Prepare layer 1:

Cook peas according to package directions. Drain. Place peas and remaining ingredients in a blender container. Blend until smooth. Spread evenly in prepared pan.

Prepare layer 2:

Cook cauliflower according to package directions. Drain. Place cauliflower in blender container with remaining ingredients. Blend until smooth. Spread evenly over pea layer.

Prepare layer 3:

Cook carrots according to package directions. Drain. Place carrots in blender container with remaining ingredients. Blend until smooth. Spread evenly over cauliflower layer.

Bake, uncovered, 55 minutes.

Let stand 10 minutes, then carefully invert onto a serving plate. Peel off wax paper. Cut into slices to serve.

Note: Be sure to rinse blender container before adding each new vegetable.

Each serving provides:

195 Calories

1/4	Protein Serving	10 g	Protein
1 1/2	Bread Servings	4 g	Fat (19% of calories)
2 1/4	Vegetable Servings	31 g	Carbohydrate
3/4	Fat Serving	188 mg	Sodium
		0 mg	Cholesterol
		6 g	Fiber

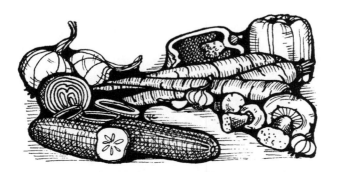

King Cabbage

Thick slices of cabbage, crowned with onions and melted cheese, make this a king of a vegetable dish.

Makes 4 servings

1	small cabbage (³/₄ pound), cut into ¹/₂ inch slices
2	teaspoons sugar
1	teaspoon caraway seeds
1	medium onion, thinly sliced (about 1 cup)
¹/₈	teaspoon salt
¹/₈	teaspoon pepper
2	ounces shredded part-skim mozzarella cheese (or reduced-fat Swiss) (¹/₂ cup)

Preheat oven to 350 degrees F.

Spray an 8-inch square baking pan with nonstick cooking spray.

Place cabbage slices in bottom of prepared pan. Sprinkle evenly with half of the sugar and half of the caraway seeds.

Place onion slices over cabbage. Sprinkle with remaining sugar and caraway seeds, and the salt and pepper.

Cover and bake 1 hour.

Uncover, sprinkle with cheese, and return to oven for 5 minutes to melt cheese.

Each serving provides:

83 Calories

¹/₂	Protein Serving	5 g	Protein
1 ¹/₄	Vegetable Servings	3 g	Fat (28% of calories)
8	Additional Calories	11 g	Carbohydrate
		152 mg	Sodium
		8 mg	Cholesterol
		3 g	Fiber

Asian Cabbage

The wonderful, aromatic sesame oil makes this dish a perfect companion for rice and your favorite Asian entrée.

Makes 6 servings

1	teaspoon vegetable oil
1	teaspoon sesame oil
1	cup sliced onion
6	cups cabbage, shredded 1/4 inch thick
2	tablespoons water
1	packet low-sodium instant beef broth mix
1	tablespoon soy sauce
1/4	teaspoon garlic powder
1/4	teaspoon ground ginger

Heat both oils in a large nonstick skillet over medium heat. Add onions and cook until tender, about 5 minutes. Reduce heat to medium-low and add cabbage.

In a small bowl, combine remaining ingredients. Pour over cabbage.

Cook, covered, until cabbage is tender, about 20 minutes. Stir occasionally while cooking.

Each serving provides:

45 Calories

2 1/4	Vegetable Servings	1 g	Protein
1/4	Fat Serving	2 g	Fat (31% of calories)
5	Additional Calories	7 g	Carbohydrate
		186 mg	Sodium
		0 mg	Cholesterol
		2 g	Fiber

Orange Broccoli

We've added orange juice to this version of stir-fried broccoli.
You're guaranteed to love it.

Makes 4 servings

1/2	cup orange juice
1	tablespoon reduced-sodium soy sauce
1	tablespoon cornstarch
2	teaspoons honey
1/4	teaspoon ground ginger
1/4	teaspoon garlic powder
1	tablespoon vegetable oil
4	cups broccoli, cut into small flowerets

In a small bowl, combine orange juice, soy sauce, cornstarch, honey, ginger, and garlic powder. Mix until cornstarch is dissolved. Set aside.

Heat oil in a large nonstick skillet over medium heat. Add broccoli. Cook, stirring frequently, until broccoli is bright green, about 2 minutes.

Stir orange juice mixture and pour over broccoli. Cook, stirring, for about 1 minute, until broccoli is evenly coated and sauce is thick and clear.

Each serving provides:

90 Calories

1	Vegetable Serving	3 g	Protein
3/4	Fat Serving	4 g	Fat (34% of calories)
3/4	Fruit Serving	13 g	Carbohydrate
8	Additional Calories	174 mg	Sodium
		0 mg	Cholesterol
		3 g	Fiber

Broccoli with Mushrooms and Walnuts

Stir-fried and laced with Cheddar cheese and sherry, this is our very favorite way to serve broccoli. Your family will love it, and your guests will rave.

Makes 6 servings

$1/2$	cup water
2	tablespoons reduced-sodium soy sauce
1	tablespoon dry sherry
1	tablespoon cornstarch
1	packet low-sodium instant chicken or vegetable broth mix
$1/2$	teaspoon dried oregano
$1/4$	teaspoon garlic powder
$1/8$	teaspoon pepper
2	teaspoons vegetable oil
3	cups sliced mushrooms
1	cup onion, cut into $1/4$-inch slices
4	cups (packed) broccoli, cut into flowerets
3	tablespoons chopped walnuts ($3/4$ ounce)
3	ounces shredded reduced-fat Cheddar cheese ($3/4$ cup)

In a small bowl, combine water, soy sauce, sherry, cornstarch, broth mix, oregano, garlic powder, and pepper. Stir to dissolve cornstarch. Set aside.

Heat oil in a large nonstick skillet over medium-high heat. Add mushrooms and onion. Cook, stirring, 5 minutes.

Add broccoli and walnuts. Cook, stirring, 3 minutes, or until broccoli turns bright green.

Stir soy sauce mixture and pour over vegetables. Cook, stirring, until vegetables are glazed and liquid has thickened and turned clear.

Remove from heat, sprinkle evenly with cheese, cover, and let stand 5 minutes before serving.

Each serving provides:

143 Calories

$1/2$	Protein Serving	10 g	Protein	
$2^3/4$	Vegetable Servings	7 g	Fat (41% of calories)	
$1/4$	Fat Serving	12 g	Carbohydrate	
40	Additional Calories	502 mg	Sodium	
		10 mg	Cholesterol	
		4 g	Fiber	

Spanish Green Beans

This dish is colorful, as well as delicious. Stir in leftover chunks of chicken and it becomes a meal in itself.

Make 6 servings

2	10-ounce packages frozen cut green beans
2	teaspoons vegetable oil
1/2	cup chopped onion
1/2	cup chopped green bell pepper
1	16-ounce can salt-free (or regular) chopped tomatoes, undrained
1/2	teaspoon dried basil
1/4	teaspoon dried rosemary, crumbled
	Salt and pepper

Cook beans according to package directions. Drain.

While beans are cooking, heat oil in a large saucepan over medium heat. Add onion and green pepper. Cook, stirring frequently, until tender, about 10 minutes.

Add beans to saucepan, along with tomatoes and spices. Cover and cook until hot and bubbly.

Each serving provides:

67 Calories

2 1/4	Vegetable Servings	3 g	Protein
1/4	Fat Serving	2 g	Fat (23% of calories)
3	Additional Calories	12 g	Carbohydrate
		13 mg	Sodium
		0 mg	Cholesterol
		3 g	Fiber

Pennsylvania Dutch Green Beans

The unique combination of flavors gives these beans a real lift. They're mildly tangy and slightly sweet.

Makes 6 servings

2	10-ounce packages frozen cut green beans
1	tablespoon margarine
1/2	cup chopped onion
1	tablespoon vinegar
1/2	teaspoon dry mustard
2	teaspoons imitation bacon bits
2	teaspoons firmly packed brown sugar
	Salt and pepper

Cook beans according to package directions, cooking until just tender-crisp. Drain.

Melt margarine in a large nonstick skillet over medium heat. Add onion and cook, stirring frequently, until tender, about 5 minutes. Reduce heat to medium-low.

Add beans and remaining ingredients to saucepan. Heat, stirring, until heated through.

Each serving provides:

63 Calories

1 1/2	Vegetable Servings	2 g	Protein
1/2	Fat Serving	2 g	Fat (29% of calories)
9	Additional Calories	10 g	Carbohydrate
		46 mg	Sodium
		0 mg	Cholesterol
		2 g	Fiber

Eggplant Supreme

Everyone who tastes this delicious dish agrees that it is indeed supreme. It can be served as a side dish, hot or cold, or on crackers or toast points as an elegant appetizer.

Makes 8 side-dish servings

1	tablespoon plus 1 teaspoon vegetable oil
1	small eggplant (about $3/4$ pound), unpeeled, finely chopped (3 cups)
$1/2$	cup finely chopped onion
$1/2$	cup finely chopped green bell pepper
1	cup chopped mushrooms
3	cloves garlic, finely minced
1	6-ounce can tomato paste
$1/2$	cup water
2	tablespoons red wine vinegar
$1^1/2$	teaspoons sugar
$1/2$	teaspoon dried oregano
$1/2$	teaspoon salt
$1/4$	teaspoon pepper
10	small, stuffed green olives, chopped
3	tablespoons sunflower seeds (raw or dry roasted)

Heat oil in a large nonstick skillet over medium heat. Add eggplant, onion, green pepper, mushrooms, and garlic. Mix well. Cover and cook 10 minutes, stirring occasionally. Add small amounts of water if necessary, a few tablespoons at a time, to prevent sticking.

Add remaining ingredients, mixing well. Reduce heat to medium-low, cover, and simmer 30 minutes, stirring occasionally.

Serve hot, or chill and serve cold.

Each serving provides:

86 Calories

$2^1/2$	Vegetable Servings	2 g	Protein
$1/2$	Fat Serving	5 g	Fat (45% of calories)
25	Additional Calories	10 g	Carbohydrate
		393 mg	Sodium
		0 mg	Cholesterol
		2 g	Fiber

Spicy Squash Pudding

Serve this all-time favorite dish hot as a vegetable or cold as a dessert. (Yes, dessert!) Either way it's spicy, sweet, and just plain delicious.

Makes 4 servings

3	cups zucchini or yellow summer squash, unpeeled, cut into small chunks
1¹/₃	cups nonfat dry milk
¹/₂	cup liquid egg substitute
3	tablespoons sugar
1	tablespoon all-purpose flour
1¹/₂	teaspoons pumpkin pie spice
1	teaspoon baking powder
1	teaspoon vanilla extract

Preheat oven to 350 degrees F.

Spray a 1-quart baking dish or a 9-inch cake pan with nonstick cooking spray.

In a blender container, combine all ingredients. Blend until smooth. Pour mixture into prepared pan.

Bake 30 minutes, or until set.

Each serving provides:

161 Calories

¹/₂	Protein Serving	12 g	Protein
1¹/₂	Vegetable Servings	1 g	Fat (3% of calories)
1	Milk Serving	27 g	Carbohydrate
44	Additional Calories	300 mg	Sodium
		4 mg	Cholesterol
		1 g	Fiber

Southern-Style Baked Squash

An adaptation of an old Southern recipe, this dish has been a family favorite for years.

Makes 6 servings

2	10-ounce packages frozen yellow summer squash
1	tablespoon minced onion flakes
2	tablespoons reduced-calorie margarine
2	egg whites
1^1/$_2$	teaspoons sugar
^{1}/$_2$	teaspoon salt
^{1}/$_8$	teaspoon pepper
3	tablespoons Italian seasoned bread crumbs

Cook squash according to package directions, cooking until it is very tender. Drain.

Preheat oven to 350 degrees F.

Spray a 1-quart baking dish with nonstick cooking spray.

Place squash in a large bowl. Mash well, using a fork or a potato masher. Add onion flakes, half of the margarine, egg whites, sugar, salt, pepper, and half of the crumbs. Mix well.

Spoon mixture into prepared baking dish. Sprinkle with remaining crumbs. Dot with remaining margarine.

Bake, uncovered, 45 minutes, or until set and lightly browned.

Each serving provides:

61 Calories

1^1/$_4$	Vegetable Servings	3 g	Protein
^{1}/$_2$	Fat Serving	2 g	Fat (32% of calories)
26	Additional Calories	8 g	Carbohydrate
		347 mg	Sodium
		0 mg	Cholesterol
		1 g	Fiber

Dilled Yellow Squash

This simple, herbed dish makes a delicious complement to almost any meal. For the best flavor, let the onions get nice and brown before adding the squash.

Makes 6 servings

2	teaspoons olive oil
1	cup chopped onion
3	cloves garlic, finely chopped
4	cups yellow summer squash, unpeeled, sliced crosswise into $1/2$-inch slices
1	teaspoon dill weed
$1/2$	teaspoon salt
$1/8$	teaspoon pepper

Heat oil in a large nonstick skillet over medium heat. Add onion and garlic. Cook, stirring frequently, until onion is lightly browned, 8 to 10 minutes.

Add squash. Sprinkle evenly with dill weed, salt, and pepper.

Cover and cook until squash is lightly browned and tender-crisp, about 5 to 7 minutes. Turn squash several times while cooking to brown both sides.

Each serving provides:

44 Calories

$1^3/4$	Vegetable Servings	1 g	Protein
$1/4$	Fat Serving	2 g	Fat (32% of calories)
3	Additional Calories	7 g	Carbohydrate
		185 mg	Sodium
		0 mg	Cholesterol
		1 g	Fiber

Italian Baked Spaghetti Squash

Kids love the spaghetti-like strands of this unique vegetable. This easy casserole can be assembled ahead, refrigerated, and baked when needed. If you have a large squash, you can easily double the recipe.

Makes 4 servings

2	cups cooked spaghetti squash*
1	8-ounce can salt-free (or regular) tomato sauce
1/2	teaspoon dried oregano
1/8	teaspoon garlic powder
	Pepper
1	tablespoon plus 1 teaspoon grated Parmesan cheese

Preheat oven to 375 degrees F.

Spray a 1-quart baking dish with nonstick cooking spray.

Place spaghetti squash in prepared baking dish. Combine tomato sauce, oregano, garlic powder, and pepper. Spoon evenly over squash.

Sprinkle with Parmesan cheese.

Bake, uncovered, 20 minutes, until hot and bubbly.

*To cook spaghetti squash, cut squash in half lengthwise. Remove seeds. Bake, cut side down in a baking pan containing 1 inch of water, at 350 degrees F, for 45 minutes, or until tender. Remove squash from pan and drain cut side down. Pull strands free with a fork.

Each serving provides:

53 Calories

2	Vegetable Servings	2 g	Protein
10	Additional Calories	1 g	Fat (19% of calories)
		10 g	Carbohydrate
		57 mg	Sodium
		1 mg	Cholesterol
		1 g	Fiber

Zucchini and Peppers

This is delicious over rice or as a topper for a baked potato. You can even add leftover cooked chicken or any type of cooked beans for a complete meal.

Makes 4 servings

2	teaspoons olive oil
1	cup chopped onion
1	cup chopped green bell pepper
2	cups zucchini, unpeeled, cut into small cubes
1/2	teaspoon dried oregano
1/4	teaspoon garlic powder
	Salt and pepper
1/2	cup salt-free (or regular) tomato sauce
	(or reduced-fat pasta sauce)

Heat oil in a large nonstick skillet over medium heat. Add onion and green pepper. Cook 5 minutes, stirring frequently.

Add zucchini. Cook, stirring frequently, 5 minutes. Add small amounts of water if necessary, about a tablespoon at a time, to prevent drying.

Reduce heat to medium-low. Stir in remaining ingredients. Cover and cook until hot and bubbly.

Each serving provides:

62 Calories

2¹/₂	Vegetable Servings	2 g	Protein
¹/₂	Fat Serving	3 g	Fat (34% of calories)
		9 g	Carbohydrate
		10 mg	Sodium
		0 mg	Cholesterol
		2 g	Fiber

Tomatoes Provençal

A delicious and colorful side dish, this one is great for a party. We usually make it in the summer when fresh, vine-ripened tomatoes are plentiful.

Makes 6 servings

1	teaspoon olive oil
1	cup chopped onion
1	cup sliced mushrooms
1/8	teaspoon garlic powder
1/2	teaspoon seasoned salt
	Pepper
1	tablespoon imitation bacon bits
2	pounds fresh, ripe tomatoes, sliced crosswise into 1/2 -inch slices (6 medium tomatoes)
2	tablespoons grated Parmesan cheese

Preheat oven to 350 degrees F.

Spray a 9-inch round or square baking dish with nonstick cooking spray.

Heat oil in a large nonstick skillet over medium heat. Add onion and mushrooms. Cook, stirring frequently, until onion is tender, about 5 minutes. Remove from heat and stir in garlic powder, seasoned salt, pepper, and bacon bits.

Place half of the tomato slices in the bottom of prepared pan. Spread onion mixture evenly over tomatoes. Sprinkle with half of the Parmesan cheese, then top with remaining tomatoes. Sprinkle with remaining cheese.

Cover tightly and bake 34 to 40 minutes.

Each serving provides:

65 Calories

2³/4	Vegetable Servings	3 g	Protein
22	Additional Calories	2 g	Fat (26% of calories)
		10 g	Carbohydrate
		98 mg	Sodium
		1 mg	Cholesterol
		3 g	Fiber

Clove-Spiced Tomatoes

The unusual blend of spices makes this one of our very favorite vegetable dishes.

Makes 4 servings

2	16-ounce cans tomatoes, undrained, coarsely chopped
$1/2$	cup chopped onion
2	tablespoons firmly packed brown sugar
$1/4$	teaspoon ground cloves
$1/8$	teaspoon pepper
1	small bay leaf
	Salt
4	slices whole wheat bread (1-ounce slices), cut into cubes

In a medium saucepan, combine all ingredients, except bread cubes. Bring to a boil over medium heat. Reduce heat to medium-low and simmer, uncovered, 30 minutes. Stir occasionally while cooking.

Remove and discard bay leaf.

Preheat oven to 375 degrees F.

Spray a $1^1/2$-quart baking dish with nonstick cooking spray.

Add bread cubes to tomato mixture and place in prepared baking dish.

Bake, uncovered, 1 hour.

Each serving provides:

151 Calories

1	Bread Serving	5 g	Protein
$1^1/4$	Vegetable Servings	2 g	Fat (11% of calories)
24	Additional Calories	31 g	Carbohydrate
		523 mg	Sodium
		0 mg	Cholesterol
		4 g	Fiber

Chinese Spinach

*The soy sauce and garlic add an Asian flair to this version of Popeye's fa-
vorite food. To dress it up for a party, sprinkle the top with slivered almonds.*

Makes 4 servings

1	10-ounce package frozen chopped spinach, thawed and drained
1	4-ounce can mushroom pieces, drained
2	tablespoons reduced-sodium (or regular) soy sauce
1	tablespoon plus 1 teaspoon reduced-calorie margarine
1/2	teaspoon sugar
1/2	packet low-sodium instant chicken broth mix
1/4	teaspoon garlic powder
	Dash ground ginger
2	tablespoons chopped green onion (green part only)

Combine all ingredients, except green onion, in a large nonstick
skillet. Heat, stirring frequently, until hot and bubbly.

Spoon into a serving bowl and top with green onion.

Each serving provides:

48 Calories

1¹/4	Vegetable Servings	3 g	Protein
¹/2	Fat Serving	2 g	Fat (35% of calories)
3	Additional Calories	6 g	Carbohydrate
		571 mg	Sodium
		0 mg	Cholesterol
		2 g	Fiber

Grilled Onions

This summertime favorite can also be made under the broiler all year round. It makes a nice extra vegetable to serve with almost any entrée.

Makes 4 servings

2   large onions, sliced 1 inch thick (Vidalia onions are superb!)
       Reduced-sodium soy sauce

Sprinkle onions evenly with soy sauce and marinate for several hours or overnight.

Grill until tender-crisp and brown on both sides, turning carefully with a spatula.

Each serving provides:

71 Calories

1¹/₂ Vegetable Servings	3 g	Protein
	trace	Fat (3% of calories)
	16 g	Carbohydrate
	168 mg	Sodium
	0 mg	Cholesterol
	3 g	Fiber

Veggie Packets

A great summer favorite, these packets of fresh vegetables are cooked on the grill. They're easy to do and won't make a mess.

Makes 6 servings

3	cups fresh tomatoes, cut into chunks
2	cups eggplant, peeled, cut into 1-inch chunks
2	cups zucchini, cut into $^1/_2$-inch slices
1	cup red or green bell pepper, cut into 1-inch chunks
$1^1/_2$	teaspoons dried oregano
$^1/_2$	teaspoon garlic powder
	Salt and pepper
1	tablespoon olive oil

Cut 6 pieces of heavy-duty aluminum foil about 12 inches square. Divide vegetables evenly and place in center of each aluminum piece.

Sprinkle with spices. Drizzle with oil. Wrap vegetables in their foil packets, folding edges to seal.

Place on preheated grill and cook for about 30 minutes, turning occasionally.

Each serving provides:

58 Calories

$2^3/_4$	Vegetable Servings	2 g	Protein
$^1/_2$	Fat Serving	3 g	Fat (37% of calories)
		9 g	Carbohydrate
		11 mg	Sodium
		0 mg	Cholesterol
		2 g	Fiber

Japanese Vegetables

Add some leftover cooked chicken or fish, serve over rice or noodles, and your dinner is done.

Makes 6 servings

2	teaspoons vegetable oil
1	cup sliced onion, broken into rings
1	cup broccoli, cut into flowerets
1	cup sliced mushrooms
1	10-ounce package frozen French-style green beans
1/4	cup water
1/4	cup reduced-sodium soy sauce
2	tablespoons cornstarch
1/4	teaspoon ground ginger
1/4	teaspoon garlic powder

Heat oil in a large nonstick skillet over medium heat. Add onion. Cook, stirring frequently, until slightly tender, about 5 minutes. Add broccoli and mushrooms, cover, and cook 5 minutes. Add small amounts of water if necessary, about a tablespoon at a time, to prevent drying.

Add green beans and water. Cover and cook 10 to 15 minutes, until beans are tender-crisp, stirring occasionally.

In a small bowl, combine remaining ingredients. Stir to dissolve cornstarch. Add to hot vegetables. Cook 2 to 3 minutes, stirring frequently.

Each serving provides:

62 Calories

1 3/4	Vegetable Servings	2 g	Protein
1/4	Fat Serving	2 g	Fat (23% of calories)
		10 g	Carbohydrate
		407 mg	Sodium
		0 mg	Cholesterol
		2 g	Fiber

Starchy Vegetables

The starchy vegetables include white potatoes, sweet potatoes, corn, peas, parsnips, and all varieties of winter squash. These vegetables are higher in carbohydrates than other vegetables and many weight-reduction organizations consider 1 serving of a starchy vegetable to be nutritionally equivalent to 1 serving of bread. Starchy vegetables, like other vegetables, are packed with vitamins, minerals, and fiber.

Some examples of winter squash are butternut, Hubbard, and acorn. We love the versatility of these types of squash. They can be served as a side dish, added to soups, stews, and casseroles, and, with some cinnamon and brown sugar, can even pass as a not-too-sweet dessert. Unlike most other vegetables, the skin on winter squash is inedible. It can be removed either before or after cooking the squash.

We always recommend leaving the skin on potatoes whenever possible, providing extra nutrients and fiber. And remember that, contrary to what our mothers may have told us, it's not the potato that is "fattening" but rather the fatty toppings and deep-frying!

Potato Flapjack

This large flapjack will be the star of any meal it accompanies. From breakfast through dinner, it adds a "homey" touch you're sure to love.

Makes 4 servings

15   ounces potatoes, unpeeled, coarsely shredded
1/2   cup finely minced onion
2   tablespoons plus 2 teaspoons reduced-calorie margarine
         Salt and pepper
         Paprika

Combine potatoes and onions, mixing well.

Melt *half* of the margarine in an 8-inch nonstick skillet over medium heat.

Add potato mixture, pressing it into the shape of a pancake, 1/2 inch thick. Sprinkle with salt, pepper, and paprika. Cook until potatoes are lightly browned on the bottom, about 8 to 10 minutes.

Loosen pancake with a spatula. Dot with remaining margarine. Invert pancake onto a large plate and then slide back into skillet so that brown side is up. Sprinkle again with salt, pepper, and paprika.

Cook 8 to 10 minutes more, until bottom is lightly browned.

Each serving provides:

119 Calories

3/4	Bread Serving	3 g	Protein
1/4	Vegetable Serving	4 g	Fat (28% of calories)
1	Fat Serving	19 g	Carbohydrate
		99 mg	Sodium
		0 mg	Cholesterol
		2 g	Fiber

Potatoes Cacciatore

This flavorful dish serves 8 as a side dish or 6 as a delicious entrée. Sprinkle it lightly with Parmesan cheese or part-skim mozzarella; if you like, add a salad with Italian dressing, and enjoy.

Makes 8 servings

2	teaspoons olive oil
2	cups sliced onions (Cut onions in half lengthwise, then slice each half crosswise into 1/4-inch slices)
2	cloves garlic, finely chopped
1	16-ounce can tomatoes, undrained, chopped
1	8-ounce can salt-free (or regular) tomato sauce
1/2	teaspoon dried oregano
1/2	teaspoon dried basil
1/2	teaspoon dried rosemary, crumbled
1/4	teaspoon pepper
11/2	pounds baking potatoes, unpeeled, sliced crosswise into 1/4-inch slices

Preheat oven to 375 degrees F.

Spray a 9 × 13-inch baking pan with nonstick cooking spray.

Heat oil in a large nonstick skillet over medium heat. Add onions and garlic and cook 5 minutes, stirring frequently, until onions are tender. Remove from heat and add remaining ingredients, except potatoes. Mix well.

Place a layer of potatoes in prepared pan. Spoon half of the tomato mixture evenly over potatoes. Add another layer of potatoes and end with remaining tomato mixture.

Cover pan tightly with aluminum foil.

Bake 50 minutes.

Each serving provides:

112 Calories

1	Bread Serving	3 g	Protein
11/4	Vegetable Servings	2 g	Fat (13% of calories)
1/4	Fat Serving	23 g	Carbohydrate
		106 mg	Sodium
		0 mg	Cholesterol
		3 g	Fiber

Parmesan Potatoes

In this recipe we've taken an old high-calorie favorite and greatly reduced the amount of cheese. For a unique serving idea, try a mound of these delicious potatoes as a "bed" for steamed or stir-fried vegetables.

Makes 4 servings

15	ounces all-purpose potatoes, unpeeled, quartered
3	tablespoons grated Parmesan cheese (1 ounce)
2	tablespoons plus 2 teaspoons reduced-calorie margarine
1/8	teaspoon garlic powder
	Pepper

Place potatoes in 2 inches of boiling water, cover, and cook over medium heat 15 to 20 minutes, or until potatoes are tender. Drain potatoes and remove skin.

In a large bowl, combine potatoes with remaining ingredients. Mash with a potato masher until smooth. Add a little skim milk if potatoes are too dry.

Each serving provides:

144 Calories

1/4	Protein Serving	5 g	Protein
3/4	Bread Serving	6 g	Fat (36% of calories)
1	Fat Serving	18 g	Carbohydrate
5	Additional Calories	230 mg	Sodium
		6 mg	Cholesterol
		2 g	Fiber

Potatoes Italiano

Leaving the skin on the potatoes adds vitamins and fiber to this classy dish.

Makes 6 servings

2	teaspoons olive oil
1¹/₂	pounds potatoes, unpeeled, cut in ¹/₈-inch slices
¹/₂	cup green or red bell pepper, thinly sliced
¹/₂	cup onion, thinly sliced
2	cloves garlic, minced
1	8-ounce can salt-free (or regular) tomato sauce
¹/₂	teaspoon dried oregano
¹/₄	teaspoon dried basil
	Salt and pepper
3	ounces shredded part-skim mozzarella cheese (³/₄ cup)

Heat oil in a large nonstick skillet over medium heat. Add potatoes, bell pepper, onion, and garlic. Cook, stirring frequently, until
vegetables are slightly tender, about 5 minutes.

Reduce heat to medium-low. Add tomato sauce and spices, cover
and cook 30 minutes, until vegetables are tender. Stir occasionally
while cooking and add small amounts of water, a few tablespoons
at a time, if necessary to prevent drying.

Remove skillet from heat. Sprinkle potatoes with cheese, cover skillet, and let stand about 3 minutes until cheese is melted.

Each serving provides:

156 Calories

¹/₂	Protein Serving	7 g	Protein
³/₄	Bread Serving	4 g	Fat (23% of calories)
1	Vegetable Serving	24 g	Carbohydrate
¹/₄	Fat Serving	83 mg	Sodium
17	Additional Calories	8 mg	Cholesterol
		3 g	Fiber

Oven-Baked French "Fries"

Can you believe it? These taste so much like the real thing, you'll make them over and over again. Just a spray of nonstick spray and you still have all of the taste without the gobs of fat.

Makes 4 servings

4   medium baking potatoes, unpeeled (about 5 ounces each)
       Nonstick cooking spray
       Salt and pepper

Preheat oven to 450 degrees F.

Spray a baking sheet with nonstick cooking spray.

Cut potatoes into strips to resemble French fries. Place on prepared sheet in a single layer. Spray potatoes lightly with nonstick spray. Sprinkle with salt and pepper.

Bake 10 minutes, then stir potatoes and bake 10 minutes more, or until desired doneness is reached.

Each serving provides:

132 Calories

1	Bread Serving	4 g	Protein
		1 g	Fat (8% of calories)
		28 g	Carbohydrate
		12 mg	Sodium
		0 mg	Cholesterol
		3 g	Fiber

Bombay Peas and Potatoes

Curry lovers will love this delicious blend of vegetables and spices. It's so pretty and colorful, too.

Makes 8 servings

2	teaspoons vegetable oil
1	cup chopped onion
2	cloves garlic, chopped
2	medium potatoes (18 ounces total), unpeeled, cut into 1/2-inch cubes
1	16-ounce can tomatoes, chopped, undrained
1	cup water
1	teaspoon curry powder
1/2	teaspoon turmeric
1/4	teaspoon chili powder
1	bay leaf
1	cup fresh or frozen peas (If using frozen peas, there's no need to thaw.)

Heat oil in a large nonstick skillet over medium heat. Add onion and garlic. Cook 10 minutes, or until onion begins to brown.

Add remaining ingredients, except peas. Mix well. Bring mixture to a boil, stirring frequently. Then cover, reduce heat to low, and simmer 15 minutes. Stir in peas, cover, and cook 20 more minutes, or until potatoes are tender.

Remove and discard bay leaf before serving.

Each serving provides:

94 Calories

1	Bread Serving	3 g	Protein
3/4	Vegetable Serving	1 g	Fat (14% of calories)
1/4	Fat Serving	18 g	Carbohydrate
		99 mg	Sodium
		0 mg	Cholesterol
		3 g	Fiber

Raspberry-Filled Sweet Potato Croquettes

There's a burst of raspberry flavor in the center of each one of these delicious croquettes. And they're so easy to make.

Makes 6 servings

1	18-ounce can sweet potatoes (vacuum packed)
2	tablespoons firmly packed brown sugar
1/2	teaspoon ground cinnamon
1	teaspoon vanilla extract
1/4	teaspoon orange extract
2	tablespoons fruit-only raspberry jam
1/2	cup plus 1 tablespoon Grape-Nuts cereal, crushed slightly* (2 1/4 ounces)
1 1/2	teaspoons vegetable oil

Preheat oven to 350 degrees F.

Spray a shallow baking pan with nonstick cooking spray.

In a large bowl, combine sweet potatoes, brown sugar, cinnamon, and extracts. Mash with a fork or potato masher until mixture is smooth and thoroughly blended.

Divide mixture into 12 equal portions. Shape each portion into a patty 1/2 inch thick. With your thumb, make an indentation in the center of the patty. Spoon 1/2 teaspoon of the jam into the indentation. Carefully form the sweet potato around the jam, molding it into the shape of a ball.

Roll each ball in crushed cereal. Place in prepared pan and drizzle lightly with the oil, using 1/8 teaspoon on each croquette.

Bake, uncovered, 30 minutes.

*An easy way to crush cereal is to place it in a plastic bag and crush it with a rolling pin.

Each serving provides:

160 Calories

1 1/2	Bread Servings	2 g	Protein
1/4	Fat Serving	2 g	Fat (9% of calories)
24	Additional Calories	35 g	Carbohydrate
		111 mg	Sodium
		0 mg	Cholesterol
		2 g	Fiber

Sweet Potato Pancakes

These moist little pancakes can be served as a side dish or as an unusual breakfast. We love them topped with applesauce and a dash of cinnamon.

Makes 4 servings

12	ounces cooked sweet potatoes, peeled and cut into chunks
1/2	cup liquid egg substitute
2	tablespoons firmly packed brown sugar
1	tablespoon all-purpose flour
2	teaspoons vegetable oil
1	teaspoon baking powder
1	teaspoon vanilla extract
1/2	teaspoon maple extract
1/4	teaspoon ground nutmeg
1/2	teaspoon ground cinnamon

Bake the sweet potatoes in a 350-degree F oven for about 1 hour, or microwave for 8 to 10 minutes, until very tender. Bake the potatoes whole and be sure to make several slits in each one to let the steam escape while cooking.

Place cooked sweet potatoes in a large bowl. Mash well, using a fork or potato masher. Add remaining ingredients. Mix well.

Spray a large nonstick skillet or griddle with nonstick cooking spray. Preheat over medium heat. Drop mixture onto skillet, making 8 pancakes, using 2 tablespoons of batter for each pancake.

Turn pancakes carefully when edges become dry and bottoms are lightly browned. Cook until browned on both sides.

Note: To make turning pancakes easier, spray both sides of your spatula with nonstick cooking spray.

Each serving provides:

165 Calories

1/2	Protein Serving	5 g	Protein
1	Bread Serving	3 g	Fat (15% of calories)
1/2	Fat Serving	30 g	Carbohydrate
32	Additional Calories	186 mg	Sodium
		0 mg	Cholesterol
		3 g	Fiber

Sweet Potato Pudding

Raisins and nuts enhance the flavor of this luscious casserole. It's definitely a "go" for any party, and the recipe can easily be doubled or tripled.

Makes 4 servings

12	ounces raw sweet potatoes, peeled, grated
1	cup grated carrots
1	small Golden Delicious apple, peeled, grated
1/2	cup orange juice (unsweetened)
1/4	cup raisins
2	tablespoons finely chopped walnuts (1/2 ounce)
2	tablespoons maple syrup
1	teaspoon vanilla extract
1	teaspoon ground cinnamon

Preheat oven to 350 degrees F.

Spray a 1-quart casserole with nonstick cooking spray.

In a large bowl, combine all ingredients. Mix well. Place in prepared casserole.

Bake, uncovered, 50 minutes.

Each serving provides:

211 Calories

3/4	Bread Serving	3 g	Protein
1/2	Vegetable Serving	3 g	Fat (12% of calories)
1	Fruit Serving	45 g	Carbohydrate
40	Additional Calories	23 mg	Sodium
		0 mg	Cholesterol
		5 g	Fiber

Sweet Potatoes and Apples

Alternating slices of sweet potatoes and apples, baked in a spiced orange sauce, create a holiday favorite that you'll want to make throughout the year.

Makes 4 servings

12	ounces cooked sweet potatoes, peeled, sliced into thin slices
2	small, sweet apples, peeled and cored, cut in half, then cut into very thin slices
1/4	cup frozen orange juice concentrate, thawed
1/4	cup water
2	tablespoons firmly packed brown sugar
1/4	teaspoon ground cinnamon
1/8	teaspoon ground nutmeg
1/8	teaspoon ground ginger
1	tablespoon plus 1 teaspoon reduced-calorie margarine

Preheat oven to 350 degrees F.

Bake the sweet potatoes for about 1 hour, or microwave for 8 to 10 minutes, until tender but not mushy.

Spray a 1-quart baking dish with nonstick cooking spray.

Arrange alternate slices of cooked sweet potatoes and apples in prepared baking dish.

Combine orange juice, water, brown sugar, and spices. Pour mixture evenly over sweet potatoes and apples. Dot with margarine.

Bake, covered, 1 hour. (If a crisper dish is desired, remove cover during second half of cooking time.)

Each serving provides:

190 Calories

1	Bread Serving	2 g	Protein
1/2	Fat Serving	3 g	Fat (12% of calories)
1	Fruit Serving	41 g	Carbohydrate
24	Additional Calories	60 mg	Sodium
		0 mg	Cholesterol
		4 g	Fiber

Corn Fritters

These delicate little pancakes are a delicious treat with any chicken or fish dinner. You'll love the leftovers cold. That is, if there are any leftovers.

Makes 4 servings

1	cup canned cream-style corn
1/2	cup liquid egg substitute
1/4	cup yellow cornmeal (1 1/2 ounces)
1/2	teaspoon baking powder
1	tablespoon all-purpose flour
	Salt and pepper

In a large bowl, combine all ingredients. Mix well with a fork or wire whisk.

Spray a nonstick griddle or skillet with nonstick cooking spray. Preheat over medium heat.

Drop corn mixture by tablespoonfuls onto skillet, making 16 small pancakes. Brown on both sides, turning carefully when edges appear dry.

Note: To make turning easier, spray both sides of spatula with nonstick cooking spray.

Each serving provides:

109 Calories

1/2	Protein Serving	5 g	Protein
1	Bread Serving	1 g	Fat (5% of calories)
8	Additional Calories	22 g	Carbohydrate
		294 mg	Sodium
		0 mg	Cholesterol
		1 g	Fiber

Roasted Corn on the Cob

What a summertime favorite!

Makes 6 servings

6   small ears of corn, in husks
1/4   cup reduced-calorie margarine
1   teaspoon dill weed (or any other favorite spice)
     Salt and pepper

Without removing husks, loosen them and remove silk. Soak corn in cold water for 30 minutes. Drain well.

In a small bowl, combine margarine, dill weed, salt and pepper. Spread evenly over corn kernels. Close husks and wrap each ear tightly in a piece of aluminum foil.

Place on grill and cook 25 minutes, turning every 5 minutes.

Remove husks to serve.

Each serving provides:

110 Calories

1	Bread Serving	3 g	Protein
1	Fat Serving	5 g	Fat (34% of calories)
		17 g	Carbohydrate
		105 mg	Sodium
		0 mg	Cholesterol
		3 g	Fiber

Mexi-Corn

The sprinkle of fresh cilantro at the end is optional, but we do hope you'll try it that way. Its unusual flavor really enhances the flavors of Mexican food. Look for cilantro in the produce section of most large grocery stores.

Makes 4 servings

2	teaspoons vegetable oil
$^1/_4$	cup finely chopped green bell pepper
$^1/_4$	cup finely chopped red bell pepper
$^1/_4$	cup finely chopped onion
$^1/_4$	cup water
1	16-ounce can salt-free (or regular) corn, drained
	Pepper
1	tablespoon chopped fresh cilantro (optional)

Heat oil in a small saucepan over medium heat. Add bell peppers and onion. Cook, stirring frequently, until vegetables are tender, about 8 minutes. Add small amounts of water if necessary, about a tablespoon at a time, to prevent sticking.

Add water and corn. Heat through and add pepper to taste. Sprinkle with cilantro, if desired.

Each serving provides:

97 Calories

1	Bread Serving	2 g	Protein
$^3/_4$	Vegetable Serving	3 g	Fat (23% of calories)
$^1/_2$	Fat Serving	18 g	Carbohydrate
		4 mg	Sodium
		0 mg	Cholesterol
		2 g	Fiber

Butternut Squash in Marmalade Sauce

Any winter squash can be substituted in this luscious dish. The flavor of the orange marmalade blends so well with the flavor and texture of the squash.

Makes 4 servings

2	cups butternut squash, peeled, cubed
$3/4$	cup water
2	tablespoons fruit-only orange marmalade
1	tablespoon cornstarch
$1/8$	teaspoon ground cinnamon

Cook squash in a small amount of boiling water, in a covered saucepan, until tender, 10 to 15 minutes. Drain. Set aside in a covered serving dish to keep warm.

In a small saucepan, combine remaining ingredients, stirring to dissolve cornstarch. Bring to a boil over medium heat, stirring constantly. Boil 1 minute, stirring. Spoon sauce over squash to serve.

Each serving provides:

60 Calories

$1/2$	Bread Serving	1 g	Protein
$1/2$	Fruit Serving	trace	Fat (1% of calories)
8	Additional Calories	15 g	Carbohydrate
		3 mg	Sodium
		0 mg	Cholesterol
		1 g	Fiber

Applesauce Acorn Squash

Acorn squash has a natural sweetness that is perfectly complemented by the applesauce, making this one of our favorite side dishes.

Makes 4 servings

2	acorn squash, 10 ounces each
1	cup applesauce (unsweetened)
2	tablespoons raisins
1	tablespoon sugar
1	teaspoon lemon juice
1/2	teaspoon maple extract
2	teaspoons margarine

Preheat oven to 375 degrees F.

Cut squash in half lengthwise and remove seeds.

In a small bowl, combine remaining ingredients, except margarine. Fill squash halves. Top each with 1/2 teaspoon of the margarine.

Place squash in a shallow baking pan. Pour hot water around squash to a depth of 1/2 inch.

Cover and bake 30 minutes. Uncover and bake 20 more minutes, until squash is tender.

Each serving provides:

113 Calories

1/2	Bread Serving	1 g	Protein
1/2	Fat Serving	2 g	Fat (15% of calories)
3/4	Fruit Serving	25 g	Carbohydrate
12	Additional Calories	28 mg	Sodium
		0 mg	Cholesterol
		5 g	Fiber

Whipped Spiced Parsnips

An often forgotten vegetable, parsnips have a wonderful flavor and texture and make a delicious side dish. They look like white carrots and can also be chopped and added to soups and stews.

Makes 4 servings

12	ounces parsnips, peeled, sliced crosswise into 1/2-inch slices
2	teaspoons firmly packed brown sugar
1	teaspoon margarine
1/4	teaspoon grated fresh orange peel
	Dash ground nutmeg or allspice
	Dash salt
1/4	cup orange juice
1/4	cup canned crushed pineapple (packed in juice), drained slightly

Place a steamer rack in the bottom of a medium saucepan. Add enough water to come almost up to the bottom of the rack. Place saucepan over medium heat. When water boils, add parsnips, cover saucepan, and cook 15 to 20 minutes, or until parsnips are very tender. Drain.

Preheat oven to 350 degrees F.

Spray a 1-quart baking dish with nonstick cooking spray.

Place parsnips in a large bowl. Add brown sugar, margarine, orange peel, nutmeg, salt, and half of the orange juice. Mash with a fork or potato masher, then beat on medium speed of an electric mixer until smooth. Add remaining orange juice as needed, until desired consistency is reached. Stir in pineapple.

Spoon mixture into prepared baking dish.

Bake, uncovered, 15 minutes, or until hot.

Each serving provides:

90 Calories

1	Bread Serving	1 g	Protein
1/4	Fat Serving	1 g	Fat (14% of calories)
1/4	Fruit Serving	19 g	Carbohydrate
8	Additional Calories	53 mg	Sodium
		0 mg	Cholesterol
		3 g	Fiber

Grains

Grains are an important building block in the foundation of a healthful diet. Many well-meaning, health-conscious eaters often eat a limited selection of grains. There is nothing wrong with the popular choices of whole wheat bread, rice, and oatmeal, but remember there are many other delicious—and nutritious—possibilities.

Grains are rich in complex carbohydrates. They also provide protein, vitamin E, B vitamins, magnesium, iron, copper, and zinc. Whole grains are an excellent source of fiber, and may help to lower blood cholesterol and maintain bowel regularity. One cup of cooked grains provides from 3 to 11 grams of fiber, depending on the grain. Grains are low in fat and calories: 1 cup of cooked grains will provide about 200 calories. And grains are versatile. Not just for dinner, cooked grains also make a filling, nutritious breakfast.

Try them all. Some popular grains are barley, cornmeal, couscous, millet, oats, rice, rye, and wheat. Many health food stores carry little-known grains such as triticale, quinoa, and teff. Be adventurous and enjoy the many delicious possibilities grains have to offer.

Spinach and Rice Bake

Rosemary lends a delicate flavor to this easy casserole. It makes 8 side-dish servings and can also be used as an entrée for 6.

Makes 8 servings

2	10-ounce packages frozen chopped spinach, thawed and drained
2	cups cooked brown rice
6	ounces shredded reduced-fat Cheddar cheese (1¹/₂ cups)
¹/₂	cup thinly sliced green onions (green and white parts)
1	teaspoon dried rosemary, crushed
¹/₂	teaspoon garlic powder
¹/₄	teaspoon salt
¹/₈	teaspoon pepper
2	cups evaporated skim milk
1	cup liquid egg substitute
1	teaspoon Worcestershire sauce

Preheat oven to 350 degrees F.

Spray an 8-inch square baking pan with nonstick cooking spray.

In a large bowl, combine spinach, rice, cheese, green onions, and rosemary. Toss to combine well. Place mixture in prepared pan.

In another bowl, combine remaining ingredients. Beat with a fork or wire whisk until blended. Pour over spinach mixture.

Bake, uncovered, 35 minutes, or until set.

Each serving provides:

200 Calories

2	Protein Servings	18 g	Protein
¹/₂	Bread Serving	5 g	Fat (21% of calories)
1	Vegetable Serving	23 g	Carbohydrate
¹/₄	Milk Serving	419 mg	Sodium
		18 mg	Cholesterol
		2 g	Fiber

Nice Spiced Rice

A delectable blend of spices makes this rice — nice.

Makes 4 servings

1	16-ounce can tomatoes, chopped, drained (Reserve liquid.)
$1/2$	cup very finely chopped onion
$1/4$	teaspoon ground cloves
$1/4$	teaspoon garlic powder
$1/2$	teaspoon ground cumin
$1/8$	teaspoon pepper
	Salt
1	bay leaf
$3/4$	cup brown rice, uncooked (5 ounces)

Place drained tomatoes in a medium saucepan. Add water to reserved tomato liquid to equal 2 cups. Add to saucepan. Add remaining ingredients, except rice. Bring to a boil over medium heat.

Stir in rice, reduce heat to low, cover, and simmer 45 minutes, until most of the liquid has been absorbed.

Remove from heat, fluff rice with a fork, replace cover, and let stand 5 minutes before serving.

Remove and discard bay leaf before serving.

Each serving provides:

164 Calories

$1^1/4$	Bread Servings	4 g	Protein
$1^1/4$	Vegetable Servings	1 g	Fat (8% of calories)
		34 g	Carbohydrate
		189 mg	Sodium
		0 mg	Cholesterol
		2 g	Fiber

Chinese Fried Rice

In fine Chinese style, this delicious dish tastes just like the fried rice in your favorite restaurant.

Makes 4 servings

2	tablespoons reduced-sodium soy sauce
1/8	teaspoon garlic powder
1/8	teaspoon ground ginger
2	teaspoons vegetable oil
1/2	cup liquid egg substitute
4	ounces cooked chicken (1 cup), cut into small pieces*
1/2	cup thinly sliced green onions
2	cups cooked white or brown rice

In a small bowl or custard cup, combine soy sauce, garlic powder, and ginger. Set aside.

Preheat a large nonstick skillet over medium heat. Add 1 teaspoon of the oil. Pour in egg substitute, tilting pan to coat bottom evenly. Cook until egg is set, then remove egg from pan and cut into 1-inch strips. Set aside.

Add remaining oil to skillet. Add chicken, green onions, and rice. Cook, stirring, until well blended. Stir in soy sauce mixture and egg. Continue to cook, stirring constantly, until rice is hot and sizzling.

*If desired, substitute cooked shrimp for the chicken.

Each serving provides:

230 Calories

1 1/2	Protein Servings	15 g	Protein
1	Bread Serving	5 g	Fat (19% of calories)
1/4	Vegetable Serving	31 g	Carbohydrate
1/2	Fat Serving	378 mg	Sodium
		25 mg	Cholesterol
		1 g	Fiber

Apple Rice Casserole

This delicious side dish is a real change of pace. The rice soaks up the juice from the apples and becomes plump and sweet. We love the leftovers for breakfast—served hot or cold with a dollop of yogurt.

Makes 8 servings

2	cups cooked brown rice
3	small, sweet apples, peeled and coarsely shredded
1/3	cup apple juice
1	tablespoon firmly packed brown sugar
2	teaspoons lemon juice
1	teaspoon vanilla extract
1/2	teaspoon ground cinnamon
1/16	teaspoon ground nutmeg

Preheat oven to 350 degrees F.

Spray a 1 1/2-quart casserole with nonstick cooking spray.

In a large bowl, combine all ingredients. Mix well. Spoon into prepared pan.

Cover tightly and bake 45 minutes.

Serve hot.

Each serving provides:

89 Calories

1/2	Bread Serving	1 g	Protein
1/2	Fruit Serving	1 g	Fat (7% of calories)
6	Additional Calories	20 g	Carbohydrate
		4 mg	Sodium
		0 mg	Cholesterol
		2 g	Fiber

Tri-Color Rice

The confetti-like appearance of the different peppers makes this a colorful dish to serve alongside almost any entrée.

Makes 4 servings

2	teaspoons vegetable oil
1/2	cup chopped onion
1/2	cup chopped green bell pepper
1/2	cup chopped red bell pepper
1/2	cup chopped yellow bell pepper
2	cups water
1	teaspoon dried oregano
1/4	teaspoon dried basil
1/4	teaspoon garlic powder
2	packets low-sodium instant chicken or vegetable broth mix
	Salt and pepper
3/4	cup converted rice, uncooked (6 ounces)

Heat oil in a medium saucepan over medium heat. Add onion and peppers. Cook 5 minutes, stirring frequently.

Add water, oregano, basil, garlic powder, and broth mix. When water boils, stir in rice. Cover, reduce heat to medium-low, and simmer 20 minutes, or until most of the water has been absorbed. Remove from heat and let stand 5 minutes.

Fluff rice with a fork before serving.

Each serving provides:

204 Calories

1 1/2	Bread Servings	4 g	Protein
1	Vegetable Serving	3 g	Fat (12% of calories)
1/2	Fat Serving	40 g	Carbohydrate
5	Additional Calories	6 mg	Sodium
		0 mg	Cholesterol
		2 g	Fiber

Couscous Sauté

Look for couscous, a wheat product consisting of tiny bits of pasta, in the grain section of most supermarkets. One of the things I like best is that it cooks in only 5 minutes.

Makes 4 servings

2	teaspoons vegetable oil
3	tablespoons reduced-sodium soy sauce
1/4	teaspoon ground ginger
2	cups finely chopped green bell pepper
1	cup finely chopped carrots
2	tablespoons firmly packed brown sugar
2/3	cup boiling water
1/2	cup couscous, uncooked (3 ounces)

Combine oil, soy sauce, and ginger in a large nonstick skillet over medium heat.

Add green pepper and carrots. Cover and cook until vegetables are tender, about 10 minutes. Add small amounts of water, a few tablespoons at a time, if necessary to prevent drying.

Stir in remaining ingredients, cover skillet, and remove from heat.

Let stand 5 minutes. Fluff with a fork before serving.

Each serving provides:

159 Calories

3/4	Bread Serving	4 g	Protein
1 1/2	Vegetable Servings	3 g	Fat (14% of calories)
1/2	Fat Serving	30 g	Carbohydrate
24	Additional Calories	465 mg	Sodium
		0 mg	Cholesterol
		2 g	Fiber

Breakfast Couscous

This is a delicious change from oatmeal and so quick to prepare.

Makes 2 servings

1/2   cup skim milk
2   tablespoons raisins
1   tablespoon maple syrup
1   teaspoon vanilla extract
1/4   cup couscous, uncooked (1 1/2 ounces)
        Ground cinnamon

In a small saucepan, combine milk, raisins, maple syrup, and vanilla. Heat, stirring constantly, until hot and steamy. Do not boil.
Stir in couscous, cover saucepan, and remove from heat.
Let stand 5 minutes.
Sprinkle with cinnamon and serve hot.

Each serving provides:

160 Calories

3/4	Bread Serving	5 g	Protein
1/2	Fruit Serving	trace	Fat (2% of calories)
1/4	Milk Serving	33 g	Carbohydrate
23	Additional Calories	36 mg	Sodium
		1 mg	Cholesterol
		1 g	Fiber

Herbed Bulgur

Bulgur (cracked wheat) is a nutritious grain that cooks in only 15 minutes. For variations, try it with other combinations of spices.

Makes 6 servings

1	cup bulgur, uncooked (6 ounces)
2	cups water
2	tablespoons minced onion flakes
1	tablespoon margarine
1	tablespoon dried parsley flakes
1/2	teaspoon ground sage
1/2	teaspoon ground savory
1/8	teaspoon garlic powder
	Salt and pepper

In a medium saucepan, combine all ingredients. Cover and bring to a boil over medium heat.

Reduce heat to low and simmer 10 minutes. Remove from heat and let stand, covered, 5 minutes.

Fluff with a fork before serving.

Each serving provides:

119 Calories

1	Bread Serving	4 g	Protein
1/2	Fat Serving	2 g	Fat (16% of calories)
		23 g	Carbohydrate
		28 mg	Sodium
		0 mg	Cholesterol
		5 g	Fiber

Date and Nut Breakfast Treat

The taste of this unique cereal is reminiscent of a moist date and nut bread.
Who says breakfast has to be boring?

Makes 4 servings

1/3	cup bulgur, uncooked (2 ounces)
1/4	cup rolled oats, uncooked (3/4 ounce)
2 1/2	tablespoons wheat germ (3/4 ounce)
1	teaspoon ground cinnamon
1/8	teaspoon ground nutmeg
2	cups water
1	tablespoon molasses
2	tablespoons chopped walnuts (1/2 ounce)
2	tablespoons raisins
2	dates, chopped (3/4 ounce)
1	teaspoon vanilla extract

In a medium saucepan, combine bulgur, oats, wheat germ, cinnamon, and nutmeg. Mix well.

Add remaining ingredients and bring to a boil over medium heat, stirring frequently.

Reduce heat to low and cook 15 minutes, until water is absorbed, stirring occasionally.

Each serving provides:

159 Calories

1	Bread Serving	5 g	Protein
1/2	Fruit Serving	3 g	Fat (18% of calories)
29	Additional Calories	29 g	Carbohydrate
		6 mg	Sodium
		0 mg	Cholesterol
		4 g	Fiber

Buckwheat–Cheese Bake

Hearty and satisfying, this is almost a meal in itself. All you really need to add is salad and a steamed vegetable and you have a filling and delicious meatless meal.

Makes 6 servings

1¹/₃	cups lowfat (1%) cottage cheese
1	cup liquid egg substitute
1	tablespoon all-purpose flour
2	teaspoons minced onion flakes
1	teaspoon dried parsley flakes
1	teaspoon dried basil
¹/₂	teaspoon dried thyme
1	packet low-sodium instant chicken broth mix
	Salt and pepper
2	cups cooked buckwheat groats (kasha)

Cook kasha according to package directions, eliminating margarine completely and using an egg white in place of the whole egg.

Preheat oven to 375 degrees F.

Spray an 8-inch square baking pan with nonstick cooking spray.

In a blender container, combine all ingredients, except buckwheat. Blend until smooth. Pour into a large bowl and stir in buckwheat. Mix well.

Pour mixture into prepared pan.

Bake, uncovered, 30 minutes, or until set and lightly browned.

Each serving provides:

132 Calories

1¹/₄	Protein Servings	13 g	Protein
¹/₂	Bread Serving	1 g	Fat (8% of calories)
25	Additional Calories	18 g	Carbohydrate
		282 mg	Sodium
		2 mg	Cholesterol
		2 g	Fiber

Kasha and Bow Ties

We've taken this traditional Jewish side dish and lowered the calories so it can be enjoyed all the time, alongside any of your favorite entrées. It uses the uniquely flavored buckwheat groats, commonly known as kasha.

Makes 6 servings

1	teaspoon vegetable oil
1/2	cup finely chopped onions
1/2	cup kasha, uncooked (3 ounces)
1	cup boiling water
1	packet low-sodium instant chicken broth mix
1/4	teaspoon salt
1/4	teaspoon pepper
3	cups cooked bow-tie noodles (If noodles are cold, put them in a strainer and pour boiling water over them to heat them.)
2	tablespoons reduced-calorie margarine

Heat oil in a medium nonstick skillet over medium heat. Add onion. Cook, stirring frequently, until lightly browned. Place onion in a small bowl, cover, and set aside.

Place kasha in pan and cook, stirring, until kasha is lightly toasted and fragrant, about 5 minutes. Add boiling water, broth mix, salt, and pepper. Cover, reduce heat to low, and simmer 10 to 15 minutes, until water is absorbed.

Stir in onion, noodles, and margarine. Toss and serve.

Each serving provides:

160 Calories

1 1/2	Bread Servings	5 g	Protein
1/4	Vegetable Serving	3 g	Fat (19% of calories)
1/2	Fat Serving	28 g	Carbohydrate
8	Additional Calories	285 mg	Sodium
		0 mg	Cholesterol
		2 g	Fiber

Buckwheat Pancakes

Buckwheat flour is available in many large supermarkets and in most health food stores. These nutritious pancakes taste great topped with cooked apples or blueberries. What a delicious brunch!

Makes 8 servings (2 pancakes each serving)

1	cup buckwheat flour
1/2	cup all-purpose flour
3 1/2	teaspoons baking powder
1	teaspoon ground cinnamon
1/8	teaspoon salt
3	tablespoons sugar
1/4	cup liquid egg substitute
2	cups skim milk
2	tablespoons vegetable oil

Sift together both types of flour, baking powder, cinnamon, and salt.

In a large bowl, combine remaining ingredients. Beat with a fork or wire whisk until blended.

Add dry ingredients to liquids. Whisk until blended.

Drop batter by 1/4 cupfuls onto a preheated nonstick griddle that has been sprayed lightly with a nonstick cooking spray.

Turn pancakes when edges appear dry, and brown lightly on both sides.

Each serving provides:

156 Calories

1	Bread Serving	6 g	Protein
3/4	Fat Serving	4 g	Fat (24% of calories)
1/4	Milk Serving	25 g	Carbohydrate
26	Additional Calories	293 mg	Sodium
		1 mg	Cholesterol
		2 g	Fiber

Bombay Millet

Millet offers a nice change of pace from rice. Its small size allows it to cook more quickly than brown rice, while offering the high quality and fiber of a whole grain. Look for millet in health food stores and many large grocery stores.

Makes 4 servings

1¹/₂	cups low-sodium chicken broth (or 1¹/₂ cups water and 1 packet low-sodium instant chicken broth mix)
¹/₂	cup millet, uncooked (3 ounces)
1	teaspoon curry powder
¹/₄	teaspoon ground cumin
¹/₄	teaspoon ground ginger
¹/₈	teaspoon ground allspice
¹/₈	teaspoon salt
¹/₈	teaspoon pepper

Bring broth to a boil in a small saucepan over medium heat. Stir in remaining ingredients. When water returns to a boil, reduce heat to medium-low, cover, and simmer 25 minutes, or until the broth has been absorbed.

Fluff with a fork before serving.

Each serving provides:

91 Calories

1	Bread Serving	3 g	Protein
8	Additional Calories	1 g	Fat (10% of calories)
		16 g	Carbohydrate
		281 mg	Sodium
		0 mg	Cholesterol
		2 g	Fiber

Tropical Millet Pudding

This milk-free pudding is a snap to make. For a special occasion, spoon it into sherbet glasses and sprinkle with a few slivered almonds.

Makes 6 servings

1¹/₂	cups water

1¹/₂   cups water
¹/₂   cup millet, uncooked (3 ounces)
1   8-ounce can crushed pineapple (packed in juice), drained
1   medium, ripe banana
2   tablespoons firmly packed brown sugar
1   teaspoon vanilla extract
¹/₂   teaspoon coconut extract
¹/₄   teaspoon almond extract
¹/₄   cup raisins
        Ground cinnamon or nutmeg

Bring water to a boil in a small saucepan over medium heat. Stir in millet. Reduce heat to medium-low, cover saucepan, and cook 20 minutes, or until water has been absorbed.

In a blender container, combine millet (while still hot), pineapple, banana, brown sugar, and extracts. Blend until smooth. (Stop blender several times to scrape sides). Stir in raisins.

Spoon pudding into a shallow serving dish and sprinkle lightly with cinnamon or nutmeg.

Chill. Or, for those who enjoy hot pudding, serve it right away.

Each serving provides:

132 Calories

¹/₂	Bread Serving	2 g	Protein
1	Fruit Serving	1 g	Fat (5% of calories)
29	Additional Calories	30 g	Carbohydrate
		4 mg	Sodium
		0 mg	Cholesterol
		2 g	Fiber

Italian Barley

A tasty side dish for almost any entrée, this filling grain reheats nicely in the microwave.

Makes 4 servings

$^1/_2$	cup finely chopped onion
$^1/_2$	cup finely chopped green bell pepper
1	clove garlic, minced
1	16-ounce can salt-free (or regular) tomatoes, undrained, chopped
$^1/_2$	teaspoon dried oregano
$^1/_2$	teaspoon dried basil
2	cups water
$5^1/_4$	ounces uncooked barley ($^3/_4$ cup)
2	tablespoons grated Parmesan cheese

In a medium saucepan, combine all ingredients, except Parmesan cheese.

Bring to a boil over medium heat, stirring occasionally. Reduce heat to medium-low, cover, and simmer 45 minutes, until barley is tender and liquid has been absorbed.

Toward the end of the cooking time, be sure to stir several times and reduce heat if necessary to prevent sticking.

To serve, spoon barley into a shallow serving bowl. Sprinkle evenly with Parmesan cheese.

Each serving provides:

179 Calories

$1^3/_4$	Bread Servings	7 g	Protein
$1^1/_2$	Vegetable Servings	2 g	Fat (9% of calories)
15	Additional Calories	35 g	Carbohydrate
		67 mg	Sodium
		2 mg	Cholesterol
		8 g	Fiber

Barley–Vegetable Casserole

The only thing better than the aroma of this casserole baking is its wonderful flavor.

Makes 6 servings

2	tablespoons reduced-calorie margarine
2/3	cup barley, uncooked (4^1/$_2$ ounces)
1	cup chopped onion
1	cup chopped cauliflower (1/4-inch pieces)
1	cup chopped mushrooms
1	cup finely shredded carrots
2^1/$_2$	cups water
2	packets low-sodium instant chicken or vegetable broth mix
1/4	teaspoon garlic powder
1/8	teaspoon pepper

Preheat oven to 350 degrees F.

Spray a 1^3/$_4$-quart casserole with nonstick cooking spray.

Melt 1 tablespoon of the margarine in a large nonstick skillet over medium heat. Add barley and cook 2 to 3 minutes, stirring frequently, until lightly browned. Place in prepared casserole.

Melt remaining margarine in skillet. Add onions and cauliflower. Cook, stirring frequently, 5 minutes. Add mushrooms and carrots. Cook 5 more minutes, stirring frequently. Add vegetables to casserole.

In a small bowl, combine water, broth mix, garlic powder, and pepper. Mix well and add to casserole.

Mix well, cover, and bake 1 hour and 15 minutes, until barley is tender and most of the liquid has been absorbed. Stir several times while baking.

Let stand 5 minutes, then mix and serve.

Each serving provides:

123 Calories

1	Bread Serving	4 g	Protein
1^1/$_4$	Vegetable Servings	3 g	Fat (18% of calories)
1/2	Fat Serving	22 g	Carbohydrate
3	Additional Calories	345 mg	Sodium
		0 mg	Cholesterol
		5 g	Fiber

Peaches 'n' Cream Casserole

This easy breakfast casserole is elegant enough for a Sunday brunch, and provides a different way to enjoy your breakfast oatmeal. It can be enjoyed as is or topped with skim milk or maple syrup.

Makes 6 servings

1¹/₂	cups rolled oats (4¹/₂ ounces)
1¹/₂	cups thinly sliced peaches, peeled (Canned peaches, packed in juice, drained, may be used.)
¹/₄	cup sugar
3	cups skim milk
2	egg whites
2	teaspoons vanilla extract
¹/₄	teaspoon almond extract

Preheat oven to 350 degrees F.

Spray an 8-inch square baking pan with nonstick cooking spray.

In a large bowl, combine oats, peaches, and sugar. In another bowl, combine remaining ingredients. Beat with a fork or wire whisk until blended. Add to oat mixture, mixing well.

Place mixture in prepared pan.

Bake, uncovered, 50 minutes.

Serve hot. (Leftovers are good cold or can be reheated in an oven or microwave.)

Each serving provides:

186 Calories

1	Bread Serving	9 g	Protein
¹/₂	Fruit Serving	2 g	Fat (8% of calories)
1	Milk Serving	34 g	Carbohydrate
38	Additional Calories	83 mg	Sodium
		2 mg	Cholesterol
		3 g	Fiber

15-Minute Muesli

This traditional Swiss breakfast is just the right way to start the day. It needs to soak for at least 15 minutes, so why not put it together and let it sit while you get dressed. There's no cooking involved and it's ready whenever you are.

Makes 2 servings

1/2	cup rolled oats, uncooked (1 1/2 ounces)
1	cup orange juice
1/3	cup nonfat dry milk
1	small apple, unpeeled, coarsely shredded
2	tablespoons raisins
2	teaspoons firmly packed brown sugar
1/2	teaspoon vanilla extract
1/4	teaspoon ground cinnamon
1/8	teaspoon almond extract
	Dash ground allspice

Combine all ingredients in a bowl and mix well. Let stand at least 15 minutes.

Stir again and serve. Leftovers should be refrigerated and can be served cold.

Each serving provides:

232 Calories

1	Bread Serving	6 g	Protein
2	Fruit Servings	2 g	Fat (6% of calories)
1/2	Milk Serving	50 g	Carbohydrate
16	Additional Calories	26 mg	Sodium
		1 mg	Cholesterol
		4 g	Fiber

Six-Grain Crock-Pot Breakfast

We've combined the taste, texture, and nutritional benefits of six grains in this truly rib-stickin' breakfast. Throw it together at night and enjoy a wonderful hot breakfast in the morning. Our selection of grains is only a suggestion—any grains will work. Just use 1 cup of grains to 3¼ cups of water.

Makes 6 servings

2½	tablespoons bulgur, uncooked (1 ounce)
2½	tablespoons brown rice, uncooked (1 ounce)
2	tablespoons barley, uncooked (³/₄ ounce)
2	tablespoons millet, uncooked (³/₄ ounce)
2	tablespoons cornmeal, uncooked (³/₄ ounce)
¹/₄	cup rolled oats, uncooked (³/₄ ounce)
³/₄	cup plus 2 tablespoons chopped dried mixed fruit (4¹/₂ ounces)
1¹/₂	teaspoons ground cinnamon
3¹/₄	cups water
1	tablespoon vanilla extract

Combine grains, dried fruit, and cinnamon in a Crock-Pot. Mix well. Stir in water and vanilla.

Cover and cook 6 to 8 hours on low setting.

Stir before serving and add more water if desired.

Serve hot, topped with brown sugar or drizzled with maple syrup.

Each serving provides:

145 Calories

1	Bread Serving	3 g	Protein
1	Fruit Serving	1 g	Fat (5% of calories)
		32 g	Carbohydrate
		6 mg	Sodium
		0 mg	Cholesterol
		4 g	Fiber

Fruits

Fruits are sweet, natural gifts from Mother Nature. Their versatility is endless, whether used as an appetizer, entrée, dessert, or in-between-meal snack. Most fruits are low in fat, high in carbohydrates, and supply our bodies with necessary vitamins, minerals, and fiber.

In preparing fruit recipes, choose varieties of fruits that are naturally sweet. The sweeter the fruit, the less sugar you need to use. Using very ripe fruit will enable you to reduce the amount of sugar in a recipe. For added nutrition, leave the skin on whenever possible.

Explore the many fruit possibilities we've created here for you, and browse through our other sections as well, to find fruits uniquely combined with unusual ingredients, and as an added bonus in many of our cakes and pies.

Quick Peaches 'n' Cream

Rich, delicious, and so easy to make, this dish makes a great snack for after school or anytime. The recipe can easily be doubled or tripled.

Makes 2 servings

1	cup plain nonfat yogurt
1	teaspoon vanilla extract
1/2	teaspoon almond extract
1/2	teaspoon ground cinnamon
1	tablespoon sugar
2	medium, ripe peaches, peeled and chopped (or 1 cup canned, unsweetened peaches, chopped)

In a small bowl, combine all ingredients. Mix well and enjoy right away or chill for a later serving.

Each serving provides:

155 Calories

1	Fruit Serving	7 g	Protein
1/2	Milk Serving	trace	Fat (2% of calories)
39	Additional Calories	30 g	Carbohydrate
		86 mg	Sodium
		2 mg	Cholesterol
		2 g	Fiber

Peach Butter

What a delicious topping for toasted bagels or English muffins!

Makes 16 servings (1½ tablespoons each serving)

2	cups canned, sliced peaches (unsweetened), drained
1	tablespoon plus 1 teaspoon cornstarch
1	tablespoon plus 1 teaspoon sugar
1/2	teaspoon vanilla extract
1/4	teaspoon ground cinnamon
1/8	teaspoon ground allspice
1/8	teaspoon ground nutmeg
	Dash ground cloves

In a blender container, combine all ingredients. Blend until smooth. Pour mixture into a medium saucepan. Cook over medium-low heat, stirring frequently, until mixture comes to a boil.

Reduce heat to low and simmer, stirring, 2 minutes.

Spoon into a jar and chill.

Each serving provides:

21 Calories

1/4	Fruit Serving	0 g	Protein
7	Additional Calories	0 g	Fat
		5 g	Carbohydrate
		1 mg	Sodium
		0 mg	Cholesterol
		0 g	Fiber

Baked Pineapple with Creamy Coconut Sauce

Baking really brings out the flavor of fresh pineapple. Served warm, this easy, refreshing dish makes a great appetizer or dessert.

Makes 8 servings

Coconut Sauce

1¹/₃   cups lowfat (1%) cottage cheese
¹/₄   cup firmly packed brown sugar
3   tablespoons skim milk
1¹/₂   teaspoons vanilla extract
¹/₄   teaspoon coconut extract

Pineapple

1   medium, ripe pineapple
4   teaspoons firmly packed brown sugar
      Ground cinnamon

In a blender container, combine all sauce ingredients. Blend until smooth. Spoon into a bowl and chill several hours, or overnight.

To prepare pineapple:

Preheat oven to 375 degrees F.

Remove and discard top of pineapple. Cut pineapple lengthwise into quarters. Remove and discard center core. Cut each quarter into chunks, but leave the chunks resting in place in the shells.

Sprinkle brown sugar along the top ledge of each quarter. (It will run down during cooking.) Sprinkle liberally with cinnamon.

Wrap each quarter tightly in aluminum foil. Bake 1 hour.

Carefully unwrap pineapple, and sprinkle with additional cinnamon. Serve hot and top each serving with 3 tablespoons of the sauce.

Each serving provides:

110 Calories

¹/₂	Protein Serving	5 g	Protein
1	Fruit Serving	1 g	Fat (6% of calories)
34	Additional Calories	22 g	Carbohydrate
		160 mg	Sodium
		2 mg	Cholesterol
		1 g	Fiber

Cherries Amandine

The flavors of cherries and almonds seem to be made for each other. In this easy fruit dish we've blended the two flavors and added an almond-laced creamy topping.

Makes 4 servings

Cherries
1	16-ounce can pitted red tart cherries, packed in water
1	tablespoon plus 1 teaspoon cornstarch
3	tablespoons sugar
1	teaspoon almond extract

Topping
3/4	cup plain nonfat yogurt
2	teaspoons sugar
1/4	teaspoon almond extract
2	tablespoons sliced almonds (1/2 ounce)

Drain cherries, reserving liquid. Place reserved liquid in a small saucepan. Add cornstarch, sugar, and almond extract. Stir to dissolve cornstarch. Add cherries to saucepan. Cook over medium heat, stirring, until mixture comes to a boil. Continue to cook, stirring, 1 minute.

Spoon cherries into a bowl and chill.

In a small bowl, combine all topping ingredients, except almonds. Mix well and chill.

To serve, divide cherries evenly into 4 individual serving bowls or sherbet glasses. Divide yogurt topping evenly and spoon over cherries. Garnish with sliced almonds.

Each serving provides:

144 Calories

1/4	Protein Serving	4 g	Protein
1/4	Fat Serving	2 g	Fat (13% of calories)
1	Fruit Serving	28 g	Carbohydrate
1/4	Milk Serving	41 mg	Sodium
54	Additional Calories	1 mg	Cholesterol
		0 g	Fiber

Mom Mom's Applesauce

This recipe was hard to duplicate, since Mom Mom doesn't measure her ingredients, but thanks to her assistance, here is our favorite applesauce. The number of servings is approximate and may vary slightly with the amount of water used and the length of cooking time.

Makes 12 servings (1/2 cup each serving)

4	pounds apples, preferably Stayman Winesap, peeled, cut into large chunks
1	whole lemon, cut into thin strips (Include rind, but remove center membrane and seeds.)
1/2	cup raisins
2	teaspoons sugar
1 1/2	teaspoons ground cinnamon

Place all ingredients in a large saucepan. Add enough water to come halfway up the apples.

Cook, uncovered, over medium heat until mixture comes to a boil. Reduce heat to low. Cook until apples are mushy and lemon is tender. Remove from heat.

Mash apples with the back of a spoon. (They will be a little lumpy.) Chill and enjoy.

Each serving provides:

97 Calories

1	Fruit Serving	0 g	Protein
3	Additional Calories	trace	Fat (4% of calories)
		26 g	Carbohydrate
		1 mg	Sodium
		0 mg	Cholesterol
		3 g	Fiber

Apple Tapioca Dessert

Using sweet apples, such as Golden Delicious, makes this succulent dessert taste even sweeter. It's a great breakfast treat.

Makes 4 servings

4	small, sweet apples, peeled, coarsely shredded
1	cup water
2	tablespoons plus 2 teaspoons quick-cooking tapioca, uncooked
1	tablespoon plus 1 teaspoon sugar
1	teaspoon vanilla extract
1/2	teaspoon ground cinnamon
1/4	teaspoon ground nutmeg

Preheat oven to 350 degrees F.

Spray a 1-quart baking dish with nonstick cooking spray.

Combine all ingredients in a large bowl and mix well. Place in prepared baking dish. Let stand 10 minutes. Smooth the top of the pudding with the back of a spoon.

Bake, uncovered, 40 minutes, until tapioca granules are clear.

Serve hot or cold.

Each serving provides:

103 Calories

1	Fruit Serving	0 g	Protein
56	Additional Calories	1 g	Fat (5% of calories)
		25 g	Carbohydrate
		30 mg	Sodium
		0 mg	Cholesterol
		2 g	Fiber

Applesauce Ambrosia

Serve this fruit combo in pretty sherbet glasses for a delicious dessert, or serve over vanilla nonfat ice cream for really elegant fare.

Makes 8 servings

2	cups applesauce (unsweetened)
2	medium, ripe bananas, sliced
1	cup canned mandarin oranges, packed in juice, drained
1	ounce slivered toasted almonds (1/4 cup)
2	tablespoons shredded coconut (unsweetened)

Combine all ingredients in a large bowl. Mix well. Chill.

Each serving provides:

98 Calories

1 1/4	Fruit Servings	1 g	Protein
21	Additional Calories	3 g	Fat (22% of calories)
		19 g	Carbohydrate
		4 mg	Sodium
		0 mg	Cholesterol
		2 g	Fiber

Blueberry and Apple Delight

We call this "delight" because it is so tasty and so versatile. Use it as a topping for cottage cheese or ice cream, spoon it over hot oatmeal, or enjoy it as is. Any way you try it, you're sure to fall in love with it.

Makes 12 servings (1/2 cup each serving)

8	cups Golden Delicious apples, peeled, sliced 1/4 inch thick
4	cups fresh or frozen blueberries (unsweetened)
1 1/2	cups water
3	tablespoons sugar
1	tablespoon plus 1 teaspoon cornstarch
1	teaspoon lemon juice
1/2	teaspoon ground cinnamon

Place apples and blueberries in a large saucepan. Combine remaining ingredients, stirring to dissolve cornstarch. Add to saucepan. Cook over medium heat, stirring occasionally, until mixture comes to a boil.

Reduce heat to low and cook, stirring frequently, until apples are tender.

Serve warm or cold.

Each serving provides:

85 Calories

1 1/4	Fruit Servings	0 g	Protein
20	Additional Calories	trace	Fat (4% of calories)
		22 g	Carbohydrate
		3 mg	Sodium
		0 mg	Cholesterol
		3 g	Fiber

Bananas New Orleans

One of our most popular dishes, this one can easily be prepared for dessert while the coffee is brewing. It's delicious by itself, and really makes a statement when served over vanilla lowfat ice cream.

Makes 4 servings

1	teaspoon margarine
1/2	cup orange juice
2	tablespoons firmly packed brown sugar
1/2	teaspoon rum extract
1/2	teaspoon vanilla butternut flavor*
2	medium, ripe bananas, cut in half lengthwise, then each piece cut in half crosswise (Choose bananas that are ripe, yet firm.) Ground cinnamon

Melt margarine in a medium nonstick skillet over medium heat. Stir in orange juice, brown sugar, and extracts.

Add bananas. Cook 2 to 3 minutes, then turn bananas carefully and cook another 1 to 2 minutes. Sprinkle with cinnamon.

Place 2 banana pieces in each of 4 individual serving bowls. Spoon sauce over bananas.

Serve right away.

*Often called "vanilla butter and nut flavor," this flavoring is found with the extracts in many large grocery stores. If you cannot locate it, use 1/2 teaspoon vanilla extract plus 1/2 teaspoon butter flavor extract in its place.

Each serving provides:

104 Calories

1/4	Fat Serving	1 g	Protein
1 1/4	Fruit Servings	1 g	Fat (10% of calories)
24	Additional Calories	23 g	Carbohydrate
		15 mg	Sodium
		0 mg	Cholesterol
		1 g	Fiber

Baked Pears with Cinnamon Creme Sauce

This dessert looks like a work of art and tastes just as good. Try the creamy sauce over other fruits as well.

Makes 4 servings

Creme Sauce
1/2	cup vanilla nonfat yogurt
1	tablespoon firmly packed brown sugar
1/2	teaspoon ground cinnamon
1/2	teaspoon vanilla extract

Pears
4	small pears
1/2	cup water
2	tablespoons firmly packed brown sugar
1	tablespoon lemon juice
1/4	teaspoon ground cinnamon

Prepare creme sauce ahead of time by combining all the ingredients and mixing well. Chill to blend flavors.

Preheat oven to 350 degrees F.

Peel pears, cut in half lengthwise, and scoop out core. Place, flat side down, in a small shallow baking dish.

Combine water, brown sugar, lemon juice, and cinnamon. Pour over pears.

Cover tightly and bake 45 minutes, or until pears are tender. Baste occasionally with pan juices while baking.

To serve, place 2 pear halves in each of 4 individual serving bowls. Spoon pan juices over pears, then top each serving with a dollop of creme sauce (about 2 tablespoons). Serve right away.

Each serving provides:

141 Calories

1	Fruit Serving	2 g	Protein
51	Additional Calories	1 g	Fat (3% of calories)
		34 g	Carbohydrate
		25 mg	Sodium
		1 mg	Cholesterol
		3 g	Fiber

Red, White, and Blueberry Parfaits

This colorful, patriotic dessert is perfect for that Fourth of July picnic. Fresh summer berries are always delicious, but frozen, unsweetened berries can easily be substituted. (Thaw and drain them before using.)

Makes 4 servings

1	cup strawberries, sliced
1/2	cup blueberries
2	tablespoons sugar
1/2	cup part-skim ricotta cheese
1/2	cup vanilla nonfat yogurt
1/2	teaspoon vanilla extract
1/8	teaspoon almond extract
1/8	teaspoon orange extract

Place strawberries and blueberries each in a separate small bowl. Toss each with 1 teaspoon of the sugar.

In another bowl, combine ricotta cheese with remaining sugar, yogurt, and extracts. Mix well.

In each of 4 parfait glasses, place 2 tablespoons of the strawberries. Top each with 2 tablespoons of the ricotta mixture. Divide blueberries evenly over the parfaits. Divide remaining ricotta mixture over blueberries. Top with remaining strawberries.

Serve right away or chill up to several hours before serving.

Each serving provides:

116 Calories

1/2	Protein Serving	5 g	Protein
1/4	Fruit Serving	3 g	Fat (20% of calories)
58	Additional Calories	18 g	Carbohydrate
		60 mg	Sodium
		10 mg	Cholesterol
		1 g	Fiber

Berries Romanoff

This dessert is so easy to prepare, and yet so elegant. Serve in tall-stemmed champagne glasses for a festive touch.

Makes 4 servings

1	cup vanilla nonfat yogurt
2	tablespoons sugar
1	teaspoon vanilla extract
1/4	teaspoon orange extract (1 tablespoon orange liqueur)
2	cups fresh strawberries

In a small bowl, combine all ingredients, except strawberries. Mix well.

Chill to blend flavors.

To serve, divide berries into individual serving bowls. Stir yogurt mixture and spoon over berries.

Each serving provides:

102 Calories

1/2	Fruit Serving	3 g	Protein
74	Additional Calories	trace	Fat (3% of calories)
		21 g	Carbohydrate
		41 mg	Sodium
		2 mg	Cholesterol
		2 g	Fiber

Raspberry Tapioca

This is a real treat when fresh summer berries are available. It's absolutely delicious as it is, and even better over nonfat vanilla ice cream.

Makes 4 servings

2   cups fresh or frozen (thawed, unsweetened) raspberries
3   tablespoons quick-cooking tapioca, uncooked
2   tablespoons plus 2 teaspoons sugar

Place berries in a blender container. Blend until smooth. Press berries through a strainer, extracting as much pulp as possible. Discard seeds.

In a small saucepan, combine puréed berries with enough water to equal 2 cups.

Stir in tapioca and sugar. Let mixture stand 5 minutes.

Bring berries to a boil over medium heat, stirring frequently. Remove from heat.

Cool in pan 20 minutes. Then stir and place in 4 custard cups. Chill.

Each serving provides:

89 Calories

1/2	Fruit Serving	1 g	Protein
87	Additional Calories	trace	Fat (3% of calories)
		22 g	Carbohydrate
		34 mg	Sodium
		0 mg	Cholesterol
		3 g	Fiber

Fruit Salad in a Watermelon Basket

Always a crowd pleaser, this elegant dish is really easy to prepare. Our fruits are just a suggestion: Feel free to fill the watermelon with whatever fresh fruits are available. Our amounts are also suggestions only, and will vary according to the size of the watermelon.

Makes 16 servings

1	medium watermelon
2	cups watermelon balls
1	cup cantaloupe balls
1	cup honeydew melon balls
1	cup strawberries, halved
1	cup blueberries
2	medium peaches, peeled, pitted, cut into chunks
24	large seedless red grapes
1/4	medium, ripe pineapple, pared, cut into chunks
3	tablespoons orange juice
1	tablespoon lime juice, preferably fresh
2	tablespoons confectioners sugar
1/2	teaspoon rum extract

To prepare basket, cut the watermelon in half lengthwise. Using a melon ball scoop, remove the pulp. Measure 2 cups of watermelon balls, reserving remaining watermelon balls for another use. Using a sharp knife, scallop the edges of the watermelon. Then slice a very thin piece off the bottom of the watermelon to keep it from tipping over.

Chill prepared watermelon basket. Also chill watermelon balls and remaining fruits, keeping them all separate.

Just before serving, combine all fruits in a large bowl. Combine orange juice, lemon juice, sugar, and rum extract. Pour over fruit and mix well. Spoon fruit into watermelon basket.

Each serving provides:

40 Calories

3/4	Fruit Serving	0 g	Protein
9	Additional Calories	trace	Fat (5% of calories)
		10 g	Carbohydrate
		3 mg	Sodium
		0 mg	Cholesterol
		1 g	Fiber

Fruit-to-Go

This is an ideal picnic treat. The fruit is neatly packed into its own disposable carrying case!

Makes 4 servings

1	medium honeydew melon (or other type of melon)
1	cup sliced strawberries
1	cup raspberries
1	tablespoon confectioners sugar
2	teaspoons lemon juice

Carefully slice off top of melon to make a "lid" about 2 inches thick. Scoop out and discard melon seeds. Scoop out flesh, using a spoon or melon baller. Place 2 cups of the melon balls in a large bowl, reserving remaining melon. Add remaining ingredients and mix well.

Spoon fruit into melon shell. (You may be able to add some of the reserved melon balls, depending on the size of the melon.) Tap melon on table top several times to help pack fruit down.

Replace "lid," wrap melon tightly, and chill several hours or overnight. (Enjoy remaining reserved melon separately.)

To serve, simply spoon fruit out of melon onto serving plates.

Each serving provides:

64 Calories

1¹/₄	Fruit Servings	1 g	Protein
12	Additional Calories	trace	Fat (5% of calories)
		16 g	Carbohydrate
		9 mg	Sodium
		0 mg	Cholesterol
		3 g	Fiber

Baked Cranberry Relish

Baking seems to bring out the color and flavor of this popular holiday treat. Hot or cold, its zesty flavor is a perfect addition to a roast chicken or turkey dinner.

Makes 12 servings

3	cups cranberries
2	small apples, peeled, cut into chunks
3	small oranges, peeled, sectioned (Discard white membranes.)
1/3	cup raisins
8	dried apricot halves
1	ounce chopped walnuts (1/4 cup)
1/4	cup sugar
3	tablespoons quick-cooking tapioca, uncooked

Preheat oven to 350 degrees F.

Spray a 1 1/2-quart casserole with nonstick cooking spray.

Combine cranberries, apples, orange sections, raisins, and apricots in a food processor. Using a steel blade, process until fruits are finely chopped. (Do not purée.)

Stir in walnuts, sugar, and tapioca. Place mixture in prepared casserole. Let stand 5 minutes.

Bake, uncovered, 40 minutes.

Serve hot or cold.

Each serving provides:

94 Calories

1	Fruit Serving	1 g	Protein
43	Additional Calories	2 g	Fat (15% of calories)
		21 g	Carbohydrate
		13 mg	Sodium
		0 mg	Cholesterol
		2 g	Fiber

Apricot–Almond Cranberry Sauce

*Why open a can of cranberry sauce when you can make your own so easily?
And this one is really special. It's laced with the flavors of apricot and almond
and is tart and delicious, as cranberries should be. (If you don't like it so tart,
add a little extra sugar.)*

Makes 9 servings (¹/₃ cup each serving)

1	cup sugar
1	cup water
3	cups cranberries
¹/₃	cup fruit-only apricot spread
¹/₂	teaspoon almond extract

Combine sugar and water in a small saucepan. Bring to a boil over
medium heat. Continue to boil, without stirring, 5 minutes.

Stir in cranberries and cook, stirring occasionally, until cranberries
burst and mixture comes to a full boil. Continue to boil 5 minutes. Remove from heat and stir in apricot spread and almond extract.

Cool slightly, then chill.

Each serving provides:

129 Calories

³/₄	Fruit Serving	0 g	Protein
96	Additional Calories	0 g	Fat
		33 g	Carbohydrate
		1 mg	Sodium
		0 mg	Cholesterol
		1 g	Fiber

Hot Spiced Fruit

A winning combination of peaches and pineapple, this dish can be used as a dessert, or as a very pretty and flavorful accompaniment for roast chicken or turkey.

Makes 4 servings

4	slices canned pineapple, packed in juice, drained (Reserve 2 tablespoons of the juice.)
1	cup canned, sliced peaches, packed in juice, drained (or fresh peaches, peeled and sliced) (If using canned peaches, reserve 2 tablespoons of the juice. If using fresh peaches, substitute with orange juice.)
1/4	teaspoon ground cinnamon
1/4	teaspoon ground cloves
1	tablespoon plus 1 teaspoon reduced-calorie margarine

Preheat oven to 350 degrees F.

Place pineapple in a shallow baking pan that has been sprayed with nonstick cooking spray. Top with peach slices.

Combine reserved juices and pour over fruit. Sprinkle evenly with cinnamon and cloves. Dot with margarine.

Bake, uncovered, 20 to 25 minutes, until hot and bubbly.

Each serving provides:

79 Calories

1/2	Fat Serving	1 g	Protein
1	Fruit Serving	2 g	Fat (20% of calories)
		16 g	Carbohydrate
		49 mg	Sodium
		0 mg	Cholesterol
		1 g	Fiber

Breads and Muffins

Breads and muffins are an excellent source of fiber in our diet. Versatile and delicious, they can be served with any meal and make great snacks. Many bakeries sell breads and muffins, but most commercial varieties are high in fat and low in fiber. When made with white flour, butter, and whole eggs, they are laden with fat and calories.

Most breads and muffins in this section are made with a combination of all-purpose flour and whole wheat flour. This, with the addition of fruits and vegetables, adds vitamins, minerals, and fiber, as well as a delectable texture, to the recipes.

To keep fat content down, we use skim milk and lowfat buttermilk. To reduce cholesterol, we use egg whites or liquid egg substitute in place of whole eggs. We add as little oil as possible and add moistness by using applesauce, yogurt, or fruit in place of most of the shortening. When we do use oil, we choose one that is mostly monounsaturated, such as canola oil.

All of our breads are quick breads. Our muffins are baked in standard muffin pans with 2 1/2-inch cups. We prefer nonstick pans for breads and muffins, and spray them lightly with nonstick cooking spray. Oven temperatures may vary slightly, so it is wise to test bread and muffins for doneness by inserting a toothpick in the center. It will come out clean when the bread or muffins are done.

Most breads and muffins taste best when served warm. If this is not possible, let them cool completely before wrapping. Because these homemade delicacies are not made with preservatives, they have a shorter shelf life than many commercially baked goods. We advise refrigerating them on the second day and reheating briefly before serving.

From Beer Bread to Rum 'n' Raisin Muffins, from sweet to savory, our wonderful variety of breads and muffins are all made "light" for you.

Orange-Raisin Tea Loaf

The chopped orange and raisins gives this bread a delicate flavor and moistness you will love. Be sure to discard the white membrane of the orange, since it is quite bitter.

Makes 10 servings

1/2	cup boiling water
1/2	cup raisins
1	small orange
1/4	cup plus 2 tablespoons sugar
2	egg whites
1	tablespoon plus 2 teaspoons vegetable oil
1	teaspoon vanilla extract
1	cup minus 2 tablespoons all-purpose flour
1	cup whole wheat flour
1	teaspoon baking powder
1	teaspoon baking soda
1	teaspoon ground cinnamon
1/2	teaspoon ground nutmeg
1/2	teaspoon ground ginger

Preheat oven to 350 degrees F.

Spray a 4 × 8-inch loaf pan with nonstick cooking spray.

Pour boiling water over raisins in a small bowl. Set aside.

Grate the orange, saving 1 tablespoon of the peel. Peel orange, discarding the white membrane. Cut up the orange pulp. Place the orange pulp, raisins, and water in a blender container. Blend for a few seconds, until raisins are just chopped. Do not purée.

In a large bowl, combine raisin mixture, orange peel, sugar, egg whites, oil, and vanilla. Mix well.

In another bowl, combine remaining ingredients. Mix well. Add to orange mixture, mixing until all ingredients are moistened. Spoon batter into prepared pan.

Bake 40 to 45 minutes, until a toothpick inserted in the center of the bread comes out clean. Cool in pan on a wire rack for 5 minutes, then turn out onto rack to finish cooling.

Each serving provides:

167 Calories

1	Bread Serving	4 g	Protein
1/2	Fat Serving	3 g	Fat (15% of calories)
1/2	Fruit Serving	33 g	Carbohydrate
33	Additional Calories	188 mg	Sodium
		0 mg	Cholesterol
		2 g	Fiber

Cranberry Nut Bread

Everyone who tastes this bread wants the recipe! Not only does it taste delicious, but it's made with healthful ingredients. It makes a wonderful holiday gift.

Makes 10 servings

$^3/_4$ cup whole wheat flour
$^1/_2$ cup plus 1 tablespoon all-purpose flour
2   teaspoons baking powder
$^1/_2$ teaspoon baking soda
$^1/_2$ cup wheat germ ($2^1/_4$ ounces)
1   teaspoon ground cinnamon
2   egg whites
1   cup buttermilk
3   tablespoons honey
1   tablespoon plus 2 teaspoons vegetable oil
1   teaspoon vanilla extract
$^1/_4$ teaspoon orange extract
1   cup cranberries
$^1/_2$ cup raisins
1   ounce chopped walnuts ($^1/_4$ cup)

Preheat oven to 350 degrees F.

Spray a 4 × 8-inch loaf pan with nonstick cooking spray.

In a large bowl, combine dry ingredients.

In a medium bowl, combine egg whites, buttermilk, honey, oil, and extracts. Beat with a fork or wire whisk until blended.

Place cranberries and raisins in a blender or food processor. Turn on and off a few times so fruit is chopped, but not puréed.

Add cranberry mixture and nuts to buttermilk mixture. Stir in dry ingredients, stirring until all ingredients are moistened.

Place batter in prepared pan.

Bake 35 minutes, until a toothpick inserted in the center of the bread comes out clean.

Cool in pan on a wire rack for 5 minutes, then invert onto rack to finish cooling.

Each serving provides:

182 Calories

3/4	Bread Serving	6 g	Protein
1/2	Fat Serving	5 g	Fat (25% of calories)
1/2	Fruit Serving	30 g	Carbohydrate
65	Additional Calories	199 mg	Sodium
		1 mg	Cholesterol
		3 g	Fiber

Beer Bread

This bread is so quick and easy, you'll make it time and again. It tastes wonderful, has almost no fat, and the texture is divine! What more could you ask for?

Makes 12 servings

1¹/₄ cups all-purpose flour
1   cup whole wheat flour
2   tablespoons sugar
2¹/₄ teaspoons baking powder
¹/₂   teaspoon salt
1   12-ounce can light beer, at room temperature

Preheat oven to 375 degrees F.

Spray a 4 × 8-inch loaf pan with nonstick cooking spray.

In a large bowl, combine both types of flour, sugar, baking powder, and salt. Mix well. Add beer. Stir until foam subsides and all ingredients are moistened.

Pour batter into prepared pan.

Bake 45 to 50 minutes, until a toothpick inserted in the center of the bread comes out clean.

Cool in pan on a wire rack for 5 minutes, then turn out onto rack to finish cooling.

Variation: For a delicious variation that tastes like rye bread, add ¹/₈ teaspoon garlic powder and 1 teaspoon caraway seeds to the dry ingredients.

Each serving provides:

99 Calories

1	Bread Serving	3 g	Protein
16	Additional Calories	trace	Fat (4% of calories)
		20 g	Carbohydrate
		184 mg	Sodium
		0 mg	Cholesterol
		2 g	Fiber

Molasses Brown Bread

This bread will definitely become a favorite! As a homemade holiday or housewarming gift, it can't be beat.

Makes 12 servings

1¹/₂   cups plus 3 tablespoons whole wheat flour
¹/₂   cup plus 1 tablespoon wheat germ
¹/₃   cup nonfat dry milk
1   teaspoon baking soda
1   teaspoon ground cinnamon
1   cup plain nonfat yogurt
¹/₄   cup plus 2 tablespoons molasses
¹/₄   cup water
2   tablespoons vegetable oil
2   egg whites
1   teaspoon vanilla extract
¹/₄   cup plus 2 tablespoons raisins

Preheat oven to 350 degrees F.

Spray a 5 × 9-inch loaf pan with nonstick cooking spray.

In a large bowl, combine flour, wheat germ, dry milk, baking soda, and cinnamon. Mix well.

In a medium bowl, combine remaining ingredients, except raisins. Beat with a fork or wire whisk until blended. Add to dry mixture, along with raisins. Stir until all ingredients are moistened.

Spoon batter into prepared pan.

Bake 40 minutes, until a toothpick inserted in the center of the bread comes out clean.

Cool in pan on a wire rack for 5 minutes, then invert onto rack to finish cooling.

Each serving provides:

160 Calories

1	Bread Serving	6 g	Protein
¹/₂	Fat Serving	3 g	Fat (18% of calories)
¹/₄	Fruit Serving	28 g	Carbohydrate
43	Additional Calories	144 mg	Sodium
		1 mg	Cholesterol
		3 g	Fiber

Skillet Cheese Corn Bread

You can bake and serve this delicious corn bread right in the skillet. For a Mexican flavor, add some chopped chilies, either fresh, dried, or canned, to the wet ingredients.

Makes 12 servings

2	cups yellow cornmeal (12 ounces)
2	teaspoons baking powder
1/2	teaspoon baking soda
1/4	teaspoon salt
1 1/4	cups buttermilk
1	16-ounce can salt-free (or regular) cream-style corn
3	egg whites
1/4	cup honey
2	tablespoons vegetable oil
1	cup shredded reduced-fat Cheddar cheese (4 ounces)

Preheat oven to 400 degrees F.

Spray a 10-inch cast-iron skillet with nonstick cooking spray.

In a large bowl, combine cornmeal, baking powder, baking soda, and salt. Mix well.

In another bowl, combine buttermilk, corn, egg whites, honey, and oil. Beat with a fork or wire whisk until blended. Stir in cheese. Add to dry mixture, stirring until all ingredients are moistened.

Heat skillet in oven for 3 minutes. Remove from oven and immediately pour in batter.

Bake 30 to 35 minutes, until a toothpick inserted in the center of the bread comes out clean.

Cut into wedges and serve hot.

Each serving provides:

215 Calories

1/2	Protein Serving	8 g	Protein
1 1/2	Bread Servings	5 g	Fat (20% of calories)
1/2	Fat Serving	36 g	Carbohydrate
44	Additional Calories	295 mg	Sodium
		8 mg	Cholesterol
		2 g	Fiber

Cinnamon Custard Corn Bread

This unique bread settles into two layers when cooked — a custard layer on the bottom and a corn bread layer on the top. It is so moist and delicious, we often eat it for dessert.

Makes 12 servings

5¹/₄	ounces yellow cornmeal
¹/₂	cup all-purpose flour
¹/₂	cup minus 1 tablespoon whole wheat flour
2	teaspoons baking powder
1	teaspoon ground cinnamon
3	cups skim milk
2	egg whites
¹/₄	cup margarine, melted
¹/₄	cup brown sugar
1¹/₂	teaspoons vanilla extract

Preheat oven to 350 degrees F.

Spray an 8-inch square glass baking pan with nonstick cooking spray.

In a large bowl, combine cornmeal, both types of flour, baking powder, and cinnamon. Mix well.

In another bowl, combine remaining ingredients. Mix with a wire whisk until blended. Add to dry mixture. Beat with whisk until lumps are gone.

Pour into prepared pan.

Bake 45 minutes, until bread is firm and bottom is lightly browned. Cool in pan on a wire rack.

Each serving provides:

158 Calories

1	Bread Serving	5 g	Protein
1	Fat Serving	4 g	Fat (25% of calories)
¹/₄	Milk Serving	25 g	Carbohydrate
19	Additional Calories	170 mg	Sodium
		1 mg	Cholesterol
		1 g	Fiber

Apple–Raisin Spice Bread

You won't believe a bread can be so tasty, tender, and moist and still be so low in fat. We serve this one warm for brunch or dessert.

Makes 8 servings

3	small, sweet apples, unpeeled, coarsely shredded (2 cups)
1/2	plus 2 tablespoons raisins
3/4	cup boiling water
1 1/2	cups whole wheat flour
1	teaspoon baking soda
1/2	teaspoon baking powder
1	teaspoon ground cinnamon
1/2	teaspoon ground allspice
1/8	teaspoon ground cloves
1/4	cup firmly packed brown sugar
1/4	cup skim milk
1	tablespoon plus 1 teaspoon vegetable oil
2	egg whites
1	teaspoon vanilla extract

In a small bowl, combine apples and raisins. Add boiling water, cover, and let stand until cool.

Preheat oven to 350 degrees F.

Spray a 4 × 8-inch loaf pan with nonstick cooking spray.

In a large bowl, combine flour, baking soda, baking powder, and spices. Mix well.

In another bowl, combine remaining ingredients. Beat with a fork or wire whisk until blended. Add to dry ingredients, along with apple mixture. Mix until all ingredients are moistened. Place mixture in prepared pan.

Bake 45 minutes, until a toothpick inserted in the center of the bread comes out clean.

Cool in pan on wire rack 5 minutes, then turn out onto rack to finish cooling.

Each serving provides:

183 Calories

1	Bread Serving	5 g	Protein
1/2	Fat Serving	3 g	Fat (14% of calories)
1	Fruit Serving	37 g	Carbohydrate
32	Additional Calories	211 mg	Sodium
		0 mg	Cholesterol
		4 g	Fiber

Orange–Currant Wheel

Similar to scones, but without the kneading, this pull-apart bread is as pretty as a picture. It's not too sweet and goes with any meal, from breakfast to midnight snack.

Makes 8 servings

3/4	cup all-purpose flour
3/4	cup whole wheat flour
1 1/2	teaspoons baking powder
1	tablespoon sugar
1/4	teaspoon salt
2	tablespoons plus 2 teaspoons margarine
1/4	cup currants (or use raisins or any chopped, dried fruit)
1/2	cup skim milk
2	teaspoons lemon juice
2	egg whites
2	teaspoons grated fresh orange peel

Topping

2	teaspoons sugar
1/8	teaspoon ground cinnamon

Preheat oven to 400 degrees F.

Spray a baking sheet with nonstick cooking spray.

In a large bowl, combine both types of flour, baking powder, sugar, and salt. Mix well.

Add margarine. Mix with a fork or pastry blender until mixture resembles coarse crumbs. Stir in currants.

Place milk in a small bowl. Add lemon juice and let stand 1 minute. Add egg whites and orange peel. Beat with a fork or wire whisk until blended. Add to dry mixture, mixing until all ingredients are moistened.

Turn dough out onto prepared baking sheet. Wetting your hands slightly, flatten dough into an 8-inch circle. With a sharp knife, cut the dough into 8 pie-shaped wedges. (Do not separate the sections.)

Combine topping ingredients and sprinkle evenly over top of bread.

Bake 15 minutes, until bottom of bread is lightly browned. Transfer to a wire rack and serve warm.

Each serving provides:

149 Calories

1	Bread Serving	4 g	Protein
1	Fat Serving	4 g	Fat (25% of calories)
1/4	Fruit Serving	24 g	Carbohydrate
20	Additional Calories	227 mg	Sodium
		0 mg	Cholesterol
		2 g	Fiber

Cheddar–Broccoli Bread Roll

We've rolled broccoli and Cheddar cheese in biscuit dough to create a visual and culinary masterpiece. Leftovers can be wrapped in foil and heated in a toasteroven, or wrapped in wax paper and heated in a microwave.

Makes 12 servings

1	10-ounce package frozen, chopped broccoli
3/4	cup all-purpose flour
3/4	cup whole wheat flour
1	tablespoon baking powder
1/2	teaspoon garlic powder
1/4	teaspoon salt
3	tablespoons margarine
1/2	cup plus 2 tablespoons skim milk
3	ounces shredded reduced-fat Cheddar cheese (3/4 cup)

Cook broccoli according to package directions. Drain.

Preheat oven to 375 degrees F. Have an ungreased baking sheet ready.

In a large bowl, combine both flours, baking powder, garlic powder, and salt. Mix well.

Add margarine. Mix with a fork or pastry blender until mixture resembles coarse crumbs.

Add milk. Stir until all ingredients are moistened.

Place dough on a floured surface and knead a few times until dough holds together in a ball. (Add a small amount of flour if dough is sticky.) Roll dough, or press with your hands, into an 8 × 14-inch rectangle.

Sprinkle cheese evenly over dough, staying 1 inch away from edges. Spread broccoli evenly over cheese.

Starting with one long side, tightly roll up dough like a jelly roll. Pinch the ends and seam together.

Place roll on prepared pan.

Bake 23 minutes, until bottom of bread is nicely browned.

Remove to a rack to cool for 5 minutes, then slice and serve warm.

Each serving provides:

113 Calories

1/4	Protein Serving	5 g	Protein
1/3	Bread Serving	4 g	Fat (34% of calories)
1/2	Vegetable Serving	14 g	Carbohydrate
3/4	Fat Serving	268 mg	Sodium
5	Additional Calories	5 mg	Cholesterol
		2 g	Fiber

Lemon Poppy Seed Muffins

You'll love the very lemony taste of these moist muffins. They work just as well without the poppy seeds, but we love the subtle crunch that they add.

Makes 8 muffins

3/4	cup all-purpose flour
3/4	cup whole wheat flour
1	tablespoon poppy seeds
2	teaspoons baking powder
1/2	teaspoon baking soda
1	cup plain nonfat yogurt
2	tablespoons vegetable oil
2	egg whites
1/4	cup sugar
2	teaspoons grated fresh lemon peel
1	teaspoon vanilla extract
1/2	teaspoon lemon extract

Preheat oven to 400 degrees F.

Spray 8 muffin cups with nonstick cooking spray.

In a large bowl, combine both types of flour, poppy seeds, baking powder, and baking soda. Mix well.

In another bowl, combine remaining ingredients. Beat with a fork or wire whisk until blended. Add to dry mixture, mixing just until all ingredients are moistened.

Divide mixture evenly into prepared muffin cups.

Bake 15 minutes, or until a toothpick inserted in the center of a muffin comes out clean.

Remove muffins to a wire rack to cool.

Each muffin provides:

167 Calories

1	Bread Serving	5 g	Protein
3/4	Fat Serving	4 g	Fat (24% of calories)
48	Additional Calories	26 g	Carbohydrate
		237 mg	Sodium
		1 mg	Cholesterol
		2 g	Fiber

Banana Date–Nut Muffins

The sweetness of bananas, teamed up with chewy dates and crunchy nuts, makes a special combination. For the sweetest muffins, make sure the bananas are super-ripe.

Makes 12 muffins

1¹/₄	cups whole wheat flour
1	cup all-purpose flour
1¹/₂	teaspoons baking powder
1	teaspoon baking soda
4	dates, chopped (1¹/₂ ounces)
2	tablespoons chopped walnuts (¹/₂ ounce)
2	egg whites
³/₄	cup skim milk
¹/₃	cup firmly packed brown sugar
2	tablespoons vegetable oil
2	teaspoons vanilla extract
2	medium, very ripe bananas, mashed (1 cup)

Preheat oven to 400 degrees F.

Spray 12 muffin cups with nonstick cooking spray.

In a large bowl, combine both types of flour, baking powder, and baking soda. Mix well. Stir in dates and nuts.

In another bowl, combine egg whites, milk, brown sugar, oil, and vanilla. Beat with a fork or wire whisk until blended. Whisk in bananas. Add to dry mixture, mixing until all ingredients are moistened. Divide mixture evenly into prepared muffin cups.

Bake 15 to 18 minutes, until a toothpick inserted in the center of a muffin comes out clean.

Remove muffins to a wire rack and serve warm for best flavor.

Each muffin provides:

170 Calories

1	Bread Serving	4 g	Protein
¹/₂	Fat Serving	4 g	Fat (19% of calories)
¹/₂	Fruit Serving	31 g	Carbohydrate
36	Additional Calories	187 mg	Sodium
		0 mg	Cholesterol
		2 g	Fiber

Jelly Muffins

These tender, egg-free muffins have a surprise burst of flavor in the center. We prefer the taste of raspberry or blackberry jam, but any flavor will work.

Makes 12 muffins

Topping
2^1/$_2$	teaspoons sugar
^{1}/$_4$	teaspoon ground cinnamon

Muffins
1^1/$_4$	cups all-purpose flour
1	cup whole wheat flour
1^1/$_2$	teaspoons baking powder
1	teaspoon baking soda
^{3}/$_4$	teaspoon ground cinnamon
2	cups skim milk
^{1}/$_3$	cup honey
2	tablespoons vegetable oil
1^1/$_2$	teaspoons vanilla extract
^{1}/$_2$	teaspoon almond extract
^{1}/$_4$	cup fruit-only raspberry or blackberry spread

Preheat oven to 400 degrees F.

Spray 12 muffin cups with nonstick cooking spray.

Combine topping ingredients in a small bowl and set aside.

In a large bowl, combine both types of flour, baking powder, baking soda, and cinnamon. Mix well.

In another bowl, combine milk, honey, oil, and extracts. Beat with a fork or wire whisk until blended. Add to dry mixture. Mix until all ingredients are moistened. (Batter will be loose.) Divide mixture evenly into prepared muffin cups. Place a teaspoon of the jam on the top center of each muffin. Sprinkle evenly with topping.

Bake 18 to 20 minutes, until a toothpick near the center of each muffin (not in the jam) comes out clean.

Remove muffins to a wire rack and serve warm for best flavor.

Each muffin provides:		
166 Calories		
1	Bread Serving	4 g	Protein
1/2	Fat Serving	3 g	Fat (15% of calories)
1/4	Fruit Serving	32 g	Carbohydrate
50	Additional Calories	188 mg	Sodium
		1 mg	Cholesterol
		2 g	Fiber

Two-Berry Muffins

What's a "two berry"? Just bite into one of these tender muffins and you'll find out!

Makes 8 muffins

1	cup all-purpose flour
1/2	cup whole wheat flour
2	teaspoons baking powder
1	teaspoon baking soda
3/4	cup skim milk
1	tablespoon lemon juice
1/4	cup sugar
2	tablespoons vegetable oil
2	egg whites
2	teaspoons vanilla extract
1/4	teaspoon lemon extract
1/2	cup fresh or frozen blueberries (If using frozen berries, there's no need to thaw.)
1/2	cup fresh or frozen raspberries (If using frozen raspberries, thaw them first and drain on paper towels.)

Preheat oven to 400 degrees F.

Spray 8 muffin cups with nonstick cooking spray.

In a large bowl, combine both types of flour, baking powder, and baking soda. Mix well.

Place milk in another bowl. Add lemon juice and let stand 1 minute. Add remaining ingredients, except berries. Beat with a fork or wire whisk until blended. Add to dry mixture, stirring until all ingredients are moistened.

Gently fold in berries.

Divide batter evenly into prepared muffin cups.

Bake 15 minutes, until a toothpick inserted in the center of a muffin comes out clean.

Remove muffins to a wire rack to cool.

Each muffin provides:

164 Calories

1	Bread Serving	4 g	Protein
3/4	Fat Serving	4 g	Fat (22% of calories)
1/4	Fruit Serving	27 g	Carbohydrate
37	Additional Calories	307 mg	Sodium
		0 mg	Cholesterol
		2 g	Fiber

Bran Muffins

These are the best ever! They're super-moist and just sweet enough.

Makes 8 muffins

$^1/_2$ cup plus 2 tablespoons all-purpose flour
$^1/_2$ cup whole wheat flour
$^3/_4$ cup bran ($1^1/_2$ ounces)
$1^1/_2$ teaspoons ground cinnamon
1   teaspoon baking soda
$1^1/_2$ cups buttermilk
$^1/_4$ cup molasses
2   egg whites
1   tablespoon plus 1 teaspoon vegetable oil
1   teaspoon vanilla extract

Preheat oven to 375 degrees F.

Spray 8 muffin cups with nonstick cooking spray.

In a medium bowl, combine both types of flour, bran, cinnamon, and baking soda. In a large bowl, combine remaining ingredients. Beat with a fork or wire whisk until blended.

Add dry ingredients to liquid mixture. Stir until all ingredients are moistened. (Batter will be thin.)

Divide mixture evenly into prepared muffin cups.

Bake 20 to 22 minutes, until a toothpick inserted in the center of a muffin comes out clean.

Remove muffins from pan and cool, upside down, on a wire rack.

Each muffin provides:

147 Calories

1	Bread Serving	5 g	Protein
$^1/_2$	Fat Serving	3 g	Fat (20% of calories)
44	Additional Calories	26 g	Carbohydrate
		224 mg	Sodium
		2 mg	Cholesterol
		3 g	Fiber

Chunky Apple Molasses Spice Muffins

Guess what the chunks are? Lots of chewy dried apples! Kids will love these and they're much more nutritious than cupcakes.

Makes 8 muffins

1	cup whole wheat flour
1/2	cup all-purpose flour
1 1/2	teaspoons baking soda
1	teaspoon ground cinnamon
1/2	teaspoon ground nutmeg
1/4	teaspoon ground cloves
1/4	teaspoon ground allspice
1	cup dried apples, cut into small pieces (3 ounces)
1	cup applesauce (unsweetened)
2	egg whites
1/4	cup skim milk
1/4	cup molasses
2	tablespoons vegetable oil
1 1/2	teaspoons vanilla extract

Preheat oven to 400 degrees F.

Spray 8 muffin cups with nonstick cooking spray.

In a large bowl, combine both flours, baking soda, and spices. Mix well. Stir in dried apples.

In another bowl, combine remaining ingredients. Beat with a fork or wire whisk until blended. Add to dry mixture, mixing until all ingredients are moistened.

Divide mixture evenly into prepared muffin cups.

Bake 15 to 18 minutes, until a toothpick inserted in the center of a muffin comes out clean.

Remove muffins to a rack to cool.

Each muffin provides:

188 Calories

1	Bread Serving	4 g	Protein
3/4	Fat Serving	4 g	Fat (19% of calories)
3/4	Fruit Serving	35 g	Carbohydrate
33	Additional Calories	268 mg	Sodium
		0 mg	Cholesterol
		3 g	Fiber

Rum 'n' Raisin Muffins

We think the combination of rum flavor and raisins is heavenly.

Makes 8 muffins

Topping
$1^1/2$	teaspoons sugar
$1/8$	teaspoon ground cinnamon

Muffins
$3/4$	cup all-purpose flour
$3/4$	cup whole wheat flour
2	teaspoons baking powder
$1/2$	teaspoon baking soda
1	cup plain nonfat yogurt
$1/4$	cup firmly packed brown sugar
2	tablespoons vegetable oil
2	egg whites
2	teaspoons grated fresh lemon peel
2	teaspoons rum extract
1	teaspoon vanilla extract
$1/2$	cup raisins

Preheat oven to 400 degrees F.

Spray 8 muffin cups with nonstick cooking spray.

Combine topping ingredients in a small bowl. Set aside.

In a large bowl, combine both flours, baking powder, and baking soda. Mix well.

In another bowl, combine remaining ingredients, except raisins. Beat with a fork or wire whisk until blended. Add to dry mixture, along with raisins, mixing just until all ingredients are moistened.

Divide mixture evenly into prepared muffin cups. Sprinkle topping evenly over muffins.

Bake 15 minutes, or until a toothpick inserted in the center of a muffin comes out clean.

Remove muffins to a wire rack to cool.

Each muffin provides:

194 Calories

1	Bread Serving	6 g	Protein
$3/4$	Fat Serving	4 g	Fat (19% of calories)
$1/2$	Fruit Serving	35 g	Carbohydrate
32	Additional Calories	240 mg	Sodium
		1 mg	Cholesterol
		2 g	Fiber

Cheddar 'n' Onion Muffins

A perfect accompaniment to a bowl of thick soup or stew, these muffins are best served hot, right out of the oven.

Makes 12 muffins

1¹/₂	cups all-purpose flour
³/₄	cup whole wheat flour
1¹/₂	teaspoons baking powder
1¹/₂	teaspoons baking soda
1	tablespoon plus 1 teaspoon dried chives
2	teaspoons onion powder
¹/₈	teaspoon salt
2	egg whites
2	tablespoons vegetable oil
2	tablespoons grated onion
1¹/₂	cups plain nonfat yogurt
4	ounces shredded reduced-fat Cheddar cheese (1 cup)

Preheat oven to 400 degrees F.

Spray 12 muffin cups with nonstick cooking spray.

In a large bowl, combine both types of flour, baking powder, baking soda, chives, onion powder, and salt. Mix well.

In another bowl, combine remining ingredients, except Cheddar cheese. Beat with a fork or wire whisk until blended. Stir in cheese. Add to dry mixture, mixing until all ingredients are moistened.

Divide mixture evenly into prepared muffin cups.

Bake 15 to 18 minutes, until tops of muffins are browned and a toothpick inserted in the center of a muffin comes out clean.

Remove muffins to a wire rack and serve right away for best flavor.

Each muffin provides:

152 Calories

¹/₄	Protein Serving	8 g	Protein
1	Bread Serving	5 g	Fat (27% of calories)
¹/₂	Fat Serving	20 g	Carbohydrate
30	Additional Calories	346 mg	Sodium
		7 mg	Cholesterol
		1 g	Fiber

Desserts

You've heard it said before, but now you can truly "have your cake and eat it, too." In this section we've created a special group of luscious desserts in which the taste has been heightened, while calories and fat have been lightened. Our secret? Substituting high-fat ingredients with their lowfat counterparts. Try this:

In place of:	Use:
whole milk	skim milk
sour cream	nonfat yogurt
cream	evaporated skim milk
baking chocolate	cocoa
whole eggs	egg whites or egg substitute
sugar	half the amount called for
chopped nuts	half the amount called for
coconut	a quarter of the amount called for
cream cheese	fat-free cream cheese
cottage cheese	lowfat (1%) cottage cheese
ricotta cheese	part-skim or fat-free ricotta cheese
pie with double crust	pie with one crust
vegetable oil in cakes and muffins	replace at least half with apple sauce or yogurt
icing on cakes	sprinkling of sugar and cinnamon

Add fiber to cakes by replacing half of the flour with whole wheat flour and using wheat germ as a topping for cakes and also as a substitute for ground nuts. Fruit adds fiber, in addition to adding flavor, moistness, and important vitamins.

And don't forget our favorite fat-free addition—extracts. Vanilla adds a sweet, rich flavor to desserts, "tricking" your taste buds into thinking foods are sweeter than they really are. Other extracts can add delectable flavors without adding unnecessary calories and fat.

Our dessert cart is overflowing with puddings, frozen desserts, cakes, pies, cobblers, and crisps. Yes, desserts can be both lean *and* luscious.

Enjoy! Enjoy! Enjoy!

Chocolate Zucchini Spice Cake

Similar to brownies, this luscious cake is moist and tender and very rich-tasting. The versatile squash reigns again!

Makes 16 servings

3/4	cup whole wheat flour
3/4	cup all-purpose flour
3	tablespoons unsweetened cocoa
1	teaspoon baking powder
1/2	teaspoon baking soda
1	teaspoon ground cinnamon
1/4	teaspoon ground nutmeg
1/8	teaspoon ground allspice
2/3	cup sugar
1/3	cup skim milk
2	tablespoons vegetable oil
2	egg whites
1	teaspoon vanilla extract
1/2	teaspoon grated fresh orange peel
1	cup (packed) finely shredded zucchini, unpeeled

Preheat oven to 350 degrees F.

Spray an 8-inch square baking pan with nonstick cooking spray.

In a large bowl, combine both types of flour, cocoa, baking powder, baking soda, and spices. Mix well.

In another bowl, combine remaining ingredients, except zucchini. Beat with a fork or wire whisk until blended. Stir in zucchini. Add to dry mixture, mixing until all ingredients are moistened. Spoon into prepared pan.

Bake 30 minutes, until a toothpick inserted in the center of the cake comes out clean.

Cool in pan on a wire rack. Cut into squares to serve.

Each serving provides:			
		98 Calories	
1/2	Bread Serving	2 g	Protein
1/4	Vegetable Serving	2 g	Fat (18% of calories)
1/4	Fat Serving	18 g	Carbohydrate
44	Additional Calories	80 mg	Sodium
		0 mg	Cholesterol
		1 g	Fiber

Banana Cake Roll

Elegant enough for any party and so easy to make, this cake will delight the banana devotees in your house.

Makes 8 servings

³/₄	cup all-purpose flour
1	teaspoon baking powder
1	teaspoon ground cinnamon
³/₄	cup liquid egg substitute
3	tablespoons plus 1 teaspoon sugar
1	tablespoon plus 1 teaspoon vegetable oil
1	teaspoon vanilla extract
¹/₂	teaspoon banana extract
2	medium, ripe bananas, mashed

Filling

1¹/₄	cups part-skim ricotta cheese
2	tablespoons sugar
1¹/₂	teaspoons vanilla extract
¹/₄	teaspoon banana extract

Preheat oven to 375 degrees F.

Spray a 10 × 15-inch jelly roll pan with nonstick cooking spray.

Sift flour, baking powder, and cinnamon into a small bowl.

In another bowl, beat egg substitute with an electric mixer on high speed. Reduce mixer to low speed and beat in sugar, oil, extracts, and bananas.

Add dry ingredients. Beat on low speed until all ingredients are moistened.

Spread batter in prepared pan.

Bake 10 minutes.

Cool in pan on wire rack for 3 minutes. Loosen sides of cake with a spatula and invert cake onto a kitchen towel. Roll up like a jelly roll and let cool completely.

Combine all filling ingredients in a small bowl.

When cake is cool, unroll and spread evenly with filling. Carefully roll cake again and chill.

Each serving provides:

194 Calories

1	Protein Serving	8 g	Protein
1/2	Bread Serving	6 g	Fat (27% of calories)
1/2	Fat Serving	27 g	Carbohydrate
1/2	Fruit Serving	147 mg	Sodium
32	Additional Calories	12 mg	Cholesterol
		1 g	Fiber

Yes—Chocolate Cake!

How can "healthy" taste so good? This cake gets its wonderful, moist texture from maple syrup, applesauce, and apple juice. And there's lots of added fiber from the oat bran.

Makes 12 servings

Cake
3/4	cup whole wheat flour
2/3	cup oat bran (3 ounces)
1/4	cup unsweetened cocoa
1	teaspoon baking powder
1	teaspoon baking soda
2/3	cup apple juice
1/2	cup unsweetened applesauce
1/2	cup pure maple syrup
2	egg whites
2	tablespoons vegetable oil
2	teaspoons vanilla extract
1/4	teaspoon almond extract

Topping
2	tablespoons chocolate chips (or carob chips)
2	tablespoons chopped walnuts (1/2 ounce)

Preheat oven to 325 degrees F.

Spray an 8-inch square baking pan with nonstick cooking spray.

In a large bowl, combine flour, oat bran, cocoa, baking powder, and baking soda. Mix well.

In another bowl, combine remaining cake ingredients. Beat with a fork or wire whisk until blended. Add to dry mixture, mixing until all ingredients are moistened.

Place in prepared pan. Sprinkle nuts and carob chips evenly over cake, pressing them lightly into the cake.

Bake 35 minutes, until a toothpick inserted in the center of the cake comes out clean.

Cool in pan on wire rack.

Cut into squares to serve.

Each serving provides:

134 Calories

1/2	Bread Serving	3 g	Protein
1/2	Fat Serving	4 g	Fat (27% of calories)
1/4	Fruit Serving	24 g	Carbohydrate
60	Additional Calories	158 mg	Sodium
		0 mg	Cholesterol
		3 g	Fiber

Most Versatile Coffee Cake

The variations of this moist, delectable cake are unlimited. In place of the peaches, try chopped apples, blueberries, cherries, or any combination of fruits. Add an extract that you like, such as almond extract if you use cherries or orange extract with blueberries. Or, leave off the fruit and just top the cake with sugar and cinnamon. The Piña Colada Upside-Down Cake on page 326 is another variation of this wonderful dessert.

Makes 8 servings

3/4	cup all-purpose flour
1	teaspoon baking powder
2	tablespoons plus 2 teaspoons reduced-calorie margarine
2/3	cup lowfat (1%) cottage cheese
1/2	cup liquid egg substitute
3	tablespoons plus 1 teaspoon sugar
2	teaspoons vanilla extract
4	medium, ripe peaches, peeled and sliced

Topping
2 1/2	teaspoons sugar
1/2	teaspoon ground cinnamon

Preheat oven to 350 degrees F.

Spray a 10-inch pie pan with nonstick cooking spray.

In a medium bowl, combine flour and baking powder. Add margarine and mix with a fork or pastry blender until mixture resembles coarse crumbs.

In another bowl, combine cottage cheese, egg substitute, sugar, and vanilla. Beat with a fork or wire whisk until blended. (Mixture will be lumpy.)

Add cottage cheese mixture to dry ingredients, stirring until all ingredients are moistened. Spoon batter into prepared pan.

Arrange peach slices evenly over batter. Press them down slightly into the batter.

Combine topping ingredients and sprinkle evenly over peaches. (If peaches are very sweet, use less sugar.)

Bake 25 to 30 minutes, until set.

Cool in pan on wire rack. Enjoy warm or cold.

Each serving provides:

138 Calories

1/2	Protein Serving	6 g	Protein
1/2	Bread Serving	2 g	Fat (15% of calories)
1/2	Fat Serving	24 g	Carbohydrate
1/2	Fruit Serving	209 mg	Sodium
25	Additional Calories	1 mg	Cholesterol
		1 g	Fiber

Piña Colada Upside-Down Cake

This cake is incredibly moist and just bursting with flavor.

Makes 8 servings

Topping
2	cups canned crushed pineapple, packed in juice, drained (Reserve juice.)
2/3	cup nonfat dry milk
1/4	cup reserved juice from pineapple
2	tablespoons cornstarch
1	tablespoon sugar
2	teaspoons shredded coconut (unsweetened)
1	teaspoon coconut extract

Cake
3/4	cup all-purpose flour
1	teaspoon baking powder
2	tablespoons plus 2 teaspoons reduced-calorie margarine
2/3	cup lowfat (1%) cottage cheese
1/2	cup liquid egg substitute
3	tablespoons sugar
2	teaspoons vanilla extract

Preheat oven to 350 degrees F.

Spray a 9-inch pie pan with nonstick cooking spray. Line the pan with wax paper. Then spray again.

In a small bowl, combine all topping ingredients, mixing well. Spread evenly in pan.

In a medium bowl, combine flour and baking powder. Add margarine and mix with a fork or pastry blender until mixture resembles coarse crumbs.

In another bowl, combine cottage cheese, egg substitute, sugar, and vanilla. Beat with a fork or wire whisk until blended. (Mixture will be lumpy.)

Add cottage cheese mixture to dry ingredients, stirring until all ingredients are moistened. Spoon batter evenly over topping in pan.

Bake 30 minutes, until golden.

Cool in pan on wire rack 15 minutes. Then loosen edges with a knife and invert cake onto a plate. Peel off wax paper.

Each serving provides:

177 Calories

1/4	Protein Serving	7 g	Protein
3/4	Bread Serving	3 g	Fat (13% of calories)
1/2	Fat Serving	31 g	Carbohydrate
1/2	Fruit Serving	241 mg	Sodium
1/4	Milk Serving	2 mg	Cholesterol
33	Additional Calories	1 g	Fiber

Best Carrot Cake

The unbelievable taste and moistness make a hit whenever we serve this delicious cake. The surprise ingredient is tofu and it makes the cake healthful, as well as delicious.

Makes 8 servings

3/4	cup whole wheat flour
1	teaspoon baking powder
1	teaspoon ground cinnamon
1/2	teaspoon ground nutmeg
1/8	teaspoon ground cloves
1/8	teaspoon ground allspice
6	ounces medium or soft tofu, sliced, drained well between towels
1/2	cup liquid egg substitute
1/4	cup honey
2	tablespoons plus 2 teaspoons vegetable oil
2	tablespoons skim milk
1	teaspoon vanilla extract
1	cup finely shredded carrots
1/2	cup raisins

Preheat oven to 350 degrees F (325 degrees F for glass pan).

Spray an 8-inch baking pan with nonstick cooking spray.

In a large bowl, combine flour, baking powder, and spices. Mix well.

In a blender container, combine tofu, egg substitute, honey, oil, milk, and vanilla. Blend until smooth. Stir in carrots and raisins.

Add tofu mixture to dry ingredients. Stir until all ingredients are moistened.

Spoon mixture into prepared pan.

Bake 25 to 30 minutes.

Cool in pan.

Each serving provides:

173 Calories

1/2	Protein Serving	5 g	Protein	
1/2	Bread Serving	6 g	Fat (30% of calories)	
1/4	Vegetable Serving	27 g	Carbohydrate	
1	Fat Serving	97 mg	Sodium	
1/2	Fruit Serving	0 mg	Cholesterol	
31	Additional Calories	3 g	Fiber	

Applesauce Wheat Bars

This moist, spicy dessert doubles as a healthful snack, and makes a perfect lunchbox treat.

Makes 10 servings

1	cup minus 1 tablespoon whole wheat flour
1	teaspoon baking soda
1	teaspoon ground cinnamon
$1/2$	teaspoon ground nutmeg
$1/4$	teaspoon ground cloves
$1/4$	teaspoon ground allspice
1	cup unsweetened applesauce
$1/4$	cup liquid egg substitute
3	tablespoons plus 1 teaspoon vegetable oil
3	tablespoons plus 1 teaspoon sugar
2	tablespoons skim milk
2	teaspoons vanilla extract
$1/4$	cup plus 2 tablespoons raisins

Preheat oven to 350 degrees F.

Spray an 8-inch square baking pan with nonstick cooking spray.

In a large bowl, combine flour, baking soda, and spices.

In a blender container, combine applesauce with remaining ingredients, except raisins. Blend until smooth.

Add applesauce mixture and raisins to dry ingredients. Mix until all ingredients are moistened.

Place batter in prepared pan

Bake 30 minutes, until a toothpick inserted in the center of the cake comes out clean.

Cool in pan on wire rack.

Each serving provides:			
	130 Calories		
$1/2$	Bread Serving	2 g	Protein
1	Fat Serving	5 g	Fat (33% of calories)
$1/2$	Fruit Serving	20 g	Carbohydrate
23	Additional Calories	140 mg	Sodium
		0 mg	Cholesterol
		2 g	Fiber

Tender-Moist Bean Cake

This recipe makes one of the most wonderful pound cakes you'll ever sink your teeth into, and it contains no flour—just high-protein beans instead. You'd better make two!

Makes 4 servings

6	ounces cooked soybeans or pinto beans, drained (Canned beans may be used.)
1/4	cup liquid egg substitute
1/2	cup orange juice (unsweetened)
1/2	teaspoon orange or lemon extract
1	teaspoon vanilla extract
1/4	cup sugar
2	egg whites
1/4	teaspoon cream of tartar
2/3	cup nonfat dry milk
1/2	teaspoon baking powder

Preheat oven to 350 degrees F.

Spray a 4 × 8-inch loaf pan with nonstick cooking spray.

In a blender container, combine soybeans, egg substitute, orange juice, extracts, and 3 tablespoons of the sugar. Blend into a paste. Place in a large bowl.

In a deep bowl, beat egg whites with an electric mixer on low speed until foamy. Add cream of tartar and beat on high speed until egg whites are stiff.

Slowly add dry milk to egg whites, continuing to beat. Beat in baking powder and remaining sugar.

Fold egg white mixture into soybean paste. Fold gently until both mixtures are combined.

Place in prepared pan.

Bake 25 to 30 minutes, until top is firm and golden.

Cool in pan on wire rack.

Each serving provides:

202 Calories

3/4	Protein Serving	15 g	Protein
1/4	Fruit Serving	4 g	Fat (18% of calories)
1/2	Milk Serving	27 g	Carbohydrate
58	Additional Calories	177 mg	Sodium
		2 mg	Cholesterol
		0 g	Fiber

Razzleberry Crisp

You can use any combination of berries for this crispy delight. Serve it warm, topped with vanilla ice milk for a dessert fit for royalty.

Makes 8 servings

1	cup fresh or frozen raspberries, unsweetened (If frozen, thaw and drain before using.)
1¹/₂	cups fresh or frozen blueberries, unsweetened (If frozen, no need to thaw.)
1¹/₂	cups frozen dark sweet cherries, unsweetened (If frozen, no need to thaw.)
¹/₄	cup sugar
2	tablespoons cornstarch

Topping

1	cup rolled oats (3 ounces)
3	tablespoons whole wheat flour
1	teaspoon ground cinnamon
3	tablespoons firmly packed brown sugar
2	tablespoons plus 2 teaspoons reduced-calorie margarine
2	tablespoons orange juice

Preheat oven to 350 degrees F.

Spray a 9-inch pie pan with nonstick cooking spray.

Place berries in a large bowl. Sprinkle with sugar and cornstarch. Toss to coat berries. Place in prepared pan.

In a medium bowl, combine oats, flour, cinnamon, and brown sugar, mixing well. Add margarine and orange juice. Mix until all ingredients are moistened. Distribute evenly over berries.

Bake, uncovered, 35 to 40 minutes, until topping is crisp and berry mixture is thick. (Frozen berries may take a little longer to cook than thawed ones.)

Serve warm or cold.

Each serving provides:

164 Calories

$^1/_2$	Bread Serving	3 g	Protein
$^1/_2$	Fat Serving	3 g	Fat (16% of calories)
1	Fruit Serving	33 g	Carbohydrate
51	Additional Calories	50 mg	Sodium
		0 mg	Cholesterol
		3 g	Fiber

Apple Crisp

Few can resist our apple crisp. The milk baked into the topping adds a delectable flavor. This is a comfort food everyone will love.

Makes 6 servings

6	small, sweet apples, peeled, cored, and sliced very thin
1	cup water
3	tablespoons sugar
2	teaspoons lemon juice
1	teaspoon vanilla extract
1	teaspoon ground cinnamon
1/8	teaspoon ground nutmeg
2	teaspoons cornstarch dissolved in 1 tablespoon water

Topping

1	cup nonfat dry milk
1	cup Grape-Nuts cereal (4^1/$_2$ ounces)
3	tablespoons sugar
1	teaspoon ground cinnamon
	Dash ground nutmeg
3	tablespoons reduced-calorie margarine
2	tablespoons water

Preheat oven to 375 degrees F.

Spray a 9-inch pie pan with nonstick cooking spray.

Place apples in a large saucepan. Add water, sugar, lemon juice, vanilla, cinnamon, and nutmeg. Toss to combine. Bring to a boil over medium heat, stirring occasionally with a tossing motion. Add cornstarch mixture. Cook, stirring constantly, until mixture has thickened and apples are slightly tender, about 5 minutes. Spoon apples into prepared pan.

In a medium bowl, combine all topping ingredients, except water. Mix with a fork until milk and margarine are evenly distributed. Add water and mix well. Sprinkle topping evenly over apples.

Bake, uncovered, 20 minutes, or until lightly browned.

For best flavor, serve warm.

Each serving provides:			
	251 Calories		
1	Bread Serving	6 g	Protein
3/4	Fat Serving	4 g	Fat (12% of calories)
1	Fruit Serving	52 g	Carbohydrate
1/2	Milk Serving	259 mg	Sodium
51	Additional Calories	2 mg	Cholesterol
		4 g	Fiber

Apple Creme Pie

We've blended cottage cheese and apples with cinnamon and nutmeg to create spectacular results!

Makes 8 servings

Crust
1	tablespoon plus 1^1/$_2$ teaspoons margarine, melted
1	tablespoon plus 1^1/$_2$ teaspoons honey
^{3}/$_4$	cup graham cracker crumbs
^{1}/$_4$	teaspoon ground cinnamon

Filling
3	small, sweet apples (such as Golden Delicious), peeled, sliced very thin
^{1}/$_3$	cup water
^{1}/$_2$	teaspoon ground cinnamon
^{1}/$_2$	teaspoon ground nutmeg
^{1}/$_3$	cup nonfat dry milk
^{3}/$_4$	cup liquid egg substitute
1	cup lowfat (1%) cottage cheese
2	teaspoons vanilla extract
^{1}/$_4$	cup sugar

Preheat oven to 350 degrees F.

Combine margarine and honey in a 9-inch pie pan. Add graham cracker crumbs and cinnamon. Mix until crumbs are moistened. Press crumbs onto bottom and sides of pan to form a crust. Bake 5 minutes.

While crust is baking, place apples and water in a large nonstick skillet. Sprinkle with cinnamon and nutmeg. Simmer apples over medium heat until slightly tender, about 10 minutes. Drain, reserving liquid.

Spread apples evenly over crust.

In a blender container, combine reserved apple liquid with remaining filling ingredients. Blend until smooth. Pour over apples.

Bake 25 minutes, until filling is set.

Chill.

Each serving provides:

168 Calories

3/4	Protein Serving	8 g	Protein
1/2	Bread Serving	3 g	Fat (18% of calories)
1/2	Fat Serving	26 g	Carbohydrate
1/4	Fruit Serving	260 mg	Sodium
57	Additional Calories	2 mg	Cholesterol
		1 g	Fiber

Coconut Custard Cheese Pie

"Rich and delicious" is the only way to describe this heavenly pie!

Makes 8 servings

Crust

1	tablespoon plus 1^1/$_2$ teaspoons margarine, melted
1	tablespoon plus 1^1/$_2$ teaspoons honey
^{3}/$_4$	cup graham cracker crumbs

Filling

2	cups part-skim ricotta cheese
1	cup liquid egg substitute
^{1}/$_2$	cup sugar
1	tablespoon all-purpose flour
2	teaspoons vanilla extract
1	teaspoon coconut extract
1	tablespoon shredded coconut (unsweetened)

Preheat oven to 350 degrees F.

Combine margarine and honey in a 9-inch pie pan. Add graham cracker crumbs; mix until crumbs are moistened. Press crumbs onto bottom and sides of pan to form crust. Bake 5 minutes.

Remove crust and increase oven temperature to 375 degrees F.

In a blender container, combine all filling ingredients, except coconut. Blend until smooth. Stir in coconut. Pour filling into crust.

Bake 25 to 30 minute, until filling is set.

Cool slightly, then chill.

Each serving provides:

236 Calories

1^1/$_2$	Protein Servings	11 g	Protein
^{1}/$_2$	Bread Serving	8 g	Fat (31% of calories)
^{1}/$_2$	Fat Serving	220 mg	Sodium
67	Additional Calories	19 mg	Cholesterol
		0 g	Fiber

Miracle Lemon Tofu Pie

There's enough protein in this pie to make it a nutritious breakfast or lunch, as well as a refreshing dessert. Imagine having a salad and a slice of pie for lunch, with no guilt!

Makes 8 servings

9	ounces medium or soft tofu, sliced, drained well between towels
1	cup evaporated skim milk
3/4	cup liquid egg substitute
1/2	cup part-skim ricotta cheese
1/4	cup plus 2 tablespoons all-purpose flour
1/4	cup plus 1 tablespoon sugar
2	teaspoons baking powder
11/2	teaspoons lemon extract
1	teaspoon vanilla extract
1/2	teaspoon vanilla butternut flavor*
1/2	teaspoon ground cinnamon

Preheat oven to 350 degrees F.

Spray a 10-inch pie pan with nonstick cooking spray.

In a blender container, combine all ingredients. Blend 2 minutes.

Pour mixture into prepared pan. Let stand 5 minutes.

Bake 30 minutes, or until set.

Cool slightly, then chill.

*Often called "vanilla butter and nut flavor," this flavoring is found with the extracts in many large grocery stores. If you cannot locate it, use 1/4 teaspoon vanilla extract plus 1/4 teaspoon butter-flavored extract in its place.

Each serving provides:

143 Calories

1	Protein Serving	10 g	Protein
1/4	Bread Serving	3 g	Fat (19% of calories)
1/4	Milk Serving	18 g	Carbohydrate
30	Additional Calories	218 mg	Sodium
		6 mg	Cholesterol
		1 g	Fiber

Maple Buttercream Cheese Pie

This luscious pie was created to please a cheesecake lover in our family. It's almost too good to be true.

Makes 8 servings

Crust
1   tablespoon plus 1¹/₂ teaspoons margarine, melted
1   tablespoon plus 1¹/₂ teaspoons honey
³/₄   cup graham cracker crumbs

Filling
2   cups part-skim ricotta cheese
1   cup liquid egg substitute
¹/₄   cup plus 1 tablespoon sugar
1   tablespoon all-purpose flour
2   teaspoons vanilla butternut flavor*
¹/₂   teaspoon maple extract

Topping
2   cups canned crushed pineapple, packed in juice, undrained
2   tablespoons water
1   tablespoon sugar
1   tablespoon cornstarch
¹/₂   teaspoon vanilla butternut flavor*

Preheat oven to 350 degrees F.

Combine margarine and honey in a 9-inch pie pan. Add graham cracker crumbs. Mix well, until crumbs are moistened. Press crumbs onto bottom and sides of pan, forming a crust. Bake 5 minutes.

Remove crust and increase oven temperature to 375 degrees F.

In a blender container, combine all filling ingredients. Blend until smooth. Pour into crust. Bake 25 to 30 minutes, until filling is set.

While pie cools, prepare topping:

Combine all topping ingredients in a small saucepan. Stir to dissolve cornstarch. Cook over medium heat, stirring constantly, until mixture boils. Boil 1 minute, stirring.

Spread topping over pie.

Chill.

---

* Often called "vanilla butter and nut flavor," this flavoring is found with the extracts in many large grocery stores. If you cannot locate it, use $^1/_4$ teaspoon vanilla extract plus $^1/_4$ teaspoon butter-flavored extract in its place.

Each serving provides:			
		261 Calories	
$1^1/_2$	Protein Servings	11 g	Protein
$^1/_2$	Bread Serving	8 g	Fat (27% of calories)
$^1/_2$	Fat Serving	36 g	Carbohydrate
$^1/_2$	Fruit Serving	220 mg	Sodium
57	Additional Calories	19 mg	Cholesterol
		1 g	Fiber

Mock Coconut Custard Pie

Eat this pie with your eyes closed and you'll think it's coconut! We've substituted the coconut, which is very high in saturated fat, with—of all things—carrots!

Makes 8 servings

2	cups skim milk
1	cup liquid egg substitute
1/4	cup plus 2 tablespoons all-purpose flour
1/4	cup plus 1 tablespoon sugar
2	tablespoons plus 2 teaspoons reduced-calorie margarine
2	teaspoons baking powder
1	teaspoon coconut extract
1	teaspoon vanilla extract
1/2	teaspoon vanilla butternut flavor*
1	cup finely shredded carrots
	Ground nutmeg

Preheat oven to 350 degrees F.

Spray a 9-inch glass pie pan with nonstick cooking spray.

In a blender container, combine all ingredients, except carrots and nutmeg. Blend 1 minute.

Stir in carrots.

Pour mixture into prepared pan. Sprinkle lightly with nutmeg. Let stand 5 minutes.

Bake 40 minutes, until pie is set and bottom is lightly browned.

Cool slightly, then chill.

*Often called "vanilla butter and nut flavor," this flavoring is found with the extracts in many large grocery stores. If you cannot locate it, use 1/4 teaspoon vanilla extract plus 1/4 teaspoon butter-flavor extract in its place.

Each serving provides:

114 Calories

1/2	Protein Serving	6 g	Protein
1/4	Bread Serving	2 g	Fat (17% of calories)
1/4	Vegetable Serving	18 g	Carbohydrate
1/2	Fat Serving	254 mg	Sodium
1/4	Milk Serving	1 mg	Cholesterol
30	Additional Calories	1 g	Fiber

Tofu Almond Creme Pie

This creamy, delectable pie has as many variations as there are flavors of extracts. In place of almond, try coconut, lemon, orange, banana. . . .

Makes 8 servings

Crust
1   tablespoon plus 1¹/₂ teaspoons margarine, melted
1   tablespoon plus 1¹/₂ teaspoons honey
³/₄   cup graham cracker crumbs

Filling
9   ounces tofu, sliced, drained well between towels
1   cup evaporated skim milk
³/₄   cup liquid egg substitute
¹/₂   cup part-skim ricotta cheese
¹/₄   cup plus 1 tablespoon sugar
2   tablespoons all-purpose flour
1¹/₂   teaspoons almond extract
1   teaspoon vanilla extract

Preheat oven to 350 degrees F.

Combine margarine and honey in a 9-inch pie pan. Add graham cracker crumbs. Mix well, until crumbs are moistened. Press crumbs onto bottom and sides of pan, forming a crust. Bake 5 minutes. Cool slightly.

In a blender container, combine all filling ingredients. Blend until smooth. Pour into cooled crust.

Bake 25 minutes, or until set.

Chill.

Each serving provides:

199 Calories

1	Protein Serving	10 g	Protein
¹/₂	Bread Serving	6 g	Fat (26% of calories)
¹/₂	Fat Serving	26 g	Carbohydrate
¹/₄	Milk Serving	189 mg	Sodium
51	Additional Calories	6 mg	Cholesterol
		1 g	Fiber

Mystery Custard Pie

The mystery ingredient is a very nutritious vegetable and it helps to make this pie a healthful, moist, and delicious treat. It has always been one of our kids' favorite breakfasts. Don't tell them it's good for them and they'll never guess what's in it!

Makes 8 servings

Crust
1	tablespoon plus 1¹/₂ teaspoons margarine, melted
1	tablespoon plus 1¹/₂ teaspoons honey
³/₄	cup graham cracker crumbs

Filling
3	cups zucchini, unpeeled, cut into ¹/₄-inch pieces
³/₄	cup liquid egg substitute
1¹/₃	cups nonfat dry milk
¹/₄	cup plus 2 tablespoons sugar
1	tablespoon all-purpose flour
1	teaspoon vanilla extract
1	teaspoon ground cinnamon
¹/₂	teaspoon ground ginger
¹/₄	teaspoon ground cloves

Preheat oven to 350 degrees F.

Combine margarine and honey in a 9-inch pie pan. Add graham cracker crumbs. Mix well, until crumbs are moistened. Press crumbs onto bottom and sides of pan, forming a crust. Bake 5 minutes. Cool slightly.

In a blender container, combine all filling ingredients. Blend until smooth. Pour into crust.

Bake 30 minutes, until set.

Cool slightly, then chill.

Each serving provides:

177 Calories

1/4	Protein Serving	8 g	Protein
1/2	Bread Serving	3 g	Fat (15% of calories)
3/4	Vegetable Serving	30 g	Carbohydrate
1/2	Fat Serving	194 mg	Sodium
1/2	Milk Serving	2 mg	Cholesterol
61	Additional Calories	1 g	Fiber

Orange Dreamsicle Dessert

The name says it all. This one's a dream! An absolute must for your next party.

Makes 12 servings

Crust

3	tablespoons honey
1	tablespoon margarine, melted
1	cup Grape-Nuts cereal, crushed slightly ($4^{1}/_{2}$ ounces)
$^{1}/_{2}$	teaspoon ground cinnamon
$^{1}/_{2}$	teaspoon freshly grated orange peel

Filling

$2^{1}/_{4}$	cups part-skim ricotta cheese
$^{3}/_{4}$	cup liquid egg substitute
$^{1}/_{4}$	cup sugar
1	tablespoon all-purpose flour
2	teaspoons vanilla extract

Topping

2	cups orange juice
$^{1}/_{4}$	cup sugar
3	tablespoons cornstarch
1	tablespoon lemon juice
$^{1}/_{2}$	teaspoon orange extract
4	cups fresh orange sections (Discard white membranes.) (Navel oranges make the best choice.)

Preheat oven to 350 degrees F.

Combine crust ingredients in a 9 × 13-inch baking pan. Press gently onto the bottom of pan to form a crust. Bake 8 minutes.

In a blender container, combine all filling ingredients. Blend until smooth. Pour over crust.

Bake 18 to 20 minutes, until set. Cool completely.

In a medium saucepan, combine orange juice, sugar, cornstarch, lemon juice, and orange extract. Stir to dissolve cornstarch. Bring mixture to a boil over medium heat, stirring constantly. Boil 1 minute, stirring. Remove from heat.

Allow to cool 5 minutes, then gently stir in orange sections. Spread mixture evenly over cooled cheese filling.

Chill. Cut into squares to serve.

Each serving provides:		
225 Calories		
1	Protein Serving	9 g	Protein
1/2	Bread Serving	5 g	Fat (19% of calories)
1/4	Fat Serving	38 g	Carbohydrate
1	Fruit Serving	159 mg	Sodium
57	Additional Calories	14 mg	Cholesterol
		2 g	Fiber

Mocha Fluff

Light as a feather, this fluffy pudding is an ideal quick dessert or after-school snack. For Chocolate Fluff, simply eliminate the coffee.

Makes 4 servings

3/4   cup water
1   envelope unflavored gelatin
2/3   cup nonfat dry milk
3   tablespoons sugar
1   tablespoon plus 1 teaspoon unsweetened cocoa
1¹/2   teaspoons vanilla extract
1/4   teaspoon rum or almond extract
1¹/2   teaspoons instant coffee granules
7   large ice cubes

Place water in a small saucepan. Sprinkle gelatin over water and let soften a few minutes. Heat over low heat, stirring frequently, until gelatin is completely dissolved. Remove from heat.

In a blender container, combine dry milk, sugar, cocoa, extracts, and coffee granules. Add gelatin mixture. Turn blender on and carefully add ice cubes, one at a time, while blending. Blend 1 minute, or until ice is gone.

Pudding may be divided into 4 serving bowls and eaten right away or, if a slightly firmer texture is desired, chilled for 15 minutes before serving.

Each serving provides:			
	95 Calories		
1/2	Milk Serving	6 g	Protein
41	Additional Calories	trace	Fat (3% of calories)
		17 g	Carbohydrate
		67 mg	Sodium
		2 mg	Cholesterol
		1 g	Fiber

Fruited No-Bake Bread Pudding

Unlike most bread puddings, this marvelous combination of bread and fruits contains no eggs. It can be made ahead and doubles as a great breakfast.

Makes 8 servings

4	slices whole wheat bread, cubed
1/2	cup orange juice
1/4	teaspoon ground cinnamon
1	medium, ripe banana, sliced
1	small orange, peeled and sectioned (Discard white membranes.)
1	envelope unflavored gelatin
3/4	cup water
11/3	cups lowfat (1%) cottage cheese
2/3	cup nonfat dry milk
3	tablespoons sugar
1	tablespoon vanilla extract
10	small ice cubes (about 1 cup)

Place bread cubes in a large bowl. Pour orange juice evenly over bread and sprinkle with cinnamon. Add banana and orange and toss to combine.

In a small saucepan, sprinkle gelatin over water. Heat over low heat, stirring frequently, until gelatin is completely dissolved.

In a blender container, combine gelatin mixture with remaining ingredients. Blend until ice cubes are completely dissolved.

Pour mixture over bread. Mix well.

Place mixture in an 8-inch square baking pan. Press bread and fruit down gently into liquid.

Chill until firm.

Each serving provides:

135 Calories

1/2	Protein Serving	9 g	Protein
1/2	Bread Serving	1 g	Fat (7% of calories)
1/2	Fruit Serving	22 g	Carbohydrate
1/4	Milk Serving	261 mg	Sodium
18	Additional Calories	3 mg	Cholesterol
		2 g	Fiber

Pumpkin Custard Cups

This moist, cheesecake-like dessert was so popular at Thanksgiving, they now ask for it all year round. Our favorite way to serve it is in tall sherbet glasses, garnished with a few orange slices and a sprig of mint. If you double the recipe it will fill a 9-inch pie crust.

Makes 4 servings

1	package orange-flavored gelatin (four $^1/_2$-cup servings)
$^3/_4$	cup boiling water
1	cup canned pumpkin
$^1/_2$	cup part-skim ricotta cheese
1	teaspoon vanilla extract
$^1/_2$	teaspoon ground cinnamon

In a small saucepan, dissolve gelatin in boiling water.

In a blender container, combine gelatin mixture with remaining ingredients. Blend until smooth.

Divide mixture evenly into 4 individual serving bowls or sherbet glasses.

Chill until firm.

Each serving provides:

148 Calories

$^1/_2$	Protein Serving	6 g	Protein
$^1/_2$	Vegetable Serving	3 g	Fat (16% of calories)
80	Additional Calories	26 g	Carbohydrate
		96 mg	Sodium
		10 mg	Cholesterol
		1 g	Fiber

Lemon Dream Parfaits

These lemony parfaits are truly a dreamy dessert, and they're a snap to make. To dress them up for a party, add a dollop of whipped topping and a few slivered almonds.

Makes 4 servings

1	cup orange juice
1	package lemon-flavored gelatin (four 1/2-cup servings)
1	cup part-skim ricotta cheese
1	cup evaporated skim milk
1 1/2	teaspoons vanilla extract

In a small saucepan, bring orange juice to a boil over medium heat. Remove from heat and stir in gelatin. Stir until gelatin is completely dissolved.

In a blender container, combine gelatin mixture with remaining ingredients. Blend until smooth.

Pour mixture into 4 parfait glasses.

Chill.

Each serving provides:

248 Calories

1	Protein Serving	14 g	Protein
1/2	Fruit Serving	5 g	Fat (18% of calories)
1/2	Milk Serving	36 g	Carbohydrate
80	Additional Calories	205 mg	Sodium
		22 mg	Cholesterol
		0 g	Fiber

Very Berry Bread Pudding

Unlike most bread puddings, this unique no-bake version has no eggs or milk—just lots of fruit and flavor. It's delicious plain or topped with vanilla ice milk.

Makes 8 servings

8	slices whole wheat bread (1-ounce slices), cut into cubes
2	cups fresh strawberries, coarsely chopped
2	cups fresh (or frozen) blueberries (If frozen, there's no need to thaw.)
1/4	cup sugar (or honey)
1/4	cup frozen orange juice concentrate, thawed
2	tablespoons water
1	teaspoon vanilla extract
1/4	teaspoon ground cinnamon

Place bread cubes and strawberries in a large bowl. Set aside.

In a small saucepan, combine blueberries with remaining ingredients. Bring to a boil over medium heat. Reduce heat to low and simmer gently 5 minutes.

Pour blueberry mixture over strawberries and bread. Mix well until bread is completely moistened. Transfer to an 8-inch square baking pan. Press pudding down into pan with the back of a spoon.

Cover and chill.

Serve cold.

Each serving provides:

141 Calories

1	Bread Serving	3 g	Protein
1	Fruit Serving	2 g	Fat (9% of calories)
24	Additional Calories	31 g	Carbohydrate
		152 mg	Sodium
		1 mg	Cholesterol
		4 g	Fiber

Indian Carrot Pudding

Don't let the seemingly long cooking time deter you. This healthful dessert is unsurpassed in flavor and well worth the effort! After all, what could be more nutritious than a dessert made out of vegetables?

Makes 4 servings

2	cups grated or finely shredded carrots
2	cups evaporated skim milk
1	ounce graham cracker crumbs (four 2^1/$_2$-inch graham crackers, crushed)
2	tablespoons plus 2 teaspoons reduced-calorie margarine
2	tablespoons firmly packed brown sugar
1	teaspoon vanilla extract
^{1}/$_8$	teaspoon ground nutmeg
^{1}/$_8$	teaspoon ground cinnamon
^{1}/$_{16}$	teaspoon saffron, crushed

In a medium saucepan, combine carrots and milk. Bring to a boil over medium heat, stirring constantly. Cook, stirring, until most of milk is absorbed, about 20 minutes.

Add remaining ingredients. Cook, stirring, 5 minutes.

Serve warm.

Each serving provides:

215 Calories

^{1}/$_4$	Bread Serving	11 g	Protein
1	Vegetable Serving	5 g	Fat (19% of calories)
1	Fat Serving	32 g	Carbohydrate
1	Milk Serving	304 mg	Sodium
31	Additional Calories	5 mg	Cholesterol
		2 g	Fiber

Tortoni

A traditional Italian dessert that is usually made with whipped cream, this version is just as refreshing as the original. And it's so creamy that you won't believe it isn't made with real cream.

Makes 4 servings

1/3	cup ice water
1/3	cup nonfat dry milk
2	tablespoons sugar
1/2	teaspoon almond extract
1/2	teaspoon rum extract
1	tablespoon graham cracker crumbs (one 2 1/2-inch square, crushed)

Place ice water and dry milk in a deep bowl. Beat with an electric mixer on medium speed for 2 minutes. Increase speed to high and continue to beat for 2 more minutes.

Add sugar and beat 2 minutes on high speed, or until mixture is thick and forms soft peaks. Add extracts, beating well.

Divide mixture evenly into 4 custard cups. Sprinkle with crumbs.

Place cups in freezer until set, at least 1 hour.

Let cups sit at room temperature for about 3 minutes before serving.

Each serving provides:

56 Calories

1/4	Milk Serving	2 g	Protein
31	Additional Calories	trace	Fat (3% of calories)
		11 g	Carbohydrate
		42 mg	Sodium
		1 mg	Cholesterol
		0 g	Fiber

Tofu Raspberry Mousse

This is a dessert you can actually encourage your family to eat. It's high in protein and tastes delicious. It's great topped with fresh berries. For variations, try other flavors of gelatin.

Makes 4 servings

1	package raspberry-flavored gelatin (four $^1/_2$-cup servings)
$^3/_4$	cup boiling water
$^2/_3$	cup nonfat dry milk
1	10-ounce package silken (or soft) tofu, drained
1	teaspoon honey
$^1/_2$	teaspoon lemon extract
$1^1/_2$	cups ice cubes

Dissolve gelatin in boiling water, stirring until completely dissolved. Pour into a blender container. Add remaining ingredients and blend until ice cubes are completely dissolved. Pour mixture into 1 large bowl or 4 individual serving bowls.

Chill.

Each serving provides:

176 Calories

$^3/_4$	Protein Serving	12 g	Protein
$^1/_2$	Milk Serving	2 g	Fat (8% of calories)
90	Additional Calories	29 g	Carbohydrate
		164 mg	Sodium
		2 mg	Cholesterol
		0 g	Fiber

Mocha Creme-Filled Meringue Nests

What an elegant dessert! And both the pudding and the nests can be made ahead and filled just before serving. For lots of other variations, the pudding can be made and eaten separately, and the nests can be used to hold any type of cold pudding or fruit.

Makes 6 servings

Mocha Creme Pudding
1	cup nonfat dry milk
1/3	cup sugar
3	tablespoons cornstarch
2	tablespoons unsweetened cocoa
1 1/2	teaspoons instant coffee (regular or decaffeinated)
2	cups water
1	teaspoon vanilla extract

Meringue Nests
3	egg whites
1/4	teaspoon cream of tartar
1/8	teaspoon salt
1/3	cup sugar
1/2	teaspoon vanilla extract

To make pudding:

In a small saucepan, combine dry milk, sugar, cornstarch, cocoa, and coffee. Mix well. Gradually stir in water. Bring mixture to a boil over medium heat, stirring constantly. Boil 2 minutes, stirring. Remove from heat and stir in vanilla.

Place pudding in a bowl and cover with wax paper, placing wax paper directly on the surface of the pudding. (This will keep a crust from forming.)

Chill.

To make meringue nests:

Preheat oven to 275 degrees F.

Line a baking sheet with wax paper.

Place egg whites in a large bowl. Beat with an electric mixer on medium speed until frothy. Add cream of tartar and salt. Beat on high speed until stiff.

Slowly beat in sugar, a tablespoon at a time, beating well after each addition. Beat in vanilla extract.

Divide mixture evenly and drop onto prepared sheet, making 6 mounds. Using a teaspoon, shape each mound into a circle 4 inches in diameter. Then build up the sides 1¹/2 inches, making a nest.

Bake 1 hour.

Turn oven off and leave nests in oven to cool. (Do not open oven door.)

To remove nests from pan, gently slide a spatula under the wax paper.

At serving time:

Place nests on a serving platter or on individual serving plates. Mix pudding well and spoon into nests, using ¹/3 cup of pudding for each nest.

Serve right away.

(Meringues can be made a day ahead and stored in an airtight container or plastic bag until needed, and pudding can be stored in the refrigerator. Unfilled shells will keep for several days.)

For Mocha Creme Pudding

Each serving provides:

105 Calories

¹/2	Milk Serving	4 g	Protein
63	Additional Calories	trace	Fat (3% of calories)
		22 g	Carbohydrate
		63 mg	Sodium
		2 mg	Cholesterol
		1 g	Fiber

For Meringue Nests

Each serving provides:

52 Calories

52	Additional Calories	2 g	Protein
		0 g	Fat
		11 g	Carbohydrate
		74 mg	Sodium
		0 mg	Cholesterol
		0 g	Fiber

Tofu Cinnamon Cheese Pudding

The mellow blending of vanilla, almond, and cinnamon make this a remarkable dessert or brunch dish. We like it drizzled lightly with maple syrup.

Makes 4 servings

6	ounces medium or soft tofu, sliced, drained well between towels
2/3	cup lowfat (1%) cottage cheese
1/2	cup liquid egg substitute
1/4	cup sugar
1	teaspoon ground cinnamon
1 1/2	teaspoons vanilla extract
1	teaspoon almond extract

Preheat oven to 350 degrees F.

Spray a 4 × 8-inch loaf pan with nonstick cooking spray.

In a blender container, combine tofu with remaining ingredients. Blend until smooth. Pour mixture into prepared pan.

Bake 35 to 40 minutes, until set.

Cool slightly. Then chill.

Cut into squares to serve.

Each serving provides:

134 Calories

1 1/2	Protein Servings	11 g	Protein
48	Additional Calories	3 g	Fat (18% of calories)
		15 g	Carbohydrate
		207 mg	Sodium
		2 mg	Cholesterol
		1 g	Fiber

Magic Strudel Bars

These delightful bars, made from a familiar breakfast cereal, make a wonderful dessert or a great snack for any time of day. When you're in a hurry, add a glass of skim milk and you have a "quickie" breakfast.

Makes 6 servings

1/2	cup water
1/2	cup canned crushed pineapple, packed in juice, drained (Reserve juice.)
2	tablespoons juice from pineapple
1 1/2	envelopes unflavored gelatin
1/2	cup plus 2 tablespoons raisins
2	tablespoons sugar
1	tablespoon shredded coconut (unsweetened)
1/4	teaspoon orange extract
1/4	teaspoon coconut extract
1/4	teaspoon ground cinnamon
1	cup Grape Nuts cereal (4 1/2 ounces)

In a medium saucepan, combine water and pineapple juice. Sprinkle with gelatin and let stand a few minutes. Heat over low heat, stirring frequently, until gelatin is completely dissolved. Add sugar. Stir until dissolved.

Add remaining ingredients, except cereal. Mix well.

Stir in cereal. Mix until cereal is moistened.

Place mixture in a 6 × 11-inch baking pan that has been sprayed with a nonstick cooking spray. Press firmly in pan.

Chill.

Cut into squares to serve.

Each serving provides:

160 Calories

1	Bread Serving	4 g	Protein
1	Fruit Serving	1 g	Fat (5% of calories)
19	Additional Calories	37 g	Carbohydrate
		134 mg	Sodium
		0 mg	Cholesterol
		3 g	Fiber

Cinnamon Whirls

These attractive pinwheels are definitely party fare!

Makes 6 servings (3 pastries each serving)

1   cup plus 2 tablespoons all-purpose flour
1^1/$_2$ teaspoons baking powder
^{1}/$_4$ teaspoon baking soda
2   tablespoons margarine
2   tablespoons sugar
1^1/$_2$ teaspoons vanilla extract
^{1}/$_4$ cup plus 1 tablespoon plain nonfat yogurt

Topping

1   tablespoon sugar
^{3}/$_4$ teaspoon ground cinnamon

Preheat oven to 425 degrees F.

Spray a baking sheet with nonstick cooking spray.

In a large bowl, combine flour, baking powder, and baking soda. Add margarine. Mix with a fork or pastry blender until mixture resembles coarse crumbs.

Stir 2 tablespoons of sugar and the vanilla into yogurt. Add to flour mixture, stirring until most of the flour is moistened. Knead dough with hands until mixture holds together.

Roll dough between 2 sheets of wax paper into a rectangle 1/4 inch thick.

Combine remaining sugar and cinnamon and sprinkle evenly over dough.

Starting with one long side, roll dough tightly into a log. With a sharp knife, cut into 18 even slices.

Place slices on prepared baking sheet.

Bake 10 minutes, until lightly browned.

Remove from pan and cool on a wire rack.

Serve warm for best flavor. Store remaining whirls in an airtight container.

Each serving provides:

156 Calories

1	Bread Serving	3 g	Protein
1	Fat Serving	4 g	Fat (25% of calories)
30	Additional Calories	26 g	Carbohydrate
		228 mg	Sodium
		0 mg	Cholesterol
		1 g	Fiber

Almond Macaroons

Wheat germ replaces the ground nuts in these crispy macaroons. It reduces the fat and calories, adds more nutrition, and still gives a delicious, nutty flavor.

Makes 10 servings (5 cookies each serving)

1   egg white
1/4   cup sugar
1   teaspoon almond extract
1/4   cup wheat germ

Preheat oven to 325 degrees F.

Spray a baking sheet with nonstick cooking spray. Dust it lightly with flour.

In a deep bowl, beat egg white with an electric mixer on low speed until frothy. Beat on high speed until stiff. Gradually beat in sugar and then almond extract.

Fold in wheat germ.

Drop mixture by 1/2 teaspoonfuls onto prepared baking sheet.

Put the cookies in the oven and immediately reduce the temperature to 200 degrees F.

Bake 1 hour.

Turn off heat and leave cookies in oven to cool. Do not open oven door until cookies are cool.

Each serving provides:

37 Calories

34 Additional Calories	1 g	Protein
	trace	Fat (10% of calories)
	7 g	Carbohydrate
	6 mg	Sodium
	0 mg	Cholesterol
	0 g	Fiber

Sauces and Toppings

Sauces can enhance even the simplest of foods. But all too often these tasty additions add lots of unwanted calories and fat. Not so if you follow a few easy rules:

- Use low-sodium broth or reduced-sodium soy sauce as a base for sauces and marinades.
- Add spices to salt-free tomato sauce to create fat-free sauces for chicken and fish.
- Combine nonfat yogurt with herbs and spoon over cooked vegetables.
- Replace butter with reduced-calorie margarine for topping pancakes and waffles.
- Use nonfat yogurt in place of sour cream for topping baked potatoes.
- Top angel food cake and pancakes with fruit toppings.
- Combine nonfat yogurt with fruit to make creamy sauces for topping desserts.
- Use evaporated skim milk to replace cream in cream sauces.

Chocolate Pineapple Sauce

Delicious, delicious, delicious! Serve over lowfat ice cream or on angel food cake and you've created an elegant dessert.

Makes 8 servings (2 tablespoons each serving)

2/3	cup nonfat dry milk
1	tablespoon plus 1 teaspoon unsweetened cocoa
1	tablespoon plus 1 teaspoon sugar
1/2	cup canned crushed pineapple (packed in juice), drained (Reserve juice.)
2	tablespoons reserved juice from pineapple
1	teaspoon vanilla extract

In a small bowl, combine dry milk and cocoa. Mix well, pressing out any lumps with the back of a spoon. Add remaining ingredients and mix well.

Chill several hours.

Each serving provides:

41 Calories

1/4	Milk Serving	2 g	Protein
18	Additional Calories	trace	Fat (4% of calories)
		8 g	Carbohydrate
		32 mg	Sodium
		1 mg	Cholesterol
		0 g	Fiber

Cinnamon Creme Sauce

This creamy sauce is great over baked apples. It's also a delicious pancake topper.

Makes 1 cup

1   cup plain nonfat yogurt
2   tablespoons firmly packed brown sugar
1   teaspoon vanilla extract
3/4   teaspoon ground cinnamon

Combine all ingredients in a small bowl, mixing well. Chill.

Each 1-tablespoon serving provides:
15 Calories

15   Additional Calories   1 g   Protein
                            trace   Fat (1% of calories)
                              3 g   Carbohydrate
                            11 mg   Sodium
                             0 mg   Cholesterol
                              0 g   Fiber

Strawberry Sauce

Make a scrumptious sundae by topping lowfat ice cream and sliced bananas with this easy sauce.

Makes 1 1/4 cups

1	cup water
1/4	cup fruit-only strawberry spread
1	tablespoon plus 1 teaspoon cornstarch
2	tablespoons sugar

Combine all ingredients in a small saucepan. Stir to dissolve cornstarch. Bring mixture to a boil over medium heat, stirring constantly. Continue to cook, stirring, for 1 minute.

Serve warm.

Each 1-tablespoon serving provides:
15 Calories

15	Additional Calories	0 g	Protein
		0 g	Fat
		4 g	Carbohydrate
		0 mg	Sodium
		0 mg	Cholesterol
		0 g	Fiber

Raspberry Melba Sauce

Serve this quick blender sauce over any type of fresh fruit. Or, for a delectable Peach Melba, spoon it over sliced peaches and vanilla lowfat ice cream.

Makes ³/₄ cup

1   10-ounce package frozen raspberries (unsweetened), thawed
3   tablespoons confectioners sugar

Place raspberries and their juice in a blender container. Blend until puréed. Pour through a strainer into a small bowl. Add sugar, stirring until it dissolves.

Serve right away or chill for later servings.

Each 3-tablespoon serving provides:
61 Calories

¹/₂	Fruit Serving	1 g	Protein
36	Additional Calories	1 g	Fat (9% of calories)
		16 g	Carbohydrate
		0 mg	Sodium
		0 mg	Cholesterol
		0 g	Fiber

Orange Creme Whip

Serve this fluffy delight over fresh fruit or make a delicious shortcake by spooning it over berry-topped angel food cake.

Makes 3 cups

1/2	cup orange juice
	Ice water
2/3	cup nonfat dry milk
2 1/2	teaspoons sugar
1	teaspoon vanilla extract

Place a medium, deep bowl and the beaters of an electric mixer in the freezer. Chill at least 1 hour.

Place orange juice in a measuring cup. Add ice water to equal 2/3 cup liquid.

Place all ingredients in the chilled bowl. Beat on high speed of electric mixer 5 minutes, until thick and creamy.

Serve right away.

Each 3/4-cup serving provides:

68 Calories

1/4	Fruit Serving	4 g	Protein
1/2	Milk Serving	trace	Fat (1% of calories)
10	Additional Calories	12 g	Carbohydrate
		63 mg	Sodium
		2 mg	Cholesterol
		0 g	Fiber

Honey Mustard Sauce

Use this delicious sauce to top sliced chicken or turkey, served either hot or cold, and either plain or on a sandwich.

Makes 3/4 cup

$^1/_2$ cup prepared yellow mustard
$^1/_4$ cup honey
2   teaspoons reduced-sodium (or regular) soy sauce

Combine all ingredients in a small bowl, mixing well.
Serve right away or chill for later servings.

Each 1-tablespoon serving provides:
30 Calories

30	Additional Calories		
		1 g	Protein
		trace	Fat (12% of calories)
		7 g	Carbohydrate
		164 mg	Sodium
		0 mg	Cholesterol
		0 g	Fiber

Chili Orange Barbecue Sauce

This is a perfect sauce to brush on chicken or meat while broiling or grilling.

Makes ½ cup

¹/4	cup plus 2 tablespoons bottled chili sauce
2	tablespoons frozen orange juice concentrate, thawed
2	teaspoons vegetable oil

Combine all ingredients in a small bowl. Mix well.

Each 1-tablespoon serving provides:
30 Calories

¹/4	Fat Serving	0 g	Protein
23	Additional Calories	1 g	Fat (33% of calories)
		5 g	Carbohydrate
		171 mg	Sodium
		0 mg	Cholesterol
		0 g	Fiber

Baked Potato Topper

Turn a baked potato into an elegant dish without adding fat. This simple mixture doubles as a salad dressing, and the herbs can be varied to accommodate everyone's taste.

Makes 4 servings (¹/₄ cup each serving)

1	cup plain nonfat yogurt
¹/₂	teaspoon dill weed
¹/₄	teaspoon salt
¹/₈	teaspoon pepper
2	teaspoons imitation bacon bits
2	teaspoons dried chives

In a small bowl, combine yogurt, dill weed, salt, and pepper. Mix well. Chill.

To serve, spoon ¹/₄ cup of the yogurt on a baked potato. Sprinkle each potato with ¹/₂ teaspoon of the bacon bits and ¹/₂ teaspoon of the chives.

Each serving provides:

37 Calories

¹/₄	Milk Serving	4 g	Protein
13	Additional Calories	trace	Fat (6% of calories)
		5 g	Carbohydrate
		209 mg	Sodium
		1 mg	Cholesterol
		0 g	Fiber

Herbed Tomato Sauce

We use this basic recipe all the time, over lots of dishes. Spoon it over cooked rice, omelets, steamed veggies, baked potatoes. . . . Its uses are endless.

Makes 1 cup

1	8-ounce can salt-free (or regular) tomato sauce
1/4	teaspoon dried basil
1/4	teaspoon dried oregano
1/8	teaspoon garlic powder

Combine all ingredients in a small saucepan and heat.

Each 1/4-cup serving provides:

21 Calories

1/2	Vegetable Serving	1 g	Protein
		trace	Fat (9% of calories)
		4 g	Carbohydrate
		12 mg	Sodium
		0 mg	Cholesterol
		1 g	Fiber

Index

A

Acorn squash, applesauce, 246
Almond
    bread puff, 178
    in cherries amandine, 274
    macaroons, 362
"Almost" lasagna, 182–183
Appetizers, 1–20. *See also* Dips *and*
    Spreads
    bagel crackers, 17
    cinnamon bread sticks, 18
    cinnamon popcorn, 20
    clams casino, 5
    crab-stuffed mushrooms, 3
    marinated mozzarella, 4
    potato chips, 19
    salmon pâté, 7
    tomato party puffs, 6
    tortilla chips, 16
    tuna mousse, 8
Apple
    blueberry and apple
        delight, 278
    chunky apple molasses spice
        muffins, 313
    creme pie, 336–337
    crisp, 334–335
    Delhi beans and, 129
    in 15-minute muesli, 267
    rice casserole, 253
    strawberry–apple mold, 58
    strudel omelet, 174
    sweet potatoes and, 241
    tapioca dessert, 278
Apple-raisin spice bread, 300–301
Applesauce
    acorn squash, 246
    ambrosia, 277

    in chunky apple molasses spice
        muffins, 313
    to replace oil in breads and muffins, 291
    wheat bars, 329
Apricot in baked cranberry relish, 287
Apricot-almond cranberry sauce, 288
Asian cabbage, 213
Asian turkey patties, 79

B

Bagel crackers, 17
Baked cranberry relish, 287
Baked herbed fish, 89
Baked pears with cinnamon crème
    sauce, 280
Baked pineapple with creamy coconut
    sauce, 273
Baked potato topper, 372
Banana
    cake roll, 320–321
    date-nut muffins, 307
    New Orleans, 279
    in tropical millet pudding, 263
Barbecue turkey loaf, 82
Barbecued shrimp, 104–105
Barley, Italian, 264
Barley-vegetable casserole, 265
Basil bean salad, 52
Bean loaf supreme, mushroom, 128
Beans, 125–139
    black bean casserole olé, 138
    butter bean and cheese squares, 134
    Cajun bean pot, 130
    and cheese quesadillas, 136
    curried lima soup, 34
    Delhi, and apples, 129
    gravy, 139

Beans, *continued*
    Italian, and cheese, 127
    kidney beans provençal, 132–133
    Mexican pinto spread, 14
    mushroom bean loaf supreme, 128
    pineapple–black bean salad, 137
    refried, 131
    salad, basil, 52
    soup, leftover, 27
    Turkish stew, 135
Beef, 109–116
    chili meat loaf, 114
    Chinese pepper steak, 111
    French meat loaf, 115
    pepper burgers, 116
    steak-kabobs, 110
    sukiyaki, 112–113
    teriyaki flank steak, 109
Beer bread, 296
Bengal seafood salad, 106
Berries Romanoff, 282
Best carrot cake, 328
Best coleslaw, 47
Black bean
    casserole olé, 138
    pineapple–black bean salad, 137
Blueberry
    and apple delight, 278
    in razzleberry crisp, 332–333
    red, white, and blueberry parfaits, 281
    in two-berry muffins, 310–311
    in very berry bread pudding, 352
Bombay millet, 262
Bombay peas and potatoes, 237
Bow tie noodles in kasha and
        bow ties, 260
Bran muffins, 312
Bread puddings. *See* Pudding
Bread sticks, cinnamon, 18
Breads, 290–305. *See also* Muffins
    apple-raisin spice, 300–301
    beer bread, 296
    Cheddar–broccoli bread roll, 304–305
    cinnamon bread sticks, 18
    cinnamon custard corn, 299
    cranberry nut, 294–295
    molasses brown, 297
    orange–current wheel, 302–303
    orange-raisin tea loaf, 292–293

    salad, Mediterranean, 53
    skillet cheese corn, 298
    testing with toothpick for
        doneness, 291
Breakfast couscous, 256
Breakfasts
    apple tapioca dessert, 276
    breakfast couscous, 256
    buckwheat pancakes, 261
    date and nut breakfast treat, 258
    15-minute muesli, 267
    fruited no-bake bread
        pudding, 349
    grains for, 249
    miracle lemon tofu pie, 339
    mystery custard pie, 344–345
    no-bake eggless noodle pudding, 166
    orange–currant wheel, 302–303
    peaches 'n' cream casserole, 266
    potato flapjack, 232
    sweet potato pancakes, 239
Broccoli
    Cheddar–broccoli bread roll,
        304–305
    in Japanese vegetables, 229
    with mushrooms and walnuts, 215
    orange, 214
    pasta and, 162
    in sesame, broccoli, and cauliflower
        salad, 43
Broth, types of, 22
Buckwheat pancakes, 261
Buckwheat-cheese bake, 259
Bulgur, herbed, 257
Burgers, pepper, 116
Butter bean and cheese squares, 134
Butternut squash
    in marmalade sauce, 245
    in millet butternut soup, 33
    in Turkish stew, 135

C

Cabbage
    Asian, 213
    king, 212
    soup, old world, 26
Cajun bean pot, 130
Cake roll, banana, 320–321

Cakes
  best carrot, 328
  chocolate zucchini spice, 319
  coffee, most versatile, 324–325
  piña colada upside-down,
    326–327
  tender-moist bean, 330–331
  yes—chocolate!, 322–323
Canned broth, 22
Canola oil, 291
Caribbean fish, 87
Caribbean rice and fruit salad, 56
Carrot
  in barley-vegetable casserole, 265
  cake, best, 328
  in couscous sauté, 255
  dilled, 49
  loaf, golden, 208
  in mock coconut custard pie, 342
  and orange salad, 55
  in party vegetable loaf, 210–211
  pudding, Indian, 353
  salad, orange, pineapple, and, 59
  soup, creamy, 23
  in Turkish stew, 135
Casseroles
  apple rice, 253
  barley-vegetable, 265
  black bean, olé, 138
  cheesy squash and rice, 185
  easy cheesy, 186
  Italian eggplant and cheese, 189
  peaches 'n' cream, 266
  potato–cheese, 181
  sweet potato pudding, 240
  tuna noodle, 99
Cauliflower
  in barley-vegetable casserole, 265
  in party vegetable loaf,
    210–211
  in sesame, broccoli, and cauliflower
    salad, 43
  soup, creamy, 32
Cheddar bread pudding, 188
Cheddar 'n' onion muffins, 316
Cheddar–broccoli bread roll, 304–305
Cheese, 180–190
  "almost" lasagna, 182–183
  banana cake roll, 320–321

bean and cheese quesadillas, 136
butter bean and cheese squares, 134
Cheddar bread pudding, 188
cheesy peaches, 190
cheesy squash and rice casserole, 185
coconut custard cheese pie, 338
easy cheesy, 186
Italian beans and, 127
Italian eggplant and cheese
    casserole, 189
Italian frittata, 180
in king cabbage, 212
in lemon dream parfaits, 351
lemon-pepper spinach puff, 184
macaroni with Cheddar and
    tomatoes, 159
maple buttercream cheese pie,
    340–341
marinated mozzarella, 4
in miracle lemon tofu pie, 339
in orange dreamsicle dessert, 346–347
pie with potato crust, 187
potato–cheese casserole, 181
pudding, tofu cinnamon, 358
in pumpkin custard cups, 350
skillet cheese corn bread, 298
spread, French herbed, 15
in tofu almond creme pie, 343
Cheesecake, maple buttercream cheese
    pie as, 340–341
Cheesy peaches, 190
Cheesy squash and rice casserole, 185
Cheesy thousand island dressing, 62
Cherries
  amandine, 274
  in razzleberry crisp, 332–333
Chick peas in Turkish stew, 135
Chicken, 66–75
  barbecue, easy, 76
  breasts, elegant stuffed, 68
  cacciatore, 71
  chow mein, 77
  corn soup, 38
  fat content of, 66
  golden crowned, 69
  Hawaiian pineapple, 74
  honey crunch, 73
  Spanish, 72
  spice-glazed, 75

Chicken, *continued,*
  topping for, 370
  with white wine and tomatoes, 70
  in wine sauce, 67
Chili con tofu, 140
Chili meat loaf, 114
Chili orange barbecue sauce, 371
Chinese fried rice, 252
Chinese pepper steak, 111
Chinese spinach, 226
Chocolate fluff, 348
Chocolate pineapple sauce, 365
Chocolate zucchini spice cake, 319
Cholesterol reduction
  using egg substitute, 172, 291
  using egg whites, 172, 291
  using grains, 249
  using reduced-fat cheese, 172
  using yolk-free noodles, 154
Chow mein, chicken, 77
Chunky apple molasses spice
    muffins, 313
Chunky tomato salad, 51
Cinnamon bread sticks, 18
Cinnamon creme sauce, 366
Cinnamon custard corn bread, 299
Cinnamon popcorn, 20
Cinnamon whirls, 360–361
Clams
  casino, 5
  chowder, Manhattan, 39
  dip, party, 11
Clove-spiced tomatoes, 225
Coconut custard cheese pie, 338
Cod à l'orange, 93
Coffee cake, most versatile, 324–325
Coleslaw, best, 47
Confetti pasta salad, 46
Convenience vegetable soup, 36–37
Cookie, almond macaroon, 362
Corn
  on the cob, roasted, 243
  fritters, 242
  Mexi-corn, 244
  soup, chicken, 38
  as starchy vegetable, 231
Corn bread
  cinnamon custard, 299
  skillet cheese, 298

Cottage cheese
  in apple creme pie, 336–337
  in buckwheat-cheese bake, 259
  in cheesy peaches, 190
  in coconut sauce, 273
  in lemon-pepper spinach puff, 184
  in most versatile coffee cake, 324–325
  and olive dip, 13
Couscous, 255–256
  breakfast, 256
Couscous sauté, 255
Crab-stuffed mushrooms, 3
Cranberry
  nut bread, 294–295
  relish, baked, 287
  sauce, apricot-almond, 288
  vinaigrette, 63
Creamy carrot soup, 23
Creamy cauliflower soup, 32
Creamy orange dressing, 64
Creamy potato soup, 28
Creamy vegetable chowder, 30
Cucumber and onion salad, 57
Curried lima soup, 34

D

Date and nut breakfast treat, 258
Dates in banana date-nut muffins, 307
Delhi beans and apples, 129
Desserts, 317–362
  almond macaroons, 362
  apple creme pie, 336–337
  apple crisp, 334–335
  apple tapioca, 276
  apple-raisin spice bread, 300–301
  applesauce ambrosia, 277
  applesauce wheat bars, 329
  banana cake roll, 320–321
  best carrot cake, 328
  chocolate zucchini spice cake, 319
  cinnamon custard corn bread, 299
  cinnamon whirls, 360–361
  coconut custard cheese pie, 338
  coffee cake, most versatile, 324–325
  creamy toppings for, 364
  fruited no-bake bread pudding, 349
  Indian carrot pudding, 353
  lemon dream parfaits, 351

magic strudel bars, 359
maple buttercream cheese pie, 340–341
miracle lemon tofu pie, 339
mocha creme-filled meringue nests, 356–357
mocha fluff, 348
mock coconut custard pie, 342
mystery custard pie, 344–345
no-bake eggless noodle pudding, 166
orange dreamsicle dessert, 346–347
piña colada upside-down cake, 326–327
pumpkin custard cups, 350
razzleberry crisp, 332–333
red, white, and blueberry parfaits, 281
spicy squash pudding, 219
substitutions for lowering fat content of, 318
tender-moist bean cake, 330–331
tofu almond creme pie, 343
tofu cinnamon cheese pudding, 358
tofu raspberry mousse, 355
tortoni, 354
very berry bread pudding, 352
yes—chocolate cake!, 322–323
Dijon dip, 10
Dijon pork steaks, 120
Dill roasted pork, 122
Dilled carrots, 49
Dilled yellow squash, 221
Dilly dip, 9
Dips. *See also* Appetizers *and* Spreads
cottage cheese and olive, 13
Dijon, 10
dilly, 9
hot pizza, 12
party clam, 11

E

Easiest shrimp salad, 103
Easy cheesy, 186
Easy chicken barbecue, 76
Egg white drop soup, 31
Eggplant
and cheese casserole, Italian, 189
supreme, 218
in veggie packets, 228

Eggs and egg substitute, 171–181, 184, 186–188, 190
almond bread puff, 178
apple strudel omelet, 174
Cheddar bread pudding, 188
cheese pie with potato crust, 187
cheesy peaches, 190
easy cheesy, 186
egg foo yung, 179
eggs suzette with strawberry sauce, 173
Italian frittata, 180
lemon-pepper spinach puff, 184
potato–cheese casserole, 181
in tomato cups, 177
Elegant stuffed chicken breasts, 68
Extracts as fat-free addition to dessert recipes, 318

F

Fajitas, tofu, 143
Fat content
of appetizers, dips, and spreads, 2
of breads and muffins, 291
of fruits, 270
of meat, 108
of sauces and toppings, 364
substitutions for lowering, 318
of vegetables, 207
Fiber content
added to cakes, 318
of breads and muffins, 291
of fruits, 270, 318
of grains, 249
of potato skins, 231
of seafood, 86
of vegetables, 207
15-minute muesli, 267
Fish, 85–99
baked herbed, 89
Caribbean, 87
cod à l'orange, 93
lemony stuffed, 90–91
Parmesan, 94
and peppers, 92
"pretend" salmon salad, 96
salmon salad, 95
salmon–potato patties, 97

Fish, *continued*
   thyme for, 88
   tuna noodle casserole, 99
   tuna-vegetable pie, 98
Franks in pungent sauce, 84
French herbed cheese spread, 15
French honey mustard, 61
French meat loaf, 115
French onion soup, 24
French toast, almond bread puff as
   version of, 178
Fried rice, Chinese, 252
Fruit salad in a watermelon basket,
   284–285
Fruited no-bake bread pudding, 349
Fruit-to-go, 286
Fruits, 269–289
   apple tapioca dessert, 276
   applesauce ambrosia, 277
   apricot-almond cranberry sauce, 288
   baked cranberry relish, 287
   baked pears with cinnamon creme
      sauce, 280
   baked pineapple with creamy
      coconut sauce, 273
   bananas New Orleans, 279
   berries Romanoff, 282
   blueberry and apple delight, 278
   Caribbean rice and fruit salad, 56
   cheesy peaches, 190
   cherries amandine, 274
   fruit salad in a watermelon basket,
      284–285
   fruit-to-go, 286
   hot spiced, 289
   and noodle kugel, 165
   peach butter, 272
   raspberry tapioca, 283
   red, white, and blueberry
      parfaits, 281
   topping for, 368

G

Garden pasta sauce, 167
Gazpacho, 35
Gelatin mold
   orange, pineapple, and carrot, 59
   strawberry–apple, 58

Golden carrot loaf, 208
Golden crowned chicken, 69
Gourmet zucchini salad, 48
Grains, 248–267. *See also*
      individual grains
   apple rice casserole, 253
   barley-vegetable casserole, 265
   Bombay millet, 262
   breakfast couscous, 256
   buckwheat pancakes, 261
   buckwheat-cheese bake, 259
   Chinese fried rice, 252
   couscous sauté, 255
   date and nut breakfast
      treat, 258
   15-minute muesli, 267
   herbed bulgur, 257
   Italian barley, 264
   kasha and bow ties, 260
   nice spiced rice, 251
   peaches 'n' cream casserole, 266
   spinach and rice bake, 250
   tri-color rice, 254
   tropical millet pudding, 263
Gravy, bean, 139
Green beans
   in Japanese vegetables, 229
   Pennsylvania Dutch, 217
Grilled ham steak, 117
Grilled onions, 227

H

Ham
   barbecue on a bun, 118–119
   steak, grilled, 117
Hawaiian pineapple chicken, 74
Herbed bulgur, 257
Herbed tomato sauce, 373
Herbed turkey roll, 83
Homemade stock, 22
Honey crunch chicken, 73
Honey mustard
   salad dressing, 61
   sauce, 370
Honeydew melon in fruit-to-
   go, 286
Hot pizza dip, 12
Hot spiced fruit, 289

I

Indian carrot pudding, 353
Instant broth mix, 22
Italian baked spaghetti squash, 222
Italian barley, 264
Italian beans and cheese, 127
Italian eggplant and cheese
casserole, 189
Italian frittata, 180
Italian macaroni salad, 158
Italian mushroom noodle bake,
160–161
Italian noodles, 163
Italian tofu squares, 146–147

J

Japanese vegetables, 229
Jelly muffins, 308–309

K

Kasha and bow ties, 260
Kidney beans
in Cajun bean pot, 130
in Delhi beans and apples, 129
in Italian beans and cheese, 127
provençal, 132–133
King cabbage, 212
Kugel, fruit and noodle, 165

L

Lamb, 123–124
leg of, roast, 124
roast, marinated, 123
Lasagne
"almost," 182–183
tofu-spinach, 156–157
Leftover bean soup, 27
Legumes. See Beans
Lemon dream parfaits, 351
Lemon poppy seed muffins, 306
Lemon-pepper spinach puff, 184
Lemony stuffed fish, 90–91
Lentils in Sicilian lentil pasta
sauce, 170
Lima beans in curried lima soup, 34

M

Macaroni verde, 155
Macaroni with Cheddar and
tomatoes, 159
Macaroons, almond, 362
Magic strudel bars, 359
Manhattan clam chowder, 39
Maple buttercream cheese pie,
340–341
Marinade for tofu kabobs, 150
Marinated lamb roast, 123
Marinated mozzarella, 4
Marinated tofu kabobs, 150–151
Marinated vegetable salad, 45
Mashed potatoes in salmon–potato
patties, 97
Meat consumption, 108
Meat loaf
chili, 114
French, 115
Mediterranean bread salad, 53
Meringue nests, mocha creme-filled,
356–357
Mexican pinto spread, 14
Mexi-corn, 244
Millet
Bombay, 262
butternut soup, 33
pudding, tropical, 263
Miracle lemon tofu pie, 339
Mocha creme-filled meringue nests,
356–357
Mocha fluff, 348
Mock coconut custard pie, 342
Mock-sausage and peppers, 80–81
Molasses brown bread, 297
Most versatile coffee cake, 324–325
Mousse, tofu raspberry, 355
Muesli, 15-minute, 267
Muffins, 306–316. See also Breads
banana date-nut, 307
bran, 312
Cheddar 'n' onion, 316
chunky apply molasses spice, 313
jelly, 308–309
lemon poppy seed, 306
rum 'n' raisin, 314–315
testing with toothpick for doneness, 291
two-berry, 310–311

Mushrooms
    in barley-vegetable
        casserole, 265
    bean loaf supreme, 128
    broccoli with mushrooms and
        walnuts, 215
    crab-stuffed, 3
    in Japanese vegetables, 229
    noodle bake, Italian, 160–161
    soup, sherried, 40
Mustard potato salad, 44
Mystery custard pie, 344–345

N

Nacho vegetable medley, 209
Nice spiced rice, 251
No-bake eggless noodle
    pudding, 166
Noodles. See also Pasta
    fruit and noodle kugel, 165
    Italian, 163
    Italian mushroom noodle bake,
        160–161
    kasha and bow ties, 260
    with peanut sauce, 164
    pudding, no-bake eggless, 166
    salad, Szechuan, 50
    tuna noodle casserole, 99
    yolk-free, 154

O

Oil, canola as monounsaturated, 291
Old world cabbage soup, 26
Omelet, apple strudel, 174
Onion
    in barley-vegetable casserole, 265
    in Bombay peas and, 237
    in Cheddar 'n' onion muffins, 316
    grilled, 227
    in Italian barley, 264
    in Japanese vegetables, 229
    in nice spiced rice, 251
    pickled, 54
    in potatoes cacciatore, 233
    salad, cucumber and, 57
    soup, French, 24
    in tri-color rice, 254

Orange
    in baked cranberry relish, 287
    baked pork chops, 121
    broccoli, 214
    creme whip, 369
    dreamsicle dessert, 346–347
    dressing, creamy, 64
    pineapple, and carrot mold, 59
    salad, carrot and, 55
Orange juice
    in Bananas New Orleans, 279
    in chili orange barbecue sauce, 371
    in cod à l'orange, 93
    in 15-minute muesli, 267
    in lemon dream parfaits, 351
    in orange baked pork chops, 121
    in orange broccoli, 214
    in orange creme whip, 369
    in sweet potatoes and apples, 241
    in tender-moist bean cake, 330–331
    in very berry bread pudding, 352
Orange marmalade in butternut squash
        in marmalade sauce, 245
Orange–currant wheel, 302–303
Orange-raisin tea loaf, 292–293
Oven-baked French "fries," 236
Oven-fried turkey cutlets, 78

P

Pacific pasta sauce with
        salmon, 168
Pancakes
    buckwheat, 261
    sweet potato, 239
    topping for, lowfat, 364
Parfaits, lemon dream, 351
Parmesan fish, 94
Parmesan potatoes, 234
Parsnips
    as starchy vegetable, 231
    whipped spiced, 247
Party clam dip, 11
Party vegetable loaf, 210–211
Pasta, 153–166. See also Noodles
    and broccoli, 162
    confetti pasta salad, 46
    fruit and noodle kugel, 165
    Italian macaroni salad, 158

Italian mushroom noodle bake, 160–161
Italian noodles, 163
macaroni with Cheddar and tomatoes, 159
macaroni verde, 155
no-bake eggless noodle pudding, 166
noodles with peanut sauce, 164
salad, confetti, 46
tofu-spinach lasagne, 156–157
Pasta sauces, 167–170
garden, 167
Pacific, with salmon, 168
Sicilian lentil, 170
spaghetti sauce Italiano, 169
Peach
butter, 272
in hot spiced fruit, 289
in most versatile coffee cake, 324–325
Peaches 'n' cream casserole, 266
Pears with cinnamon creme sauce, baked, 280
Peas
Bombay peas and potatoes, 237
in party vegetable loaf, 210–211
as starchy vegetable, 231
Pennsylvania Dutch green beans, 217
Pepper, bell
burgers, 116
in couscous sauté, 255
fish and, 92
in Italian barley, 264
in Mexi-corn, 244
mock-sausage and, 80–81
in tri-color rice, 254
in veggie packets, 228
zucchini and, 223
Pickled onions, 54
Pies
apple creme, 336–337
coconut custard, 338
maple buttercream cheese, 340–341
miracle lemon tofu, 339
mock coconut custard, 342
mystery custard, 344
tofu almond creme, 343
Piña colada upside-down cake, 326–327

Pineapple
baked, with creamy coconut sauce, 273
chicken, Hawaiian, 74
in hot spiced fruit, 289
in maple buttercream cheese pie, 340–341
in orange, pineapple, and carrot mold, 59
in piña colada upside-down, 326–327
sauce, chocolate, 365
in tropical millet pudding, 26
Pineapple–black bean salad, 137
Pinto beans in refried beans, 131
Pinwheels, cinnamon whirls, 360–361
Pizza dip, hot, 12
Popcorn, cinnamon, 20
Pork, 108, 117–122
chops, orange baked, 121
dill roasted, 122
grilled ham steak, 117
ham barbecue on a bun, 118–119
orange baked pork chops, 121
steak, Dijon, 120
Potato
Bombay peas and, 237
cheese pie with potato crust, 187
flapjack, 232
oven-baked French "fries," 236
Parmesan, 234
salad, mustard, 44
salmon–potato patties, 97
soup, creamy, 28
as starchy vegetable, 231
tofu stuffed, 152
topping for, 364, 372
Potato chips, 19
Potato–cheese casserole, 181
Potatoes cacciatore, 233
Potatoes Italiano, 235
Poultry, 65–84
"Pretend" salmon salad, 96
Pudding
Cheddar bread, 188
fruited no-bake bread, 349
Indian carrot, 353
no-bake eggless noodle, 166
spicy squash, 219
sweet potato, 240

Pudding, *continued*
  tofu cinnamon cheese, 358
  tropical millet, 263
  very berry bread, 352
Pumpkin custard cup, 350

Q

Quesadillas, bean and cheese, 136

R

Raspberry
  in fruit-to-go, 286
  melba sauce, 368
  in razzleberry crisp, 332–333
  tapioca, 283
  in two-berry muffins, 310–311
Raspberry-filled sweet potato cro-
    quettes, 238
Razzleberry crisp, 332–333
Red, white, and blueberry parfaits, 281
Refried beans, 131
Rice, 249–254
  apple rice casserole, 253
  cheesy squash and rice casserole, 185
  fried, Chinese, 252
  and fruit salad, Caribbean, 56
  nice spiced, 251
  spinach and rice bake, 250
  tofu raisin and rice patties, 148–149
  tofu–rice patties with sweet and sour
      sauce, 142
  tri-color, 254
Roast leg of lamb, 124
Roasted corn on the cob, 243
Rolled oats
  in 15-minute muesli, 267
  in peaches 'n' cream casserole, 266
Rum 'n' raisin muffins, 314–315

S

Salad dressings, 60–64
  cheesy thousand island, 62
  cranberry vinaigrette, 63
  creamy orange, 64
  French honey mustard, 61
  zesty tomato, 60

Salads, 41–59
  basil bean, 52
  Bengal seafood, 106
  best coleslaw, 47
  Caribbean rice and fruit, 56
  carrot and orange, 55
  chunky tomato, 51
  confetti pasta, 46
  cucumber and onion, 57
  dilled carrots, 49
  easiest shrimp, 103
  fruit, in a watermelon basket,
      284–285
  gourmet zucchini, 48
  Italian macaroni, 158
  marinated vegetable, 45
  Mediterranean bread, 53
  mustard potato, 44
  orange, pineapple, and carrot
      mold, 59
  pickled onions, 54
  pineapple–black bean, 137
  "pretend" salmon, 96
  salmon, 95
  sesame, broccoli, and cauliflower, 43
  strawberry–apple mold, 58
  Szechuan noodle, 50
Salmon
  Pacific pasta sauce with, 168
  pâté, 7
  salad, 95
  salad, "pretend," 96
Salmon–potato patties, 97
Sauces, 363–373
  baked potato topper, 372
  chili orange barbecue, 371
  chocolate pineapple, 365
  cinnamon creme, 366
  coconut, 273
  cranberry, apricot-almond, 288
  creme, 280
  herbed tomato, 373
  honey mustard, 370
  lowfat, low-calorie bases for, 364
  orange creme whip, 369
  peanut, 164
  raspberry melba, 368
  strawberry, 173, 367
  sweet and sour, 142

Seafood, 101–106
  barbecued shrimp, 104–105
  easiest shrimp salad, 103
  salad, Bengal, 106
  shrimp teriyaki, 101
  and water chestnuts, 102
  whole grain added to meal of, 86
Sesame, broccoli, and cauliflower
    salad, 43
Sherried mushroom soup, 40
Shrimp
  barbecued, 104–105
  salad, easiest, 103
  teriyaki, 101
  and water chestnuts, 102
Sicilian lentil pasta sauce, 170
Skillet cheese corn bread, 298
Snacks
  applesauce wheat bars, 329
  bagel crackers, 17
  cinnamon popcorn, 20
  magic strudel bars, 359
  orange–currant wheel, 302–303
  potato chips, 19
  tortilla chips, 16
Soups, 21–40
  chicken corn, 8
  convenience vegetable, 36–37
  creamy carrot, 23
  creamy cauliflower, 32
  creamy potato, 28
  creamy vegetable chowder, 30
  curried lima, 34
  egg white drop, 31
  French onion, 24
  gazpacho, 35
  leftover bean, 27
  Manhattan clam chowder, 39
  millet butternut, 33
  old world cabbage, 26
  sherried mushroom, 40
  spiced tomato, 29
  split pea, 25
Southern-style baked squash, 220
Spaghetti sauce Italiano, 169
Spaghetti squash, Italian baked, 222
Spanish chicken, 72
Spice-glazed chicken, 75
Spiced tomato soup, 29

Spicy squash pudding, 219
Spinach
  Chinese, 226
  and rice bake, 250
Split pea soup, 25
Spreads
  French herbed cheese, 15
  Mexican pinto, 14
Starchy vegetables. See Vegetables,
    starchy
Steak
  Chinese pepper, 111
  teriyaki flank, 109
Steak-kabobs, 110
Strawberry
  in berries Romanoff, 282
  in fruit-to-go, 286
  red, white, and blueberry parfaits, 281
  sauce, 367
  in very berry bread pudding, 352
Strawberry–apple mold, 58
Strudel bars, magic, 359
Substitutions for high-fat ingredients, list
    of, 318, 364
Sukiyaki, 112–113
Summer squash, yellow
  in cheesy squash and rice casserole,
    185
  dilled, 221
  Southern-style baked squash, 220
Sweet and spicy tofu and vegetables, 141
Sweet potato
  and apples, 241
  croquettes, raspberry-filled, 238
  pancakes, 239
  pudding, 240
  as starchy vegetable, 231
  in Turkish stew, 135
Szechuan noodle salad, 50

T

Tender-moist bean cake, 330–331
Teriyaki flank steak, 109
Thousand island dressing, cheesy, 62
Thyme for fish, 88
Tofu, 140–152
  almond creme pie, 343
  chili con, 140

Tofu, *continued*
  cinnamon cheese pudding, 358
  Creole, 144
  description of, 126
  fajitas, 143
  fritters, tropical, 145
  kabobs, marinated, 150–151
  pie, miracle lemon, 339
  raisin and rice patties, 148–149
  raspberry mousse, 355
  squares, Italian, 146–147
  stuffed potatoes, 152
  sweet and spicy, and vegetables, 141
  tofu–rice patties with sweet and sour
      sauce, 142
  tofu-spinach lasagne, 156–157
Tomato
  chicken with white wine and, 70
  clove-spiced, 225
  cups, eggs in, 177
  dressing, zesty, 60
  in gazpacho, 35
  macaroni with Cheddar and, 159
  in nice spiced rice, 251
  party puffs, 6
  salad, chunky, 51
  sauce, herbed, 373
  soup, spiced, 29
  in veggie packets, 228
Tomatoes provençal, 224
Toppings. *See* Sauces
Tortilla chips, 16
Tortoni, 354
Tri-color rice, 254
Tropical millet pudding, 263
Tropical tofu fritters, 145
Tuna mousse, 8
Tuna noodle casserole, 99
Tuna-vegetable pie, 98
Turkey, 66, 78–84
  cutlets, oven-fried, 78
  franks in pungent sauce, 84
  loaf, barbecue, 82
  mock-sausage and peppers, 80–81
  patties, Asian, 79
  roll, herbed, 83
  topping for, 370
Turkish stew, 135
Two-berry muffins, 310–311

V
Vegetable loaf, party, 210–211
Vegetables, 206–229
  Asian cabbage, 213
  broccoli with mushrooms and wal-
      nuts, 215
  Chinese spinach, 226
  chowder, creamy, 30
  clove-spice tomatoes, 225
  cooking, 207
  dilled yellow squash, 221
  eggplant supreme, 218
  in garden pasta sauce, 167
  golden carrot loaf, 208
  grilled onions, 227
  Italian basked spaghetti squash, 222
  Japanese, 229
  king cabbage, 212
  medley, nacho, 209
  nacho vegetable medley, 209
  orange broccoli, 214
  party vegetable loaf, 210–211
  Pennsylvania Dutch green beans, 217
  salad, marinated, 45
  soup, convenience, 36–37
  Southern-style baked squash, 220
  spicy squash pudding, 219
  sweet and spicy tofu and, 141
  tomatoes provençal, 224
  topping for, 364
  tuna-vegetable pie, 98
  veggie packets, 228
  zucchini and peppers, 223
Vegetables, starchy, 230–247
  applesauce acorn squash, 246
  Bombay peas and potatoes, 237
  butternut squash in marmalade
      sauce, 245
  corn fritters, 242
  Mexi-corn, 244
  oven-baked French fries, 236
  Parmesan potatoes, 234
  potato flapjack, 232
  potatoes cacciatore, 233
  potatoes Italiano, 235
  raspberry-filled sweet potato cro-
      quettes, 238
  roasted corn on the cob, 243
  sweet potato pancakes, 239

sweet potato pudding, 240
sweet potatoes and apples, 241
whipped spiced parsnips, 247
Veggie packets, 228
Very berry bread pudding, 352

W

Walnuts
in baked cranberry relish, 287
in banana-date nut muffins, 307
broccoli with mushrooms and, 215
in cranberry nut bread, 294–295
in yes—chocolate cake!, 322–323
Water chestnuts, shrimp and, 102
Watermelon basket, fruit salad in, 284–285
Whipped spiced parsnips, 247
White wine, chicken with tomatoes and, 70

Wine sauce, chicken in, 67
Winter squash, 231

Y

Yes—chocolate cake!, 322–323

Z

Zesty tomato dressing, 60
Zucchini
in cheesy squash and rice casserole, 185
in mystery custard pie, 344–345
and peppers, 223
salad, gourmet, 48
spice cake, chocolate, 319
in veggie packets, 228

International Conversion Chart

These are not exact equivalents: they have been slightly rounded to make measuring easier.

LIQUID MEASUREMENTS

American	Imperial	Metric	Australian
2 tablespoons (1 oz.)	1 fl. oz.	30 ml	1 tablespoon
1/4 cup (2 oz.)	2 fl. oz.	60 ml	2 tablespoons
1/3 cup (3 oz.)	3 fl. oz.	80 ml	1/4 cup
1/2 cup (4 oz.)	4 fl. oz.	125 ml	1/3 cup
2/3 cup (5 oz.)	5 fl. oz.	165 ml	1/2 cup
3/4 cup (6 oz.)	6 fl. oz.	185 ml	2/3 cup
1 cup (8 oz.)	8 fl. oz.	250 ml	3/4 cup

SPOON MEASUREMENTS

American	Metric
1/4 teaspoon	1 ml
1/2 teaspoon	2 ml
1 teaspoon	5 ml
1 tablespoon	15 ml

WEIGHTS

US/UK	Metric
1 oz.	30 grams (g)
2 oz.	60 g
4 oz. (1/4 lb)	125 g
5 oz. (1/3 lb)	155 g
6 oz.	185 g
7 oz.	220 g
8 oz. (1/2 lb)	250 g
10 oz.	315 g
12 oz. (3/4 lb)	375 g
14 oz.	440 g
16 oz. (1 lb)	500 g
2 lbs	1 kg

OVEN TEMPERATURES

Farenheit	Centigrade	Gas
250	120	1/2
300	150	2
325	160	3
350	180	4
375	190	5
400	200	6
450	230	8

Bobbie Hinman

Bobbie Hinman has been a pioneer in the field of lowfat cooking. She has been preparing healthful meals since she discovered, over twenty years ago, that her family had a hereditary cholesterol problem. She jokes about the fact that the rest of the world is "finally catching up to her." Determined to raise her family on a healthful lowfat diet, and aware that there were few, if any, teaching cookbooks available when she began, Bobbie set out to find ways to make healthful meals that were also tasty meals. Her unique contribution to healthful cooking comes from her masterful ability to create lowfat meals that taste delicious.

Bobbie is in constant demand as a speaker and cooking teacher and has been a guest on numerous television and radio shows, including *The Regis Philbin Show* and *The Low Cholesterol Gourmet*. She also completed a media tour for General Mills where she discussed the benefits of eating a lowfat, high-fiber diet. Bobbie is the author of *The Meatless Gourmet: Favorite Recipes from Around the World*, *The Meatless Gourmet: Easy Lowfat Favorites*, and *Burgers 'n' Fries 'n' Cinnamon Buns*. In addition to writing cooking columns for several monthly publications, Bobbie travels extensively, teaching classes and speaking to hospital groups, cardiac centers, weight management centers, colleges, and private organizations.

Bobbie resides in Delaware with her husband Harry. They have four grown children.

Millie Snyder

For thirty-one years, Millie Snyder has devoted the majority of her time and interest to helping individuals with weight control problems. In her leadership role with Weight Watchers of West Virginia, Inc., she expresses her belief that it is not that people don't want to change; they simply don't know how. To that end, she has made a professional life as a public speaker, encouraging those with weight problems to "listen up" and "lighten up." Because of her concern for people, Millie has established a reputation for enhancing the quality of life by teaching people how to change.

Millie has also managed, amidst a busy schedule, to create a large line of low-calorie foods, which she markets through her wholesale/retail business. Her frozen confectionery bar "Dippy Do" will soon be available over the World Wide Web delivered on dry ice by overnight service.

Millie also finds time to co-author cookbooks such as *Light Fantastic!* with Alyssa Alia, following 15 years of success with the LEAN AND LUSCIOUS series upon which *Lean and Luscious Favorites* is based.

Millie believes that humor is a necessary requirement for change. Her personality, both serious and comic, is one reason why she has become a much sought-after public speaker on the subject of self-image and weight control.

Millie is the parent of two married children. She is listed in *Who's Who of American Women* and *Who's Who Finance and Industry*. She continues to live life according to her own formula for success: "One day at a time."

ALSO FROM PRIMA

The Meatless Gourmet
Easy Lowfat Favorites

Bobbie Hinman

U.S. $18.00
Can. $24.95
ISBN: 0-7615-0059-6
comb bound / 512 pages

Bobbie Hinman, coauthor of the bestselling LEAN AND LUSCIOUS cookbooks, has an endless supply of lowfat, high-flavor meal ideas that will appeal to the entire family. *The Meatless Gourmet* offers over 300 tantalizing, easy-to-prepare dishes featuring a rich variety of whole grains and fresh fruits and vegetables. Recipes include:

- Corn and Red Pepper Chowder
- Pizza-Style Pasta
- Banana Corn Bread
- Iced Maple Coffee Float
- Fabulous Berry Party Trifle
- And hundreds more!

Each recipe includes the detailed nutrition information, ease of preparation, and great taste you expect from Prima.

Visit us online at www.primapublishing.com

ALSO FROM PRIMA

Low-Fat Gourmet Chicken

Jackie Eddy and Eleanor Clark

U.S. $14.95
Can. $19.95
ISBN 1-55958-139-5
comb bound / 288 pages

Bestselling authors and gourmet cooks Jackie Eddy and Eleanor Clark present over 200 delicious, versatile recipes for chicken that are high in fiber and low in calories and cholesterol. This rich variety of soups, salads, and entrées includes:

- Sweet Red Pepper Chicken
- Thai Noodles and Chicken
- Easy Leftover Chicken Soup
- And many more!

Special sections boast recipes for the barbecue, stovetop, microwave, stir-fry, and oven. Others focus on chicken and pasta dishes, leftovers, and low-fat accompaniments, such as pastries, sauces, and seasonings. Each recipe has a complete nutritional analysis.

Visit us online at www.primapublishing.com

Also from Prima

Fat Free 2

More Fat Free and Ultra Lowfat Recipes—
No Butter, No Oil, No Margarine!

Doris Cross

U.S. $15.95
Can. $21.95
ISBN: 0-7615-0129-0
comb bound / 272 pages

Bestselling author Doris Cross has made it her life's work to prove that there's no end to the great flavor and homestyle variety available in lowfat foods. The unbelievably fat-free and ultra lowfat recipes in this collection include:

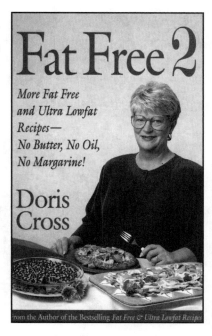

- Chicken Gumbo
- Sausage and Rice Casserole
- Stuffed Potato Skins
- Chili Dogs in a Blanket
- Deviled Eggs
- Pumpkin Cheesecake
- Banana Cream Pudding
- And many more!

Each easy-to-prepare recipe includes a breakdown of fat and calorie content per serving.

Visit us online at www.primapublishing.com

To Order Books

Please send me the following items:

Quantity	Title	Unit Price	Total
_____	The Meatless Gourmet: Easy Lowfat Favorites	$ 18.00	$ _____
_____	Low-Fat Gourmet Chicken	$ 14.95	$ _____
_____	Fat Free & Ultra Lowfat Recipes	$ 14.95	$ _____
_____	Fat Free 2	$ 15.95	$ _____
_____	_____	$ _____	$ _____

*Shipping and Handling depend on Subtotal.

Subtotal	Shipping/Handling
$0.00–$14.99	$3.00
$15.00–$29.99	$4.00
$30.00–$49.99	$6.00
$50.00–$99.99	$10.00
$100.00–$199.99	$13.50
$200.00+	Call for Quote

Foreign and all Priority Request orders:
Call Order Entry department
for price quote at 916-632-4400

This chart represents the total retail price of books only (before applicable discounts are taken).

Subtotal $ _____

Deduct 10% when ordering 3-5 books $ _____

7.25% Sales Tax (CA only) $ _____

8.25% Sales Tax (TN only) $ _____

5.0% Sales Tax (MD and IN only) $ _____

7.0% G.S.T. Tax (Canada only) $ _____

Shipping and Handling* $ _____

Total Order $ _____

By Telephone: With MC or Visa, call 800-632-8676 or 916-632-4400.
Mon–Fri, 8:30-4:30.

WWW: http://www.primapublishing.com

By Internet E-mail: sales@primapub.com

By Mail: Just fill out the information below and send with your remittance to:

Prima Publishing
P.O. Box 1260BK
Rocklin, CA 95677

My name is _____

I live at _____

City _____ State _____ ZIP_____

MC/Visa#_____ Exp. _____

Check/money order enclosed for $_____ Payable to Prima Publishing

Daytime telephone _____

Signature _____